What Does WoMan Want?

What Does WoMan Want?

by

Timothy Leary

1988
Falcon Press
Phoenix, Arizona 85012
U.S.A.

Hardbound Collector's Edition ISBN: 0-941404-76-5
Softbound Edition ISBN: 0-941404-62-5

Limited Collectors Edition by Timothy Leary—1976

First Revised Falcon Press Edition Hardbound—1988
First Revised Falcon Press Edition Softbound—1988

Cover Design Clara Cohan

Falcon Press
3660 N. 3rd St.
Phoenix, Arizona 85012
(602) 246-3546

FURTHER CONSPIRACIES?!

If you would like to read further on the New Age Conspiracy to elevate Human Consciousness on this Planet and elsewhere — don't simply ask your book dealer to order the following titles — **Demand that S/He do so!** They are:

THE FUTURE HISTORY SERIES
By Timothy Leary, Ph.D.
Exo-Psychology
Neuropolitics
The Intelligence Agents
The Game Of Life

ROBERT ANTON WILSON SERIES

The Cosmic Trigger
Sex and Drugs
Wilhelm Reich In Hell
Prometheus Rising
Coincidance -- A New Anthology
The New Inquisition

The Future Is NOW Series

Breaking The GodSpell: Genetic Evolution By Neil Freer. Introduced by Zecharia Sitchin.
The Sapiens System — The Illuminati Conspiracy: Their Objectives, Methods and Who They Are! by Donald Holmes, M.D. With an extensive introduction by Robert Anton Wilson.
UnDoing Yourself with Energized Meditation and Other Devices by Christopher S. Hyatt. Introduced by Israel Regardie, with an extensive Foreword by Robert Anton Wilson.
Angel Tech — A Modern Shaman's Guide to Reality Selection by Antero Alli, Preface by Robert Anton Wilson.
An Interview with Israel Regardie — His Final Thoughts Edited by Christopher S. Hyatt.
Zen Without Zen Masters by Camden Benares.
Monsters and Magical Sticks: There Is No Such Thing As Hypnosis? by Steven Heller, Ph.D. Introduced by Robert Anton Wilson.
An Extraterrestrial Conspiracy By Marian Greenberg. Not Introduced by Robert Anton Wilson.
The Shaman Warrior by Gini Graham Scott, Ph.D.

-1-

OPENING CREDITS

Geneva Airport, May 1971

Commodore Tom Dylan, now impersonating a Fugitive Philosopher (male), steps out of the long-distance audio-transceiver booth in the Geneva Airport of SOL-3, colliding gently with a technicolor biped, silver hair, pink face, portly body covered with well-tailored artificial fabric, dress and groomed to play the Bank that broke the Man at Montecarlo. Most probably a Frenchman named Franc or a German named Mark.

WHAT DOES WOMAN WANT?

"Pardonez-moi," says the Pink man seizing the Alchemist gently by the arm. The accent is Parisian.

"Einstein hat ihr gepardoned," replies Dylan carefully. *"Vorein fur Raumschiffahrt?"*
"So? You are not American?" says the Pink Man in surprise. He gently removes his tentacle. "I thought you were someone else. *Je Suis desole.*"
Resonance exchanged, he nods politely and spins away with a puzzled look.

> THE OUTLAW GNOSTIC, GUITAR-STRUMMING PHILOSOPHER WAS ON THE RUN AGAIN. HE HELD NO ILLUSIONS ABOUT HIS ASSIGNMENT— TO SEARCH ALONG THE RISKY SCHWARTZCHILD RADIUS AND FIND THE ENCODED SECRET THAT THE BORING PLANET HUNGERED FOR.
>
> HIS GENETIC TASK IS COMPLICATED WHEN HE DISCOVERS THAT HIS OWN NAME HEADS THE WANTED LIST OF THE DREAD NIXON-LIDDY GANG ...

The ex-convict Bard, whose genetic-code number is Eight, walks to the other side of the room where his Binary Companion waits with legs crossed. She is currently impersonating the eternal cosmetic commerical, open mouth of the year juicy with color; petal skin moist with dew, big eyes watching him with ingenue expectation (Female!).

ROSAMUND AS DEMETER—3

HIS BINARY COMPANION AND OBSESSION IS A VERITABLE DAR DAR. HER MYSTERIOUS EGG WISDOM PULLS HIM INTO A FUSION ORBIT IMPOSSIBLE TO ESCAPE!
HER MISSION: TO TEACH DYLAN THE ANSWER TO THE ULTIMATE QUESTION.

What a neurosurgical task to disconnect the billion fibers that join us, he laments. The hair, now scarlet-brown with henna sheen, for example, not to mention Her cream-white membrane covering.

"What did Pierre have to say?"

"He and Anita left Copenhagen. They're back in Paris. He advises against going to Denmark. The prices are high and it's dangerous. He says there are too many people there who don't want me to give the lecture."

MICHEL HAUCHARD AS HERMES — 4

SUAVE FRENCH CONFIDANCE MAN, GEMINI ARMS MERCHANT, GOURMET GANGSTER. AT HOME EQUALLY IN THE BACK ROOMS OF THE CORSICAN MAFIA, THE ELEGANT SMUGGLER PENTHOUSES OF BEIRUT, THE SWANK RESTUARANTS OF JET-SET SWITZERLAND . . .COMPELLED (BY WHOSE POWER?) TO OPPOSE THE HEDONIC FUTURE HE CAN NEVER EXPERIENCE.

She nods thoughtfully. "I'm not surprised. Politics makes people so mean. Who's uptight now?"

"Pierre says that my lecture there is sponsored by an anarchist group led by Red Rudi."

"That doesn't sound good."

"The Danish government promises to protect us from extradition but there are rumors that the CIA may try to kidnap us from the International Section of the airport."

"How ungrateful of the CIA," She complains, "after all the oriental marital counseling we gave the silly agent Muktar and his wife in Algiers. And we left our rugs and silverware with that nice CIA lady at Point Pescade. And our music machine and tapes with that sweet snoopy hotel manager with the American briefcase. Not to mention the furs."

DR. CHRISTOPHER S. HYATT AS APOLLO — 6

MYSTERIOUS CYBER-DIPLOMAT. GENETIC ENGI-
NEER. ONE TIME NEURO-PSYCHOLOGIST NOW
SUFFERING FROM AMNESIA. SENSITIVE, TOUGH
ESPIONAGE AGENT WHOSE UNDERSTANDING
OF THE NEURO-GENETIC FORCES AT PLAY MAKES
HIM A TREACHEROUS ENEMY OR CRUCIAL ALLY?

The soft fur thing cannot be denied, nor the fact that Her skin is so tender
She must wear soft-leather shoes and smooth silk things around Her.

"We have a shopping list of angry crazies to avoid there," he says. "A
Maoist action group is planning to picket. They don't like our changing the
title from Revolution to Revelation. They say we de-politicize young larvals,
seduce them away from dialectic materialism."

"That's as good a reason to seduce them as any," She muses.

"Are you ready for a right-wing neo-Nazi group denouncing us for
politicizing young people? They say LSD means *Links Social Democratische.*"

"What's that?"

"Anthony Burgess says it's a selfish way of attaining the view of ultimate
reality. Pierre's bored with Denmark. He doesn't want me to speak either. I
don't know what's happening down here. I always have trouble adjusting to
these slow altitudes.

RAM POONA AS NEPTUNE — 14

> ADEPT IN TANTRIC YOGA, WHO TRANSMITS TO DYLAN THE BENGALI SCROLL WHICH REVEALS THE SECRET OF IRRESISTABLE EROTICA ATTRACTION AND THE TWENTY-FOUR STAGES OF NEURO-SOMATIC FUSION.

Well, this much is obvious," She says briskly. "Now that he's become President of the U.N. Board of Experts, Pierre thinks he has too much cargo to lose. No one wants the game to get any bigger than themselves. Will you buy me a drink while you think?"

They are still within the International Section of the airport, protected from no one. There are Interpol warrants for their arrest and they are travelling exposed using their own passports. All the Eye-nets and Heat-Detectors are tracking their flight from Algiers to Denmark. They are not expected to stay in Geneva so they will remain off the screen until they don't walk off the plane at Copenhagen.

She sips Dubonnet, puts Her finger on Her moist lower lip and speaks in a low voice. "I knew we shouldn't have left the music and the rugs in Algiers. What now Eight?"

INNOCENT, BIG-EYED "GIRL" SENT TO PLANET EARTH (BY WAY OF ENID, OKLAHOMA) TO FIND AND MUTATE DYLAN OUT OF FOUR-BRAINED HARVARD CAPTIVITY. FROM HER RINGSIDE TABLE AT BIRDLAND (WHERE SHE DEALT CARDS FOR THE GLOBAL BEAUTY GAME) AND FROM HER PLEASURE PALACE ON THE HUDSON, SHE TAUGHT, IN A LOW CURVY WHISPER, THE CIRCLING OF THE SQUARE

"Pierre called the Swiss Banker. He's expecting us. We'll hide out in Geneva until Pierre arrives to rescue us."

"Who was that silver-haired pink-faced dude? He looked like the owner of the casino. He asked me to pardon him and said he was desolated. I gave him a password from behind a *Peenemunde* screen."

"He was watching you very closely. He materialized out of Booth number Four. That's Gemini. What does that mean here? He looked like an elegant arms dealer."

"Probably French. But he could be CIA."

"Pierre is too. Gemini, I mean. My Playgirl is in Four so I'm ready to be amused. How do you feel? It seemed like a long reality jump."

"I felt only a slight click as the transmission ended. The booth's lights didn't even flicker."

"What are conditions like in this Zone?"

"The reports indicate that the natives are Stage 11. Peaceable, familial-domestic and very materialistic. However, they explode easily when they sense a threat."

"Excellent," She exclaims. "There'll be good dress shops. I like the silk-money scent in the atmosphere. I'm burnt out on veils, Eight. I want mini-skirts and clacking high-heels. When will we score?"

"Geneva's the place for high heels."

AND INTRODUCING

She hated Algeria for the male chauvinism and the veils and the leering and the lack of style.

The Commodore is wearing the brown business suit bought for him by the Witch Bomber Bernadine Baez, when they were with the Weather Underground in Seattle, His hair is moderate. People vaguely remember seeing his face and assume he is a folk-rock singer from the 20th Century.

KATHERINE ANNE PORTER O'SHEA AS JUNO — 11

WHOSE SCRIPT FOR A HIGHLY SUCCESSFUL MOVIE (THE NUCLEAR CAFE?) MADE THIS NOT-SO-SIMPLE GIRL FROM ST. MORITZ PART OF THE INTER-NATIONAL FILM SET.

ANNA KATE'S BIG PROJECT IS TO FIND A MAN WORTH CARING ABOUT, BUT WHEN HER DREAM AT LAST BEGINS TO COME TRUE, IT ALMOST DESTROYS HER.

"I read an article on the plane about sexual fantasies," She confides.

"I'm having one right now." He wonders how long it will take him to get over his Her habit, *Solve et coagule*.

"Rape fantasies, harem fantasies, Catherine the Great wishes. She depoliticized 108 men in a single night. If you call such a night single. Trying to top Cleopatra's record. Do you want to hear my fantasy? A smart, funny call-girl goes to a fraternity house at Harvard. . ."

"Harvard doesn't have fraternity houses."

"That's your reality. In mine it does. And She initiates every one of the twenty four eager, downy-cheeked, clear-eyed young men. She shows them how to make love slowly and elegantly. They're very thankful. They worship Her and don't want Her to leave. But She walks out and they never find out who I am."

"Hmm. Is that little dark man still watching us?"

"He was watching *me*. He left chasing an Air France stewardess."

"What a simple planet. Politics, sex, and money. Let's see what the Swiss banker looks like."

"I've always wanted a Swiss banker."

"You remember the procedures?"

"Locate the narrow mind-band frequency used by the natives and transmit within its limits. Remain ready to take any role, adapt to any situation. Stay as comfortable as possible, and. . ."

"I do love you."

"Yes, it's too bad. Well, you know what I want. Just get me out of this heavy-G turbulance to a house in the Alps with a white picket fence and make me some babies and you'll give me another chance. If I feel up to it. We've had so many."

Their departure from the Airport is noted by seventeen Agents of thirteen Intelligence Bureaus.

-2-

COMMODORE

1. *an Evolutionary Agent responsible for a squardron of larval planets;*
2. *chief officer of a yacht club;*
3. *commander of a flotilla of Pleasure Craft.*

from Manual for Evolutionary Agents

A JUMPY PAIR

El Djamila, Algeria, April 1971

Think of them as impersonating Cary Grant and Marilyn Monroe, now cast as ex-members of the first group of Political Exiles from the American Empire, led by fugitive Eldridge Cleaver, whose *Panthers Noir* had been officially recognized by the bewildered Algerian government as an Authentic Liberation Front and given an embassy building in the hills of El Biar formerly occupied by the rightist Government of South Vietnam.

The glamour of belonging to an Official Government in Exile was soon dashed by the Generalissimo fantasies of Cleaver who turned out to be an avid admirer of General Amin Dada. Having escaped the custody and assassination threats of the would-be Papa Doc, they had found refuge in a hide-out beach hotel near Algiers where they lived under the menacing scrutiny of the CIA, protected both left and right by the ambidexterous Algerian government which had given them political asylum.

Home-less, country-less, species-less, carrying as concealed weapons only their six calibre brains, it is not surprising that they were forced to recognize their status as aliens to this warlike period, evolutionary scouts, as it were, trapped by gravity in a time warp, searching, not for a place to live but for a hospitable time.

These adventures had triggered a reaction common to those who have shared dangerous ordeals on galactic peripheries. They had become jumpy.

-3-

"The ability to time-jump across chrono-gaps from the freedom of high-velocity to the fixed whirlpool of star-systems, from the wave to the sandy shore, from the roll to the rock, without confusing frequencies is the mark of the Wizard. 'The Cosmic Dancer,' declares Joseph Campbell, 'does not rest heavily in a single spot, but gaily, lightly turns and leaps from one position to another.'"

Millenium Madness

AT THE BANKER'S HOUSE

Geneva, May 1971

In the seventh decade of the Roaring 20th Century there was to be found among the successful male impersonators of Geneva a polished young banker named Marcel Quenon, more prudent than ambitious and yet more ambitious than talented, who lived with his wife in an apartment built of solid stone.

"Ah there," says Marcel opening his door. "The famous Rock Star and his ravishing wife. Welcome, *mes amis.*"

Marcel smiles cynically and offers his soft dexterity. He is a sleek seal with plump cheeks.

"And may I present my wife, Lena?"

"We are honored to have such distinguished guests," says Lena, a wiry slim seal with soft blond pelt and arctic eyes (female). "Pierre has told us much about you. Did you come alone? Were you followed?"

"Our crew is two in number. And we were not followed as far as we can tell," replies the Commodore sending a Significant Glance to Her while Marcel and Lena are exchanging a Meaningful Nod of their own.

"You came in on your own passports? Please forgive our impertinent questions. You are most welcome. But we are not eager for publicity. We Swiss are so stuffy. Let me show you to your room."

The deep-carpet hallway is lined with Daumier engravings. Marcel waves his hand carelessly as they pass the enormous living room, lush with deep sofas, gleaming woodwork, glass coffee table and two Renoirs splashing colors off the wall.

"*Tres Bourgeois,* you are thinking. We Swiss are so addicted to tawdry comfort."

The bedroom is large. Fur-rugs and acres of light blue silk on a king-size bed.

"Some change from stern Arab socialism," says Eight.

"I'm ready for a decadent streak." She lights a cigarette, coughs, kicks off Her shoes and carefully arranges Herself on the sahara folds of the bed. "You plotted the coordinates of this time-jump very skillfully, my husband. Your unconventional approach to eight-dimensional solitaire seems to have some advantages. What's the scattering amplitude?"

"Forty-four, I think. Four-brained organisms, very domesticated, late industrial society. Family style. Weekend hedonism. Suburban wife-swapping. One generation away from singularity. And bear in mind that this sector is the base for every espionage agency and counter-intelligence network in the world.

"Pierre says this is where Sophia Loren came to get her baby," She sighs shyly.

-4-

Proverbs for Paranoids, 1: You may never get to touch the Master, but you can tickle his creatures.

Thomas Pynchon
in GRAVITY'S RAINBOW

THE PHILOSPHER IS CONFUSED, AGAIN!

El Djamila, Algeria, April 1971

Each morning Dylan would rise, bathe in the liquid medium of the planet, remove his whiskers with a teflon blade, dress in the artificial covering favored by the natives, walk across the village square to the sea-side restaurant and continue his shuffling of the neurogenetic cards that could map them out of captivity.

He would sit at a table next to the glass windows overlooking the Middle-earth Sea, tide-flecked with sliver spume and shiny black scallops of oil-tar flushed from ballast tanks. The waiter, Mohammed himself, a thin, sallow Kabyl from the Rif mountains with wispy mustache and greasy apron brought two white pots containing thick black coffee and milk steaming with bubbles. And a felt pen, an ancient device used for inscribing manual hieroglphics.

The Philosopher would deal 48 icon-cards of the Hesse Bead Game in the seven present slots and make the linkages. Playing the Game of Life to find the navigational coordinates for the next move on the dangerous political board. A flight which had become necessary after several futile and frustrating debates with Black Panthers who stubbornly claimed that there was only one Revolution, copyrighted by them, featuring their new offensive tactic—Violent Rhetoric.

The Commodore's protests that this was simplistic Newtonian thinking enraged the suspicious Cleaverites who were, at the time, exchanging intercontinental extinction threats with one Huey Newton (no relation) for control of the miniscule party. Equally intolerable were the Song Writer's Einsteinian precriptions for non-violent political change lyricized in the ancient Gurdjieffian campaign slogan, *Revolution Without Revelation is Tyranny. Revelation Without Revolution is Slavery.* At which, taking him at his word, the Cleaverites promptly clapped the Alien Prophet and his Luscious Co-reveler into a home-made prison using primitive tactics rigoroulsy rehearsed by the six-man armed force of the Panther Field Marshall, who rejoiced in his chance to put White Soul in Black Hole. It was just a training exercise, he joked later.

Back in the restaurant Eight watched extraterrestrial seagulls wheel over the bay in graceful winged defiance of the Laws of Land and small fishing smacks slide out of port past stone breakwaters along the old pirate-slaver coast.

-5-

FOOLISHNESS FIRST

"Few events can have carried such a clear cosmic message as the running of the Kentucky Derby, May 12, 1975. While two horses fought for the lead, a third came up from behind and walked away with the purse. The two horses intent only on bumping each other for the favored position were Avatar and Diabolo. Avatar means a deity. Diabolo means devil. So while the deity contended with Lucifer, who dashed home first? Foolish Pleasure. Let that be a happy lesson for us all."

Letter to Time by Richard Goldwater

EXPLORERS OF THE NEWLY DISCOVERED BRAIN

Michael Horowitz Archives

The Agent Dylan discovered his brain during a "magic mushroom" ceremony in Mexico, August 1960. This neural activation was standard psyber-flash, long-term memory gain, standard retrieval of reincarnation memories. The sudden revelation of the neuro-verse formerly described in vague Buddhist concepts, basic Hindu brain disorder. Wall-to-wall erotics ignored in the cosmological hurricane. Flash distracting flesh.

He lay on couch next to lush bikini girl, her hand slid into his taffy musculature setting off membrane bombs beyond orgasm. Her divinity emerges as a classic Semetic statue alive and wiggling.

First time he had ventured out beyond body brain into gene grids. Every tense organ cheerfully alert.

The focus kept sliding down kaleidoscopic brain drains.

Rapture signals drowned in Niagras of data. Data.

After this discovery, the Agent Dylan paddled back, as everyone did in that crude exploratory period, to the comforting shores of social role. The young song writer from Minnesota with a head full of ideas that were driving him sane.

Back at Cambridge, in the laboratory founded by Woody Guthrie, he joined a team of graduate students and young instructors to explore these uncharted continents of inner-geography.

They jokingly called themselves cyber-nauts. (The word "cyber" is the Greek word for "pilot" one who navigates skillfully and thinks for him or herself.)

The maps of mysticism, Buddhism, gnosticism, and fruit-loopy occultism were studied and noted as confirmation of the infinite complexity of the info-world.

Aldous Huxley, Alan Watts, Georges Gurdjieff, Jayne Loader and Aleister Crowley, John Lilly, Richard Alpert, Ralph Metzner were seen as the Columbus, Vespucci and Magellans of the brain.

The Harvard Psychedelic Research Projectors were launching out with the drug psilocybin in the context of philosophic discovery and psychological research. They quickly learned the basic lessons of "set-and-setting," the effect of the external environment on vulnerable, exposed brain-film. They played Vivaldi, furnished the experiment rooms with "Art"—oriental rugs, paintings by great masters, flowers, sea-shells.

Records indicate that Dylan took psilocybin more than a hundred times during the first two years of his research but he apparently never engaged his erotic machinery. He had predictably imprinted the role of species-pilot, gyroscopic figure navigating his mind in the "search for truth" and to the benevolent role of protector-guide.

Then Flora Lu Ferguson arrived to change all that.

WHAT DOES WOMAN WANT?

-6-

"The Rapture Imprint discovers the Body as instrument of freedom-pleasure, as hover-craft to be used, not just for survival, not for power, not to work for the gene-pool, not for sexual status, but for brain exploration. Joy-riding the body becomes an hedonic art. The aesthetic of the natural."

Jerry Casale in Info-Psychology

A GUIDED TOUR OF SWITZERLAND

Geneva, May 1971

The Banker Marcel leads the fugitives into the white and gold regency dining-room. After the women are seated he nests himself at the head of the table and nods to the Italian servant.

"I've a veritable mania for really good smoked salmon," says Marcel, his pink face smiling. "And some ice-cold Vodka? Not the watery stuff you Americans serve in your martinis. This is the true Wolfschmidt from Riga. You'll have some with your smoked salmon?"

"If you please," She says shyly.

The maid puts racks of fresh toast on the linen table cloth and a silver dish of Danish butter.

"And some champagne to celebrate your liberation from the Socialists and your welcome arrival in the Land of Democracy. Some Dom Perignon has been awaiting you on ice."

"You two have had an adventurous life, to say the least," says Lena through a mouthful of buttered toast.

Eight reaches for another slice of smoked salmon from the silver dish. It has the sharp, cold-sea flavor of Scandinavia—very different from the weak glutinous texture of the Highland curers. The vodka in the frosted glass is fire on ice.

"We are about ready to come in from the cold," She answers cunningly.

Marcel tilts the vodka glass to his mouth and pats his face with a napkin.

"Good," he says. "Switzerland is the right place for you. We think of our land as an island of peace and sanity in a troubled world. Here, I regret to say, we have no excitement. We are, let me confess, a rather boring folk. What have we contributed to the world? The Cuckoo clock? The Pulsar Watch? William Tell is our only claim to fame. After Tell can you name one Swiss who has contributed anything to world culture?"

"I can," says the Philosopher, warming to the challenge.

"Carl Jung, perhaps the greatest psychologist of his time. Piaget. Duhrematt. Calvin. Zwingli. Bill. Bernouilli. Alain Tanner. Not to forget Paracelsus, certainly one of the most perceptive minds the west has produced. I wonder if your modesty is playful, my dear Marcel."

"Not to mention Basel drug firms like Sandoz, Leonardo, Giotto and Raphael," She says sweetly, "as mentioned in the Orson Welles Script. Didn't Orson live in Switzerland?"

Lena and Marcel exchange a quick glance.

"Very good," continues Marcel. "I am glad to see you like good movies. Now can you name any Swiss politicians or military leaders? You can't? Exactly. You see, we prefer to keep everything quite boring. Elimination of friction is the ideal of the engineered society. When we want excitement, there's no problem, Gods know, to find it. It's an hour to Paris. A short flight to Rome or Beirut of Tangier, or even Belfast. Lots of our youngsters rushed off to join both sides in the Six Day War. Arriving there on the seventh day, happily."

"We get the message," she says, smiling, to dull the primates' suspicions. "We'd like to enroll in a Swiss Boring School and learn how."

"You have made a wise choice. We Swiss are not very creative. We don't have to be. The Creator did it all for us. Perched us up here in these high valleys surrounded by the loftiest peaks in Europe. Let me speak frankly. We think of Switzerland as an intelligence test. If you are clever enough to figure out how to scale the mountains and find your way here, you will discover what the philosophers have said to be the goals of life—peace, tranquility, health, wealth, comfort, natural beauty, unobtrusive technological efficiency.

"You make planetary life sound like a paradise," She says. "And you were too modest to mention the cooking. The cutlets are superb. I could cut them with a fork. And the Hollandaise sauce is cerebellar."

"But I must say," continues the host, "we do not go in for Valhalla-Olympian adventures! Let Jupiter rule the world from Moscow or Washington. Let Mars have the Middle-East; Vulcan, Pittsburg; Copenhagen, naked Venus. Let us say that Switzerland is a paradise for retired heroes and beautiful heroines to relax after their triumphs. To enjoy the material fruits of their success."

"Exactly what I want," She says. "To taste the fruits of success."

"It was my impression," says the burnt-out Pop Star, "that Switzerland was famous for the asylum offered to philosophic exiles: Vladimir Ilyich Lenin, Jean Jacques Rousseau, Thomas Pynchon, Hermann Hess, Jayne Loader, Charlie Chaplin, James Joyce, Miguel Servatus."

"And King Farouk," adds Lena.

After the asparagus the Folk Singer has little appetite for the thin slivers of fresh pineapple. He spills the last of the ice-cold champagne into his glass, holds it high in toast to host.

"Have you thought of which part of the country you would like to live in?" asks Lena. "The south has combined the best of Italy with the essence of *La Suisse*. The north is really like a different land to us. Swiss-German. But really every Swiss city—like the Italian city-states—has its own flavor. Bern is truly the land of the mystical melancholy bear. Basel is like your San Francisco, liberal, *avant-garde*, intellectual. Zurich, hard, smooth, money and machines. And we here, around the lake, I fear, are not much more than suburbanites of Paris."

"I believe Pierre wishes us to stay here in Geneva," replied the Minstrel. "Is it difficult to find housing?"

"No problem at all," says Marcel. "As a banker I shall be glad to help you get your money here. And my dear Lena can arrange for you to spend it.

Did you know she is a real-estate agent and manager of several new apartments?"

"How perfect for us," She whispers, turning Her petal towards Lena. Marcel clasps his plump hands in pleasure.

"*Parfait*. Now I suppose that we move to the living room for coffee and brandy. Lena can show you pictures of her flats and you can decide on a place to live."

-7-

"*Bliss can become an addiction. Certain sense organs can be fixated as 'rapture-islands'. Aesthetically pleasing stimuli become associated with hedonic rewards: sensory chauvinism. Special sounds, ordors, tastes, touches, somatic reactions. The marijuana ritual. Erotic sequences. Hedonic styles. Stage 13 can become a repetitious satin-trap as the history of leisure classes testifies.*"

Larry Flint in Exo-Psychology

EXIT VISAS!

El Djamila, Algeria, April 1971

She was a Temple Dancer running gracefully across the square, smiling joyfull, waving to catch the attention of the Exiled Prince. Your dream girl from the menthol cigarette ads. She was Honeymoon in Picturesque Algeria. Fly me to the Mediterranean.

The Minstrel Philosopher and Mohammed waved back in sincere appreciation. So it was, making the daily movie with Her, endless Marilyn Love Scenes, breathless entree, the call-girl jokes, agile exits with wry throw-away lines and the ever-changing stamen-petal commericals.

Mohammed returned with four white pots and rubbed his brown hand on the back of the empty chair as he smiled at Her.

She leaned Her head on Husband Shoulder and whispered innocently in his ear. "What are those cards you are shuffling comrade Pavlov? Explain everything. It's what I always wanted."

"What have you always wanted, woman?"

"To be a Professor's Fred Mac Murray's wife, you lucky man."

"But you are not Comrade Ivanova," he said sharply.

"I am."

"You are not. Although my pattern-recognition circuits are not complete, they have distinguished several distinct differences between you and Comrade Ivanova. You are much more beautiful! Who are you? What do you really want?"

"I want you to take me to a place where I'll feel good all the time. I WoMan want you to perfect your anti-gravity machine."

The Commodore points to the cards lined up on the table cloth.

"Well, the first step will be to go to Denmark where we are invited to give a lecture on Political Revolution."

"If the Algerians give us an exit visa."

"But we have stumbled on the secret of Neurological Immigration.

"Which offends the Revolting Politicians."

"You cannot imagine the thrill," he said pointing to the cards," to see the perfection of this numerical code which plots the course of human evolution. The deciphering will soon be finished. The Revolutionary Fundamentalists must not be allowed to censor this information."

"Pour me some coffee and continue," She murmured reverently.

"The First Phase of Terrestrial Evolution is Biological Survival. Amoeboid politics. Kill or be killed. 'Off the Pig,' as our erstwhile captors would say. The colonel's junta. But Violent Revolutions lasts only as long as Victor keeps his itchy finger on the trigger and that's all it changes. We have succeeded in escaping our armed captors. Thus we have evolved from line one to line two. Do you understand?"

"Do not be deceived by my appearance, Professor. Just because my dimensions seem to have been worked out by a well-programmed computer and my equally spectacular brain does not show beneath my sun-streaked coppery hair. Pray continue."

"The Second Phase of Terrestrial Evolution is Barnyard Politics. Change the power-system and the downs become the new leaders of the pack. Politics changes only the name of the tax-collector and the possessor of the key to the prison cell, the exec. bathroom and the key to the black Jag-Cad that goes with it. Mammalian push-pull to get on top. That's where we are trapped right now. Trying to get exit visas—can you believe that cosmic concept;—*Exit visas*, from an animal farm government."

"Exist visas? Is this a prison?

-8-

"How did Rotwang meet the Aliens? Well, one day a very simple thing happened; Rotwang got stoned! The Aliens gassed him through the open window. Now the Aliens had been doing this sort of thing for years. It was part of their scientific study of the Earth thing. They developed a gas which put Earthlings into a light trance state."

ROTWANG by Tim Hildebrand

NEAL CASSADAY TAKES CHARGE

Harvard University, Cambridge, Massachusetts, October, 1960

Commodore Dylan who, to the amazement and amusement of the knowledgeable, had been offically designated and widely renowned as Spokeman for the Harvard Psychedelic Research Project, sat behind the desk of his large corner office and observed the physiology of his secretary, a lovely Chinese woman. Jewel, as she was called, stood in the doorway and looked down at the Philosopher with affectionate concern.

"Are you braced for your next appointment?"

"Who?"

"He's the poet from New York who was so insistent and dropped all those names. Says he's a friend of Ginsberg, Kerouac, Burroughs, and Baudelaire. I must warn you. He's horny and disreputable." He certainly is, thought the Commodore, as his vistor entered. Swaggering, handsome, macho, longish hair, blue jeans, baseball jacket. (This was, in 1960, most anachronistic garb, especially in an Ivy League setting. Ed.)

"I am Neal Cassady. I'm a beatnik. Ever met one before?"

"Can't say that I have," said the bewildered Alchemist.

"I wanna talk to you about this here research your doing. It interests my people."

"I appreciate your support. But what can Scientific Exploration of the Brain and Altered States of Consciousness have to do with poetry, jazz, existential nihilism and Naked Lunches?"

"We've been using dope for poetic purposes for centuries, man. Don't you know that?"

"Marijuana and opium take one to such low altitudes. Have a Salem?"

"Don't mind if I do," said Cassady. "Or could I turn you on to some heavy gauge?"

"I beg your pardon?"

"Gauge. Boo. Mary Jane. Muggles. Would you like to smoke a reefer?"

"I'm afraid not. We use only legal drugs in our experimentation."

The Commodore and his guest lit filter-tip mentholated cigarettes and regarded each other uneasily.

"What is this research you are doing?"

"We are giving a series of new drugs, consciousness-expanding substances to volunteers under a variety of sets and settings to chart unknown phenomenological territories to explore the info-worlds of the brain."

"What new drugs?" asked the vistor, brightening up.

"Psilocybin. Mescaline. Lysergic acid."

"Groovy. I've done the Magic Mushrooms in Oaxaca. And I've done peyote with the Navaho. But LSD is new. And I'd really dig taking the pill form of the mushrooms. Psilocybin you call it? Can you lay some on me?"

"I can't give you the drug. But perhaps you could become a volunteer pilot in one of our experiments. We are interested in administering the experience to artists because they seem more articulate in describing post-literal experiences.

"What are these experiments?"

"We have a staff of about twenty-five young professors and graduate students — mainly from the behavioral sciences and the Divinity School. We are training them to conduct psychedelic sessions."

"Shaman training, eh? Sounds good. How do you do it?"

"Mainly by having them take the drug with the novitiate pilots they are guiding."

"Teaching them to turn on, eh?"

"Turn on?"

"The art of getting high."

"I see what you mean," said the Bard. "We've found that with adequate preparation, subjects have little trouble and can master the fears involved."

"Fears? How do you prepare them for that?"

"We have them read some of the literature. And protocols written by other subjects."

Cassady shook his head dubiously. "You make it soud so dangerous."

"Yes," admitted the Folk Singer. "You are right. My first experience with these substances was in a garden next to a swimming pool with a pretty woman. I was too unprepared to have anything but a good time. But the atmosphere, even in an enlightened place like Harvard, reeks with fear of the strange, the new and particularly of the word drug. There is a deep-seated taboo against brain exploration. It violates their notion of artifical predictability. Gene-pool worship. So we've had to deal with that reality. We've had to build up the aura of safeguards and guidance to counter-act the taboo. Otherwise no one would want the experience."

At this the eccentric visitor clapped both of his hands together in glee and hooted with laughter. "Dread! Not want the experience! Man, what are you talking about? I should think you'd be driving away candidates with sticks."

"It's true that the undergraduates are eager for the experience, but we aren't allowed to use them as subjects. The older the subject, the more fear seems to exist. I guess they're afraid of losing something that the young haven't gotten attached to. We have had some dramatic scenes before the sessions, I can tell you."

"What do you mean?"

"Well, last Saturday morning, for example, I drove to the home of a faculty member in the Divinity School to pick him up. We don't allow subjects to drive their own cars to the sessions so that they don't have to drive home under the influence. When the young professor opened the door he was pale and sweating with fear. The parting scene with his family was tragic. He wife was in tears. His kids were grabbing him by the legs begging him not to do it. Mass hysteria."

"About taking a day off to get high? Man, you gotta be kidding. What are they afraid of?"

"You must realize that the cybernetic experience is totally new to this culture. They sense that they are going to be changed and they both want this desperately and fear it."

"That's terrible. You've got to stop this nonsense. You're defiling and corrupting something that is beautiful and should be spontaneous. Why, you're running a defloration clinic where people can regain their spiritual virginity in a sanitized, mental health situation."

"I hear you," said the Commodore glumly. "But what can I do? If we weren't doing it this way, it wouldn't be done at all. No one knows anything about this kind of experimental mysticism. We're doing our best. We've read everything that's been written in the last four thousand years on the subject."

"That's a laugh. It's oral history, man. Almost nothing gets printed about what really happens in history. What you read is genetic fantasy."

"What do you mean?"

"Sex and drugs. The history books and philosophers write about meaningless, public events like wars and elections and revolutions. But the only important things that happen to individuals are bodily wisdom and brain exploration. And that's the great secret of human life that they never talk about."

"I didn't know that," said the Pop Star.

-9-

"Resurrection of the Body—the amused, liberation retracting the body from terrestrial imprints, the discovery that one is not a robot, that the body can be experienced as a self-directed time-machine.

The Game of Life

MR. TERROR KNOCKS ON THE DOOR! AGAIN!

Geneva, May 1971

Lena presides at breakfast. Fluffy scrambled eggs, crisp golden bacon, flaky French rolls, tall glasses of thick, creamy milk, fresh roast coffee brewed dark and pungent.

"The confiture comes from a farm we own in the Vallais," says Lena.

"Alive," She says, "every mouthful."

"Fresh and homegrown," says Lena. "We hope we can keep it that way." She motions to a manila folder next to her plate. "And now let's plan our day. We'll spend what's left of the morning looking at the apartments you liked last night. Then we'll meet Marcel for lunch. And then some shopping. *Apres* Algeria you'll enjoy the boutiques."

"And perhaps, the hairdressers," She murmurs tossing her head shyly.

"Of course. I've made us appointments for five at Atila's. Marcel spoke of driving down the lake to a charming country restaurant. And, oh yes, Pierre Bensousan called before you were awake. He and Anita will be here tomorrow to make business plans about your record albums, the book and publishers and posters and some movie offers Pierre has been exploring. Now that you're becoming an adopted Swiss we're going to put you to work making money like the rest of us."

Lena pauses in her cheerful narration and frowns. "That's strange. I just heard the front door open."

Marcel walks in the dining room looking haggard, mopping his face with a white handkerchief. He sits down heavily.

"Terrible news," he gasps. "It's in the afternoon paper. I just saw an early edition. The university people in Denmark. The fools. When you didn't show up as expected they notified the Danish government and the press that you've been kidnapped by the CIA. Disappeared mysteriously between

Algiers and Copenhagen. Interpol is looking for you. The American embassy denies any knowledge. The Swiss police will be combing the country. *Quel scandal!*"

"That sounds dangerous," says Lena biting her lip thoughtfully.

"Dangerous? What could happen to us?" asks Dylan.

"Dangerous for us," exclaims Marcel. "I'm sorry. I must apologize. But you must realize our delicate situation. I am a banker you know. We like you and would have enjoyed having you as our guests here in Geneva. But in my business. . .and the government is so strict."

"What do you propose?" asks Lena.

"I've just talked to Pierre in Paris. He says we should take them to Michel Hauchard in Lausanne. He can hide them until they find out what the situation is."

"Who is Michel Hauchard?"

"He's a French millionaire. Well-know International operator. Arms merchant. Smuggler. He's wanted himself by the French police and has arranged some sort of asylum here in Switzerland. Pierre said he might do the same for you. So, if you don't mind, I think you should pack your bags. I've taken the day off work and I'll run you down to Lausanne."

"Has Pierre called Michel?" Lena's voice is business like. "Are you sure he's there? He's always going off to Morocco or Beirut on business."

"Pierre doesn't risk phoning him. His wire is surely tapped. If he's not there we'll have to figure out something else."

"And our plans for the apartment and shopping and the wife-swapping party?"

"Must be postponed, I fear," says Marcel shaking his face. "And I forgot to mention; the dollar fell the day you arrived in Geneva. Figures, doesn't it?"

Then The Terror hits the Harassed Fugitive!

The Electricity of Panic overrides his circuits, paralyzing throat-thought, stopping flow of warm juice as blood drains away from comfort organs and paranoia hardens him into a worried stone-posture.

He looks at Marcel who has become the eternal, Pitiless Spectator at the Roman Colosseum (male) and Lena whose soft fibers are retracting into a cold coral reef (neuter).

Time to flick the dial, he thinks, staggering to the control panel.

He joins the thumb and index finger of his right hand to form a circle, and, like movie director framing-the-shot, peers through the digital aperture. He places Marcel's pink-face in the center of the circle then moves his eye-focus to his own hand examining his thumb nail, the black hair on his fore-finger, his tanned wrist. Marcel's face has now dissolved into two pink blobs shimmering liquidly in the background.

The relieved Fugitive then snaps his fingers and ends the scene. She watches, nodding in approval. "Clear it?"

-10-

"With a spontaneous sense of recognition, Rotwang welcomed them into his home. . .'Relax, I'm your friend. I knew you'd be coming to Earth some day, but I didn't know when. Welcome to our part of the Universe.' The Aliens had never run into a person like Rotwang before. Usually the subjects behaved as if they were drugged or happy. Most could hardly talk at all—they'd lay there smirking and smiling while the Aliens took memory shots and entered their minds looking for a few answers or maybe some music. Rotwang wasn't at all passive. His body had been slowed down and his mind speeded up. He was more than ready for them."

from ROTWANG by Tim Hildebrand

A LECTURE BY NEAL CASSADY

Harvard University, Cambridge, Massachusetts, October 1960

"This is most fascinating," exclaimed the innocent spokesman of the Harvard University Psychedelic Research Project, in response to his visitor's enigmatic remarks about neuroerotics. "I'd like to know more about this, ah, theory."

"I take it," said Cassady, "that you are not aware of the fact that all modern religions and philosophies derive from pre-monotheistic drug-cults and sex-magic rites?"

"I've read a bit of Frazier," replied the Commodore, a bit defensively. "But that's all primitive stuff. And Robert Gordon Wasson is an impressionable fool."

"You're not aware of the fact that English literature of the 19th Century was almost entirely drug inspired? Not to mention dopers like Poe, Samuel Clemens, Robert Louis Stevenson. Nor to mention the main stream of English poetry for the last three centures. Didn't you know that the great minds of the last generation—Freud, Joyce, Gurdjieff, Crowley—derived their wisdom from the same alchemy? My God, man, don't you know that there are several thousand of the wisest human beings who ever lived hanging around New York City right now waiting to try your drugs? People who really know how to use chemicals and move neurons around like chess-masters?"

"Why, that's fantastic," cried the Bard. "I freely admit that we don't know what we're doing with these drugs. If it's true that people exist who have this kind of inner skill, I want to meet them and learn from them."

"I assure you that will be no problem," answered Cassady dryly. "Do you ever go to New York?"

"I'll come at a moment's notice," said the goodhearted Academician. "How can I contact these authorities?"

"Here," said Cassady scribbling on a piece of paper, "is a number in New York where you can contact me. Phone a day in advance and I'll set up a, shall we say, seminar, for you?"

"I'll come down next Saturday. Will that be convenient?"

"Groovy. In the meantime, why don't I fuck your head up with a few little corny Sufi tricks. Will you be turning on before Saturday?"

"As a matter of fact, we have an experiment planned for tomorrow night."

"Okay. During your voyage take out this piece of paper and meditate about these words."

Cassady wrote:
"LIVE—EVIL"

"Have you ever seen that before?"

"I can't say I've seen that palindrome before," replied the straight-minded Professor.

"Then ponder this one."
"LIVED—DEVIL"

"And this one."
"GOD—DOG"

"And this one."
"DNA—AND"

"These words will have more meaning for you when your brain is accelerated and loosened fom lettered servitude," said the Beatnik, noticing the puzzled look on the Professor's face.

"And IRELAND breaks down to I RE—LAND. That should be enough clues for your next, ah, experiment."

"Well," says Dylan. "Ireland, is a strange and fascinating place."

Cassidy smiles, takes a look at the clock, jitters a bit strangely and replies, "There is more to Ireland than meets the eye. A genetic truth, almost yet unrecognized is emerging there. I am no sooth-sayer, but you are deeply linked to its past and future."

-11-

"It is unwise to seek admirers when one is falling to bits."

Jayne Loader in "Between Pictures"

A VERY FRIGHTENED SWISS BANKER

Geneva, May 1971

Marcel trembles as they carry the bags to the car, which he has craftily parked in the rear of his building. As they drive along the freeway he glances nervously in the rear view mirror (always a dubious maneuver) and chain-smokes. Slient in thought.

Suddenly, with muttered curse, he leans on the horn and pulls out to pass a red Fiat, shaking his fist and making throwing motions out the window.

"What's happening?" asks Eight.

"*Salaud.* Irresponsible criminal! Did you see what he did?"

Marcel's jowls quiver in outrage. "He threw a cigarette package out of the window of his car."

"Good grief," She gasps. "What's the crime? What was in the package?"

"Empty. What crime? Don't you understand? Out the window— on the road. Littering! We don't like that here."

"Speaking of crime," She says, "can you tell us anything more about this man upon whose mercy we are about to throw ourselves?"

"Hauchard? A scoundrel, I suppose. Euro-trash adventurer. But he's rich and that makes him respectable enough. Guns are more legal than drugs, you know. He's one of the most flamboyant spenders in Switzerland. Rolls Royce. Big boat on the lake. Chalet in Gstaad. Private airplanes."

"Well that's a relief," She sighs. "I mean, I guess it's a relief. I'd been imagining a shabby heroin dealer's pad down by the railroad station."

"If he likes you, he can do much for you. He's unpredictable. Most people despise him for his arrogance. Rather French you know. But he spends like a sultan and that tends to excuse many sins."

"Listen," continues Marcel. "I have a sincere request to make. I hope you'll understand. If it should happen that you are questioned by the Swiss police, if possible, would you not mention my name? Or say you stayed with us? My business, you know, is so delicate. And if they were to know we harbored you, the could cause us trouble."

Marcel shakes his head in a shuddering motion.

"They might come to our apartment to search and rip open the furniture, tear up the floors, anything."

"Looking for us?" She asked in surprise.

"Looking for you? No. Looking for drugs, or communist literature, Hong Kong chocolate bars, fake stock certificates, Japanese Cuckoo clocks, ANYTHING!"

"My dear Marcel," says the Doctor reassuringly. "We are most grateful to you and Lena for your hospitality. We understand your situation and will do nothing to burn you."

"*Merci bien,*" mutters Marcel hunched over the wheel and darting looks in the rear-view mirror. "We're being followed, you realize."

-12-

"The most striking symbol of the Tarot Card (Empress) is the stylized Valentine 'Heart' which is the Disneyland pop symbol of Love. The real meaning of this ritual icon, (which has little resemblance to the cardiac structure) would be shocking to those who flaunt it for commercial purposes. THe Valentine Heart is obviously a hieroglyphic for the Female rapture-organ, engorged, distended, pink-with-arousal, bisceted on top by the clitoral dimple."

Jim Goode in The Game of Life

STILL ANOTHER FLIGHT PLAN

El Djamila, Algeria, April 1971

She arched Her spine, stretched Her back muscles and wished they were in bed. She looked out at the sea and wished it were July lying on the hot sand, feeling warm sun-tongue on Her body and the welcome cold shock of salt water.

She watched Mohammed setting up the luncheon self-serve tables, cold-slaw already wilted, tired pickled herring, muddy-pink shrimp, yesterday's sliced beets, dessicated disks of salami, grey rubble-piles of potato salad and flies circling in anticipation.

Regular patrons, they had long since exhausted the novelty of government menus. Socialist cuisine. She thought. The French taught them form but the aesthetic sense and style can't be imposed on slaves. Shabby, ersatz, muddle-class technical socialism pasted over Arab slave-master harsh, desert simplicity.

She tried to get Mohammed to fling Her across his saddle and gallop across the pure desert where sand-dune brilliance hurts Her eyes, to the dark, cavern-cool of skin tent, soft with Ethiope rugs, piles of dates on burnished plates and Her cunt moist like a camel in heat.

But the flies kept circling around the goat-milk, warm and sour in hairy skin-sacks and no hot water.

She looked at Eight's face smiling with alchemical excitement and felt at home again. It was the only home She had in that solar system.

"It's a brilliant revelation," She said, "but it's too Eight for me. I'm stuck at fleshy Thirteen. Can we put just a tiny touch of common sense around it? How does it feel? What's its flavor? Let's get some more hot coffee. The baker just arrived with the bread warm from his oven and the strawberry jam is fresh. How strange, I feel optimistic again. Wanna fly me to Geneva?"

-13-

"Soon after the first contact, the Aliens were busy helping Rotwang with the dishes. Rotwang washed and they dried. Rotwang began whistling a song, 'Call Me up In Dreamland', and the Aliens immediately turned on their recording equipment. They told Rotwang they had over 100 million hours of Earth music in their collection. Rotwang kept whistling and the dishes were done in no time."

ROTWANG *by Time Hildebrand*

AN ANTHROPOLGICAL VISIT TO THE HIPPIES

New York, N.Y., October 1960.

The door to the apartment was opened by a slim young female disguised as a New York model. She wore tight blue jeans, tight sweater, long black hair falling down her back. Her feel were bare. She focused her cool grey eyes on the Professor.

"Come in, man, we've been waiting for you. I'm Salinas."

In the living room apartment Neal Cassady sprawled in an easy chair, waved a casual hand. "Greetings, doctor. Meet Bennie."

Bennie, a stocky young man with long hair, stands in the corner, hands held behind him, rocking back and forth solemnly; nodding. "Welcome, man. We're glad you're here."

Salinas moved to the wide couch and folded her legs under her.

"I've heard of you from Neal Cassady and from Betty Ann."

"Betty Ann from Vassar," said the Commodore.

"She was my room-mate there last year. She talked about you all the time."

"But now you're in New York."

"Yes, I decided to become a person. And everything. So I'm a model. And learning about life. And all. I'm chattering this way, man, because we've been freaking out waiting for your visit. We can't wait to begin, can we Bennie?"

Bennie rocked back and forth on his heels and nodded. "We've never done this psilocybin, man. We've done everything else. Every dope we've heard of, we've done."

"Done?"

"He means to do a drug; to take it," explained Schwartzenspeil. "Salinas and Bennie have had a great deal of experience in brain exploration, getting high. They're very eager to try your brain fuel."

"Very good," said Dylan nodding his head. "I have come to suspect that drugs open up important areas of the brain, areas that psychologists know almost nothing about."

"You're really too much, man," said Salinas leaning back against the couch gracefully. "You're just now turning on to the dimensions of the head?" She shot an amused look towards Cassady. "But I've got to hand that to you. At least you're beginning to realize what's left out of the text books. I was a Psych Major at Vassar for three years. Can you believe that?"

Bennie giggled and continued to rock.

"Did Cassady tell you about the experimental contract?"

"The what?" asked Salinas.

The Philosopher regarded her with admiration. She was the most beautiful and sophisticated creature he had ever seen.

"The contract. I'll provide you with the drugs. You take them and tell me what you experienced. I'm particularly interested in how psilocybin compares with other drugs you have taken. I don't think that any other psychopharamocologist has been able to collect this kind of phenomenological comparative data."

"You mean, man you want us to get off on your thing and then compare it with other drugs we've done?"

"Exactly. The opinion of experienced subjects is invaluable."

"And you get paid by Harvard for doing this kind of research? Is he putting us on Neal?" she said looking to Cassady.

"When you took Introductory Psychology, didn't they teach you about the Introspectionist experiments of Wundt, Fechner and Titchener?" said the Philosopher.

"You mean comparing colors and weights and sounds," said Salinas dubiously. "That always seemed so dull."

"They called it psychophysics. It was the first scientific psychology; the first attempt to systematically correlate external stimuli with internal sensation."

"But where are your brass instruments, Professor?"

"The stimulus in this experiment is a chemical. It's external. See, here it is. You can see it, touch it, measure it in milligrams. We'll simply apply the stimulus. It opens up new synaptic areas of your brain.

The Commodore took a small vial from his pocket and spilled out a few dozen sky blue pills on the coffee table. Salinas gasped in surprise and leaned forward wetting Her lips. Bennie moved quickly from the corner and, hands still clasped behind his back, leaned over the table in fascination. Cassady knelt in front of the table and poked the blue pills with his finger. His dark eyes were glittering.

"How much is a dose," he said hoarsely.

"One pill is the dose Sandoz suggests. Two is what most experimenters have used. Six is what we have found to be a moderate dose. Ten takes you where no human has been before.

"What's the most anyone has taken?" asked Salinas.

"Twelve."

"Who took twelve?"

"I did."

"Then I want twelve," She said.

"Body weight is a factor," added the Philosopher. He measured the svelte lines of the slender model. "I'd say twelve for me would be eight for you."

"Are you going to tell us how many to take?" asked Bennie.

"No. We try to avoid Doctor-patient games."

"You mean you'll turn on with us?" said Salinas in surprise.

"Of course. I want my brain to be operating at the same speed and elevation as yours."

"Wow. You're too much, man. You're blowing my mind."

"I beg your pardon," said the Commodore who found it difficult to comprehend the new patois.

"You're copping my head, man. I confess I underestimated you. Okay, man, you're the dealer. Tell us what to take. Right Neal?"

Cassady smiled and nodded.

"All right," said the Philosopher briskly. "None of us know what we are doing, but we've established a crude sort of trust. So I suggest that, based on body weight, we three men take ten pills and Salinas six. Well, let's say eight. All right? Do you have any fruit juice?"

"Yeah, man," said Salinas softly.

"And some crystal glasses with long stems."

Salinas stopped at the door to the kitchen. "This is getting more interesting by the moment. Tell me, man, what else would you like for your experiment?"

"Candle light would be pleasant," said the Alchemist. "This 60 cycle frequency gets to be a bore."

"Groovy," said Bennie with unexpected emotion.

Neal Cassady smiled.

-14-

Proverbs for Paranoids, 2: The innocence of the creatures is in inverse proportion to the immorality of the Master.

Thomas Pynchon in "Gravity's Rainbow"

POLITICAL ASYLUM IN THE LAP OF LUXURY

Lausanne, May 1971

As the highway enters Lausanne, Marcel swings right following the sign *Port d'Ouchy* down a road which runs by the lake. He parks in front of a new, luxurious highrise building surrounded by lush landscaping.

"We'll leave your bags in the car until we find out what happens."

Marcel studies the bell panel in the foyer, pushes a button and then speaks in low French. The buzzer rasps. The fugitives enter the elegant lobby and quickly move to the lift. Marcel punches the button PH-D.

"That's me," says Dylan. "U.C. Berkeley. 1950."

"What's you?" asks Marcel absently.

"Penthouse D. In psychology. Is he home?"

Marcel smiles nervously. The elevator opens onto a private landing. Marcel rings the bell. The door opens immediately. Standing tall in the entrance, a cold appraising look on his face, is the ruddy-faced, silver-maned biped from the Geneva airport. He bows formally and waves them in. A huge German police dog thunders up quivering with menace.

"Kay Beck, Alle," commands Monsieur Hauchard. The dog drops its tail and slinks to the corner.

"What an unusual name," She says hopefully. "Is it Belgian?"

"It's a city in Canada," whispers the Commodore.

Monsieur Hauchard leads them down a hundred foot living room which faces out through glass doors to a terrace overlooking Lac Leman. At the end of the room two beautiful female earthlings sit lifting flower faces in expectation.

Monsieur Hauchard stands with his back to the windows, a pensive look in his petulant face.

"How strange," he hisses to the Philosopher. "I thought Pierre said you were Algerian and I mistook you for German. German!"

Turning to the room Monsieur Hauchard waves his hand and draws back his facial muscles to show his teeth.

"May I present Dee Dee and our charming visitor from Rome, Antonia. You remember Marcel Guinon from Geneva? And now his distinguished American guests."

Dee Dee, young, fresh, given to undulating curves and bursting fruit-blossoms, reclining on the soft cushions of the voluptuous sofa watches the scene with aristocratic amusement. Antonia, Italian starlet-style, nods silently and turns her sullen face to look at the lake. Beautiful and stoned thinks the Philosopher, glancing for confirmation at his Companion who has suddenly become a starlet herself, no other than Marilyn waiting with breathless timidity to be cast in *How to Marry a Millionaire*. The philosopher raises his eyebrows and She suddenly becomes Jaqueline Kennedy paying a state visit to Charles de Gaulle.

Dee Dee, a natural born female impersonator (Stage 3, Taurus) rubs her silken finger across her nose. "Haven't I seen you somewhere? At Deauville last season was it?"

"No, I don't think so," She says, turning up the candle-power. "We were at El Djamila."

"El Djamila! How chic! I've never heard of it." Dee Dee's English is British nanny-finishing school. Monsieur Hauchard watches the scene with the appraising approval of a thoroughbred owner. Antonia swings her sultry face in a lazy indolent loop, licks her lips and turns back to the lake. Mandrax, decides the Bard; lustful Italian quaaludes.

"It's an undiscovered fishing port outside of Algiers. And, I must confess, it may have been discovered and deliberately un-discovered."

Somewhat reluctantly Monsieur Hauchard interrupts the charming proton exchange.

"Dee dee, *ma cher*, we men have something urgent to discuss in the study. Would you see if our charming visitor from El Djamila would like a drink?"

Sitting behind his desk Monsieur Hauchard turns to the Wizard and lifts his cheek muscles into a charming smile.

"I'm afraid I didn't get your name. I should know you by sight, but one tends to get provincial here."

Marcel takes over. "The Spokesman for His generation. The American Philosopher. The Maggie's Farm Scandal."

Hauchard pretends to look puzzled, but the Minstrel is not deceived by the feigned ignorance of the wily Frenchman.

Marcel switches to French explaining rapidly, Harvard, Hibbing, Minnesota, the Twins, the campaign for governor of California, the escape from Algeria, the influence of Woody Guthrie, the CIA, Pierre, the books, record albums, a movie, very famous and rich; the need for underground protection.

Suddenly Monsieur Hauchard's face explodes in pretended revelation. He turns to the Minstrel, face wreathed in smiles, stands up and holds out his hand.

"Of course. *Mais naturalment*. I am so slow. The famous philosopher from Minnesota and Woodstock with the Rimbaud drugs. Le Grands Hashishine, eh! Ha. Ha. My dear Philosopher, I am honored to have made your acquaintance. I understand you situation very well. I am totally sympathetique. It is our obligation to protect philosophers. I ask you and your beautiful wife to be my guests here for as long as necessary and I pledge you my assistance in taking care of these petty little disagreeable things with the police. Pouf! *Pas de probleme*, eh Marcel?"

Marcel slumps in visible relief.

'And Dee Dee will be so pleased," continues Hauchard. "She is an admirer of yours. She finds Lausanne less amusing than Paris so she'll be enchanted to have you stay with us."

Marcel stands up and clasps the hand of the host. "You cannot imagine how happy this makes me. I have been so worried about this problem."

"*Mais oui*, I can understand exactly how you are happy, my dear Marcel."

Marcel turns to the Fugitive. "*Eh bien*. Now that this has transpired so well I can excuse myself. Lena is waiting to hear the good news.'

Monsieur Hauchard moves to the desk and picks up the phone, which is wired to a stainless steel box flowered with knobs and dials. A most modern recording device notes the Exile.

"I am calling the porter who will meet you at the lobby and bring our visitors' bags up."

The three men return to the salon. Marcel bows to the women and receives with modesty the round of gratitude. Monsieur Hauchard flings his arm around the banker and turning him vigorously towards the door moves down the long room whsipering conspiratorially.

He returns in a moment, his pink face glowing with pleasure.

"You know who our guests are, cheri?"

Dee Dee nods her black head with charming French vitality. *Mon Dieu!* I can't tell you how glad I am to find some excitement. Lausanne is such a desert. This country is the most boring place in the world. I don't want to frighten you away, God knows, but I imagine you generate your own electricity; wherever you go. So it won't be a problem."

Hauchard suddenly bursts into rapid, giggling, confidences.

"Ah, yes, these Swiss are horrible. They are so petty and bourgeois. Did you see that little frightened banker? How he was sweating, eh! *Incroyable!* All they think of is money. *Oui, c'est vrani, n'est-ce pas, Dee Dee?* Let me tell you one thing, Tom. May I call you Tom? *Bon*. Money. Money. Money. Dollars. Francs. Marks. Pounds. Dinars. Yen.

"Yes," says the Minstrel, "like Crowley's poem about money. It went like this, 'Money, Money." Money, Money, Money, Money, Money, Money, Money, Money, Money, Money, Money Money, Money Money, Money Money, Money Money, Money.'"

Hauchard laughs deeply, "*Merci*. Wonderful poem. A brilliant poet. That's all they think about. I find it so boring. *Mais alors*. Let us forget these little vexations." He clasps his hands again in pleasure. "Champagne! Let us show some Parisian hospitality and welcome our enchanting guests."

He swings on his heel, marches, shoulders back, fifty paces down the living room and calls, "Yo Yo!"

A pretty young woman in a mini-skirt appears from the end of the room and Monsieur Hauchard, now Napoleon at the Nile, gives rapid commands, pointing to the kitchen with outstretched arms. Yo Yo glances at the fugitives, and trots off.

Dee Dee turns provocatively to the expensive high-fi set and turns up *Pink Floyd*.

"Michel can't stand rock'n roll," She smiles. "But *tant pis*. If he likes the sight of young people, he must put up with the sound."

-15-

"I run to the john, crying. Two English girls are at the mirror, making up their eyes.
"He wants me to fuck his dog," I hear one whisper. "Blimey."
I wipe my face with a wet paper towel, take a deep breath.
"But. . .was the dog cute?" I say sweetly. "Cuter than the guy?"

from BETWEEN PICTURES by Jayne Loader

THE POLITICS OF THAT TIME

El Djamila, Algeria, April 1971

As a rule the Philosopher was not given to pronouncements about revolution, his political experience having been limited to running for governor of Minnesota for which campaign he had prepared a conservative 1999 political program calling for the total elimination of taxes. ("No government is tolerable until it pays at least for its own expense," he said.) Making crime pay is the function of government with license fees for victimless crime and heavy fines for robbery. The practicing of law for profit to be prohibited. Trial by jury eliminated. Politicians outlawed. Representative government, unnecessary in an electronic age, replaced by direct telephone-computer ballot. Cash eliminated. The Foreign policy of Switzerland unashamedly imitated.

The inevitable result of this injection of futique orthodoxy into the primitive 1970 vein of body politic was predictable. A week before filing date for candidacy he was brought before the judges who enthusiastically slapped him with two tenners, as Solzhenitsyn would say, or in the argot of the California Archipelago, downed for two dimes running wild, remained without bail to prison, an eventuality for which he was well prepared having noted in his extensive reading of interstellar literature that those who are assigned to work on Backward Planets often end up in dungeons for the Genetic Crime of being in the right place at exactly the wrong time, for acting out scripts written for audiences that weren't scheduled to be born for at least two decades, as it were. If ever.

There were warnings enough. In addition to the science fiction scripts, there was Aldous Huxley, who having lived to see Brave New World grow old, had turned his blank, blue future eyes towards the Bard and said with precise Oxford concern, "You must not forget, Dylan, that you are an

Anthropologist visiting very primitive tribles." Not to mention Walter Lippman's grim neo-Spenglerian comment that the election of Richard Nixon would swing the pendulum back to a Period of Repression, and provide a needed check on the Alarming Growth of Permissiveness, a necessary return to Forbiddingness, or, as *Time* magazine might solemnly declare, a Healthy No Nonsense antidote to the Demand-Feeding practices inculcated by Dr. Spock which produced a generation who had never been told NO, but told to KNOW! A deprived youth which had not yet felt the fat-trimming discipline of economic depression with its sphincter-tightening of the National Mood and the added advantage of teaching the Value of a Dollar, assuming recession with no inflation.

There had been other warnings of the ominous trend of the National Psych-Cycle in the pop-cult heroes popping up in books and television. One of most significant diagnostic clues to the spirit of the times was to be found in President John F. Kennedy's addiction to James Bond espionage stories with assassination plots, betraying a closet *machismo* which led directly to Cuban complicities and the ascendence of Hard-Line Cold Warriors like Rusk, McNamara and Brezhnev over the aimiable Kruschev who had wept while reading *A Day in the Life of Ivan Denisovich*.

Another ominous indication of the Paranoia-As-Public-Policy from which they fled was the elevation to the Special White House Police Force one E. Howard Hunt, an ex-agent of the CIA and *an author himself of Espionage Stories!* Not to neglect G. Gordon Liddy, another true believer in the Micky Spillane-John le Carre school of politics whose promotion to the secret executive-branch police squad, another thrilling example of the power of fantasy to create reality, resulted from his successful 1967 campaign to drive the harassed Wizard from Dutchess County, N.Y. where Liddy had served as pistol-packing Assistant D.A. and, according to the story he himself prepared for the Creative Writing Class in the Terminal Island Federal Prison, had made it his practice to crouch in the bushes outside the Songwriter's Millbrook estate, peering through windows to watch psyche-delic light shows, in surveillance preparation for an illegal midnight raid, the failure of which qualified him for future illegal entries of greater notoriety.

Still another warning signal of the return of the Sterner Morality from which they were offically in exile, came from John Mitchell, the nation's "Top Cop," who, under the influence of a Dangerous Drug which it was his custom to ingest from a glass half-filled with ice cubes, boasted to a lady reporter, "We'll take this country so Far Right you won't believe it."

Not to forget the popular Vice President, Spiro Agnew speaking darkly about the necessity of removing a few Rotten Apples from the National Barrel.

In spite of these many road signs predicting a sharp U-turn to the wrong, the Minstrel found himself, perhaps in the grasp of some neurosocial version of the law of Spin Parity, being accelerated like a charged psi particle through dark prison tunnels of the Minnesota Department of Corrections, out over the fence at Escape Velocity, pulled by some sinister attraction into the gravitational field of the Weathermen, around whose neo-Narodnik planet the Wizard, now joined by His beautiful wife, hurtled at super-orbital speed into the path of the Black Panthers, themselves satellites of the militant socialist government of the Colonel with the shiny white false teeth, Houari Boumedienne, rule of the Fierce hick Moslem Tribesmen of Algeria.

-16-

"The Aliens finally arrived. They have definitely changed my life. One of the Aliens, John, tells me on their planet they don't understand everything that happens either. But they still know a lot. Just the other day he told me the truth about tomatoes. According to popular legend, the tomato was brought over to the Old world from the New by Columbus and his friends. Spaghetti was then developed in Spain and Italy. But this story isn't the true origin of spaghetti, according to John. The Aliens claimed to have discovered spaghetti thousands of years ago and it was they who first introduced tomatoes to Earth. Spaghetti is an Alien dish; they always have it on their festival days. It seems that one day back in 1092 the Aliens accidentally contaminated Earth with tomatoes and the rest is history."

Rotwang's Journal March 18
By Tim Hildebrand

THE EXPERIMENTAL SUBJECTS FILE THEIR REPORT

New York, N.Y., October 1960

The Commodore was fascinated to witness the devotion, the total commitment of the three Beatniks to the Ingestion Process. He was used to the giggling nervousness, the uneasy rationalization, the concealed panic which the Harvard intellectuals manifested in approaching the drug. Salinas, Neal Cassady, and Bennie, by contrast, were wise connoisseiur children, experienced space-travellers approaching a promising planet.

For the first hour little was said. Salinas remained curled in the corner of the couch occasionally scanning the room with her gorgeous blue binoculars, more often eyes closed. Cassady had folded his body into some oriental meditation pose and seemed to be concentrating on his breathing-navel. Bennie sat wit his legs ourstretched, arms folded on his chest. In this atmosphere of serenity, the Doctor found himself reclining on some ledge of Darwiniam tissue from whence he could leisurely examine the relentless cellular clicking of evolutionary events passing by. No tell what next tick of clock will bring. He could hear new Info-worlds being born in grey tissue.

Suddenly Bernie leaped to his feet and began pacing the room. His face was flushed, radiating benificence.

"This stuff is incredible! Are your sure it's legal?"

The Commodore nodded.

The Commodore Smiled.

The Commodore giggled.

Salinas opened her sloe-eyes and smiled enigmatically. "It does seem too heavenly to be true. There's got to be a catch. Admit it, man, it's addictive, isn't it?"

The Commodore shook his head and said, "Must everything beautiful be a sin?"

Cassady opened his eyes with a beautific grin. "You want a report on this experience? Well, I'll give you the expert's opinion. Man, this perfect! What you have here is the ultimate luxury, the flawless wisdom-pleasure experience."

Bennie chanted, his face still shining. "Man, can you dig it, we're here. We've arrived! This is it! There's no place to go and nothing more to do. And it's legal!"

Waves of warm love rippled around the room.

"Incredible, man," murmured Salinas. "This is what I've always looked for."

Ribbons of peace and congeniality linked the time travellers in the hushed room. The candle burned silently.

"I'm trying to think of a problem or an unanswered question," said Bennie quietly.

"Eventually, we'll need some more candles." answered Cassady.

-17-

"He remembers his father's last words:
Stay out of churches, son. All they got a key to is the shit-house. And Swear to me you'll never
wear a lawman's badge."

William S. Burroughs, in THE PLACE OF DEAD ROADS

THE EXILES MAKE PLANS

Lausanne, May 1971

Yo Yo arrives with glasses, caviar and crackers. Michel appears from the study carrying the champagne. Welcome toasts proposed. Michel encourages the Philosopher to talk about Algeria, listening carefully, bursting into thunderous laughter at the jokes. Suddenly he stands, assumes St. Cyr posture and issues commands for the next colonial maneuver.

"Perhaps the ladies would like to prepare themselves for dinner. I've reserved a table at a superb restaurant. Absolutely the best meat in Switzerland. And you, come, let me show the view to France."

Placing his huge hand on the Song Writer's shoulder he turns him towards the terrace and pushes with firmness in the direction of the glass doors. The sun has just set and lights twinkle across the lake.

"There, the lights! France! Some night we'll take my boat and cross over to gamble in the casino. Some more champagne? *Pas mal, eh? Bien,* tonight we shall enjoy a fine dinner, without which life is not amusing and tomorrow we shall go to work on your affair. I've been thinking about our meeting at the airport. *Quel coincidence!* That our lives should intersect like that. The hand of destiny directing us. Do you beieve in such things?"

"It happens all the time," agrees Eight. "The trick is to recognize the moment and to act. To sieze the time." He is not proud of the banal script but it is the best his stir-fried-brain can produce.

"You will understand what an extraordinary coincidence when I tell you that I myself have been in your position. I came to Switzerland as a fugitive." He makes a brushing movement with his hand. "A ridiculous misunderstanding with the French government about taxes, and the Swiss police come and put me in jail. Intolerable. No? Can you beieve it, right here in Lausanne? The famous *Bois Mermet* prison. Stupid lawyers. I detest them. *Alors,* finally I ask around and found the best criminal lawyer in Switzerland. Maitre Mastronardi.

"Expensive, yes, *Mon Dieu* how these Swiss love money! But good. He knows the right people. He says the right things. And *voila*, I am free. Now they adore me here in Switzerland. I have paid their dues and I produce francs for them. I was the new kid on the block. So, my dear Tom, you see how perfect it is that you have come to me. Tomorrow we shall go to Bern and consult with Maitre Mastronardi. I have phoned him already and we shall meet him for lunch. And I have already contacted a Very Important Person in Geneva who will tell us what is really going on with your case. His name is Hyatt."

"Hyatt? What do you mean, Hyatt?"

"The police. Interpol. You must understand, Tom, I detest the police. Pouf. Money lovers! Greedy scoundrels, one and all. They are so Arab-Jewish. But we must use them, *n'est-ce pas?* To us they are a necessary evil. Like waiters or barbers. I would not receive policemen socially at my house, but it is necessary to do business with them to survive comfortably. And that is what we want, eh?

"I can tell you that Hyatt is a man who will tell us what your status is. Are there warrants for you? Who is it specifically who wants you? Who can help you? We must have certain facts to present to the *avocat* so that he will know what to do. So tomorrow at nine we meet this man Dr. Hyatt who will tell us what your legal situation is. I am sure that Maitre Mastionardi will be able to arrange for you to stay in Switzerland. Why not? It's a comfortable place to live. The Swiss themselves we shall have nothing to do with. They are here to serve us. Pouf! A few francs in their pocket and they are in our pockets. But if, by some chance, there complications, I tell you not to worry Tom. I have many connections. Beirut. Malta. Africa. Morocco, the royal family are my close friends. Luxembourg. Turkey. Even Italy."

"Italy? The government is very close to the Americans. Why, the police there are riddled with Italians!"

"Perhaps. But proper diplomacy can work miracles. I have many police on my payroll in Italy. I pay ten, sometimes fifteen thousand pounds a month to the proper people in Italy. I tell you because you are an outlaw fighting for your freedom and what you believe. You are a Gentleman, a Professor, a musical composer, and a Man of Individual. It is a matter of honor for me to help you. I receive very few people in my house. But I have learned this from the Arabs. Once you are my guest, everything I have is at your command."

Michel Hauchard bows and extends his hand smiling broadly. The two men shake hands formally.

"I thank you," said the Philosopher. "We are delighted to be here and we shall do our best to make our meeting a memorable one for you."

-18-

"It has been recorded that Mrs. Theresa Vaughan (or Vaughn) aged 24, while on trial in Sheffield, Yorkshire, England on December 19, 1922, confessed to 61 bigamous marriages within five years. No confirmation of this case is obtainable from police records. A male record of 72 has been claimed."

Michael Horowitz, Book of Records

A LUSTY LADY WITH TALENT TOO

The Tatler, June 1973

There are days when Anna Kate sighs in resignation at the suggestion that her book BETWEEN ENGAGEMENTS is autobiographical. "Frankly I doubt if I'm quite that funny."

But there are late-night-clubbings when Anna Kate will confess that she laughs at what the critics say.

"Except for my mother, who always expected the best, everybody expected the worst for yours truly, expected me to die in a cheap motel room with a needle in my veins and a red neon light clicking on and off over my syphilitic body saying Dew Drop Inn."

Like Joanna, she was raised on Switzerland's Upper Best Side, excelled in Gstadd's select Marie Jose school, expelled from the best convent seminaries of France, ran away with the raffish French gangster Michel Hauchard when she was thirteen, married the son of an Egyptian diplomat when she was fourteen, the heir to a Greek shipping fortune when she was eighteen and emerged on the Washington scene at age 30 impersonating a smallish, sveltly rounded, voraciously sensual "short showgirl or starlet, a bottled blonde a second rate Forties pinup whose face will one day show vestiges of weary beauty".

She had "the same face at 30 that she had at five, same sulky mouth, Kewpie-doll cheeks" and darting eyes that miss nothing.

Anna Kate is an intensity-addict with the funniest, smartest mind in town.

And she laughs wickedly at her gossipy detractors.

"They expected me to be carved like a turkey by one of my boyfriends--the number is thought to be infinite--driven beserk, poor slob, by my obstinacy, promiscuity, and nose-in-the-air high-class bitchiness. I should have at least picked up some incurable disease, like Saigon Rose or herpes, or numerous messy abortions."

And look! Now she's off to Geneva on a mysterious quest the purpose of which not even the TATLER can reveal.

Yet.

-19-

" 'As many as 300,000 women are believed to have been executed for witchcraft between the years of 1484 and 1782,' said Rotwang. He was speaking to 140,000 women in a huge auditorium."

ROTWANG
By Tim Hildebrand

THE PHILOSOPHER LEARNS A NEW WORD!

New York, N.Y., October 1960

Dawn flushing the windows and walls of the room found the four experimenters floating serenely in the laboratory. Little had been said during the night but much had been communicated.

Salinas untwined herself from the couch and stood looking at the Commodore quizzically.

"I gotta shower and dress and paint my egg for the cameras. I got an eight o'clock appointment. But I must say, man, that I haven't a clue as to what you're all about. When I first heard about you I thought you might be looking for a little hippy-whore girl to play Dr. John with. Or maybe you were coming down to dope me up and ball me into some Ivy-League stupor. What do you want, man?"

"I want to thank you Salinas, and you two as well, for teaching me so much last night."

"What did we teach you?"

"Don't you see, Salinas?" interjected Cassady. "While the Professor has run many consciousness expansion experiments, he had never seen anyone getting high before last night. Right?"

"Right," agreed Dylan. "You have provided a smashing demonstration of the Set-Setting hypothesis."

"What?"

"That the drug has no specific effect. It propels you into the brain. And where you go depends on you."

"You mean you never turned on like this before?"

"Our experiments are a bit more formal and prepared. And our subjects haven't been as experienced. I've witnessed two hundred people crack through the hedonic gap and get into inner space. I've heard the post-literal Brain described in every possible metaphor, the gasping responses, the standard cliches, 'It's all one! It's all vibrations! Nirvana. Now I understand God's design! Ecstasy. Wow! Revelation! Blah! Blah! Blah! But I must confess that you are the first professional alchemists, the first brain veterans who can give me precise neuronaut navigational coordinates, psycho-pharmacological read-outs."

"We helped you, huh?"

"I was most impressed by your lack of fear. By the absence of surprise. You seemed to me like professional mathematicians who see the correct formula written on the blackboard and nod quietly. Equation solved."

"You mean we're the first hippies you've met?"

"Hippies?"

"Druggies. People who keep their heads loose and free. You know, that float around unattached."

"I see," replied the Philosopher.

"Dig, man. Do you want to engage in more of these, ah, experiments?"

"I very much want to expand our range of subjects. I can see after tonight that we've been much too restricted in our selection."

"Groovy," said Salinas. You've just hired yourself an informal research assistant. Leave me your phone number and I'll arrange to expand your range of subjects."

"Groovy?"

-20-

"Money SHOULD grow on trees."

Jayne Loader in BETWEEN PICTURES

SOCIOLOGICAL CHIT-CHAT AT THE GOURMET RESTAURANT

Lausanne, May 1971

The Rolls Royce rolls smoothly down the highway. Michel Hauchard drives with elegant distraction while Dee Dee curls in the front seat chatting up Lausanne gossip. Antonia, who has requested to sit in the middle of the back seat to protect her from cold uses her right hand to stroke the Song Writer's genitals. Antonia's left hand is holding Rosamund's right hand tracing sensual designs on her palm with Roman finger. The affectionate girl says nothing but licks bottom lip with tongue from time to time.

As the car pulls up in front of the restaurant the doorman leaps to open the door. After the passengers descend he runs to the driver's side, greeting Michel Hauchard with effusive enthusiasm.

The owner waits at the door, flanked by the *maitre d'* and three waiters, all bowing and shouting passionate welcome. Michel Houchard, his shoulders high, his head tossed back, sweeps forward to lead his troops within, rattling cheerful French and rubbing his hands in pleasure. The party is escorted to a corner table and seated with flourish. Waiters swarm around the table arranging candles, presenting menus, lighting cigarettes. Dee Dee grins sagely.

"Quite a show, eh? Michel is one of the last great non-Arabic flamboyant spenders. He plays the part so well. They love him in these places because he knows how to be a rich man. So few people these days care enough. Me, I'm too lazy. I could never do it."

"Do what?" She asks.

"Be the Rich Man. It requires so much work. Arranging to have his special cigars made to order and shipped from Havana. Stocking his own personal wine cellar in the six restaurants he prefers in the Romande. Even to pick out the six best restaurants is a complicated research. Then the ordering of the meals. He spent a half hour this morning planning the menu for tonight."

"They really light up when he sweeps on the scene."

Dee Dee shrugs. "It's non-taxable money, of course. Non-taxable money makes it happen and Michel has it. He's living beyond his means, but apparently he can afford it."

Michel, who has been conferring with the owner, turns to the guest.

"And to celebrate this splendid occasion, let us sacrifice a stately Chateau Lafitte Rothchild. And let me propose a toast. To France. And to America. Although we are exiles we are still patriots, eh Dylan?"

"Have you been to the United States?" asks the Fugitive.

"*Mais oui*, we spent a week there in New York. Saw everything worth seeing. My friends said there was no point in going further. After all, what is France but Paris?"

"Tell them what you saw, Michel," commands Dee Dee with a shrug.

"La Cote Basque, of course. Then La Caravelle; superb *Foie gras truffe*. La Grenouille, *naturalment* for *escargots*. Le Mistral for the *bouillabaisse*. La Poiniere du Soir for *filets de boeuf perigourdine.* Lutece for the *pigeonneau mascotte.* Le Manoir for *truite au bleu.*"

A stone drag," says Dee Dee reprovingly. "I couldn't extract him from those six tightly-packed blocks in mid-Manhattan. We never spoke anything but French and didn't hear a note of rock & roll. And I begged him to take me to San Francisco."

"Dee Dee is right," admits the bon vivant. "We were too restricted. But I shall make arrangements with my friend J. Edgar Hoover and we shall return to America with you as our guides and meet the natives."

"Oh, we'd love to do that," Rosamund says wistfully. "We could show a side of America you've missed."

"Disneyland?"

"There are thousands of real-life Disneylands," says the Dar Dar.

"*Alors,*" says Monsieur Hauchard, "all joking aside, *mes amis,* shall we discuss the meal? Does the menu tempt you?"

"Why don't we let you select our dinner," answers the Commodore. "I'm sure you know the pitfalls better than we."

"*Exactement,*" replies the Frenchman wagging his pink wattles in approval. "This restaurant, like all the others, is a merciless jungle loaded with traps for the unwary. *Mon Dieu,* if I could tell you about the *cannelloni, specialita della casa* that brutally ambushed us just yesterday afternoon. The pitiful but pitiless dish had been allowed to sit for several minutes and a film had formed over the entire thing plus there were spots around the edge of the plate where sauce had splashed. I commanded that the monstrosity be put out of its misery at once, so that it cannot contaminate our memories. But let us discuss more pleasant prospects."

"*D'accord,*" the Dar Dar murmurs timidly.

"To begin, I beg you to try a little *crepe farci* with lobster and crab *armoricaine.* Tom, I swear to you this is proof absolute of telepathy. Three days ago, not knowing you were coming, I arranged to have some lobster of Maine flown across the Atlantic for tonight's dinner. I swear this to you! *Fantastique! Non?* They were alive swimming in Maine sea-water just this afternoon when I made conference with the chef."

"I trust this is not a grim reminder of the fate of fugitives," says the Bard with a watery, wintery smile.

"And after, in honor of our good *avocat* Maitre Mastronardi we shall have a simple, sincere, hard-working sirloin steak with *sauce bernaise.*"

-21-

*". . . right is a concept that continues to elude me. I never want to mess with decency again.
Given the company I keep, this is an easy goal to meet. We use each other's bodies, then hold
them like Teddy bears. Sleep is a problem, for all of us."*

Jayne Loader in BETWEEN PICTURES

A FINE MIND IN A STRONG BODY

Marbella, Spain, May 1970

Katherine Anne Porter O'Shea has that look of someone who is someone
else. Folks, indeed, often mistake Her for Audrey Hepburn, Jayne Loader,
Brigette Bardot, Joanna Ulam, or Lauren Bacall's younger sister Nan.

"I just sign Bardot's name when they ask for autographs. It's much easier
than explaining," She said with a husky Dietrich-like laugh.

Anna Kate is the St. Moritz-born girl who has been out-witting
European society just by being eager and wanting to meet everyone and
doing everything ten-times speedier than anyone else.

Anna Kate boasts: "I take lots of drugs, of course, proud of being an
informed consumer, the kind who buys in bulk. We use drugs to simulate
the feelings we don't have for each other. But my body is strong with good
Irish genes. My moderate self-abuse, still under nominal control, is nothing
compared to the plague or the potato famines, to the stinking holds of the
ships that brought my clan to America."

Anna Kate who is engaged to Clement Goodman of the famous
Washington real-estate combine, has also found time to work over the years.

For some time She was the behind-the-scenes social advisor to Bruno
Aitken, owner of London's *Daily Express.*

She is currently a tour operator for Costa del Sol, Anonymous,
promoting pandemoniums in Malaga.

"I believe we were placed on this earth to perform some evolutionary
task. Sure I love money. And certainly I love clothes," She admits. Her
favorite designers are Ron Bernstein, Saint Laurent, Nikhail Bulgakov, and
Pierre Mattheissen. "But I'm mainly comfortable with my familiar old Hot
Genes," she quips, referring to the genetic responsibilities she carries as the
descendant of Stanislaus Ulam, the shadowy figure who designed the
Hydrogen Bomb and Arpad Plesch, furtive collector of rare plants and hot
currencies.

Although She weighs only 103 pounds, Mademoiselle O'Shea insists that She devours life like a boa-constrictor (Her zodiac Sign is Hera-ine), and awaits, coiled majestically in Her mountain retreat above Malaga, hoarding Her chromosomes, bathed in $225-an-ounce Jean Patou 1000, waiting for a Mediterranean man worth caring for.

-22-

"The Aliens gave Rotwang one of their wave-guns. This gun could send out any one of 10 different waves; cosmic waves, light waves, heat waves, atomic waves, pleasure waves, night waves, X-waves, right waves, blank waves, and reality waves."

ROTWANG
By Tim Hildebrand

MANY SINGULARITIES, BUT NOT ONE GOD

Newton Centre, Massachusetts, October 1960.

Dylan drove along Charles River towards Boston and tunnel. Thin Islam moon rode low in cloudless sky. The night humid, cool. Through tunnel he drove rapidly to Logan Field, swung car into transient zone, turned off six cylinder gas-fed engine and sat for a moment, hands lightly gripping the molded plastic steering wheel. Huge flashing neon sign above terminal building flooded red light over sidewalk, car and rugged face of Agent. Sign spelled out words, TRANSWORLD AIRLINES. He could hear whine of jet engines and roar of planes hurtling down wide cement runway. Airport pulsed with Newtonian energy. Self-propelled ground cars discharged and picked up Primates, most of whom carried imitation leather plastic luggage. He got out, entered building and walked through lobby to tunnel which led to small waiting rooms for individual flights. Just in time to see New York—Boston shuttle plane taxi ponderously into place.

In two minutes he caught sight of his visitors. Salinas still in blue jeans, swinging along with the loose gait of the Beatnik (or as she called herself, the Hippie). With her was a slender woman about thirty, smartly dressed with blonde hair parted in the middle and lying in long waves down her shoulders. She wore no makeup. Her dark blue eyes flashed with alert intelligence. She exuded world-weary wisdom.

"This is Flora Lu."

The blonde woman dropped her light suitcase and stood looking up at the Professor examining his face with frank curiosity. Her skin was smooth, her mouth full, her eyes enormous, her voice a subtle Marilyn whisper. There was a wisdom look on her face which she wiped away with a Starlet smile and a quick batting of eyes.

"I'm glad to meet you," she murmured. "Salinas made it sound as though you might be the One." She turned to Salinas and giggled. "God, would you believe it, I'm shaky and trembling. Isn't that too much?"

The Philosopher, somewhat abashed, reached for the two suitcases and led the way to his ground car.

Flora Lu was in the back seat and Salinas in front as the Folksinger dextrously piloted the swift, pneumatic-tired, four-wheeled vehicle through tunnel, around dock area of Boston and along Charles River. He kept up a running tourist-guide commentary pointing out historic spots, meanwhile sensing that his two guests were paying more attention to him and to their reactions to him than to his words.

"Flora Lu," said the professor talking over his shoulder to the back seat, "I am not The One. There is no, The One."

"I can dig it" replied Flora Lu in bright, self-confident voice. "I've lived a full life myself and put in a lot of time in Hollywood and New York watching the most successful, beautiful people in the world do their thing. And I'm left with this funny feeling that no one knows what they're doing. And that includes me. And I don't dig that feeling."

The Commodore piloted ground car around curve in river, past low domes of Harvard and coliseum bulk of Soldier's Field, his brain computing the curious words of his blonde visitor.

"So," continued Flora Lu, "when Salinas told me about this Harvard psychologist who is studying drugs that zoom you around in your brain, it sounded like one of those rare Magellan signals that comes along not so often in a lifetime. You know?

-23-

"Hippies, dropped-out hedonists, are premature brain-explorers. Their passive receptive style is ill-adapted for survival in assemly-line, industrial cultures. These sensory consumers paddle around in the spinal canals waiting to be towed up the frontal lobes of the west-brain."

from The Periodic Table of Energy

WHAT IS THE QUESTION?

Lausanne, May 1971

"A most enjoyable meal," murmured the Folksinger, "but I wonder, is it safe?"

"To be eating with me in public this way is fattening but quite safe," says Michel Hauchard. "Do not worry. I have made arrangements. You will be spirited away to safety."

"I hope you do better than Michel," says Dee Dee. "I'll never forget the morning the Swiss police came for him. He rushed into the bedroom to say good-bye to me. 'Where are you going?' 'Down the back elevator,' said Michel. 'You meet me in Malta.' That's where I drew the line. Lausanne is the most boring place in the civilized world. But Malta! Really, that's not even civilized."

"But you are right, Dylan," says Michel Hauchard. "People will be asking who you are and we should have some cover names. What shall we call you?"

"Our code names in Algeria were Nino and Maya Baraka."

"Superb," exclaimed Michel. "Let's drink some cognac to our new friends, Nino and Maya. Antonia, do you want some cognac?" Antonia shrugs.

Michel, who is leaning to offer the bottle, falls back in his chair and throws up his hands.

"Nino, you are a psychologist. What shall we do with this silent flower from Rome? She never knows what she wants. I ask her, what would you want to drink? She shrugs. I ask her what do you want to do? She shrugs. Who do you want to fuck? She shrugs again."

"I think she may know what she wants," answers the Philosopher. "But really can man ever know what woman wants? Do you know the legend?"

"A legend about What Woman Wants? Splendid! I've never heard it, but I must."

"Let me tell you then. Perhaps you can help with an answer. The story goes like this. The year is 1976. On a warm summer night the radar-tracking stations in America, Russia, China record an Unidentified Flying Object hurtling into our atmosphere. Suddenly every radio and television station in the world picks up a message to humanity. The U.F.O. announces that it has come from the Galactic Network to determine if intelligent life exists on earth. Evolution here has reached the stage where, if the required level of intelligence has not manifested, then the genetic experiment of Sol—3 must be considered a failure and the planet wiped clean to prepare for a new genesis. You can imagine the chaos. Military types propose and even attempt offensive meaures against the interstellar visitor. These hostile moves are easily neutralized and humanity is confronted with the aweful reality that it must demonstrate its maturity. And fast! Forty-eight of the most brilliant scholars and scientists meet in the United Nations to respond to the challenge. The world is watching over satellite T.V. as the UFO beams down the first question humanity must answer."

Michel and Dee Dee are leaning forward in fascination. Even Antonia shows a flicker of interest.

Maya laughs in delight. "Forty-eight! Oh, that's good."

"Haven't you heard this story?" asks Michel.

"I don't think so. Not in this form at least. Do continue, Eight. What is the question?"

"How beautiful and wise you are," says Eight. "That was the question."

"What?" shouts Michel. "What is the Question?"

"*What is The Question* is the First Question. Let me give you the exact wording. The voice of Higher Intelligence boomed through the loud-speakers in the U.N. Assembly Hall and said: **WHAT IS THE QUESTION FOR WHICH LIFE IS THE ANSWER?**"

In the employees' dressing room of the restaurant a thin weasly waiter is writing eavedrops in a small notebook. "Rocket ships. Genetic experiments." He wipes his damp forehead with a napkin and wets the pencil tip in his mouth. He is trembling with excitement. "Military offensive weapons." This is really hot stuff. "Scientists from the United Nations."

Replacing the notebook in his breast pocket he returns to the dining room and begins refilling wine glasses at the table of Monsieur Hauchard.

-24-

*"LEVITY; lightness, buoyancy, weightlessness, volatility, frivolity, flippancy.
go to LIGHT, CHANGEABLENESS"*

Interplanetary Thesaurus

GOSSIP BY MILITARY WIVES

Alexandria, Virginia, May 1971

The Silenus Club is a remodeled Virginia colonial of worn pink brick with manicured lawns rolling down to the shores of the Potomac. It is a country-club, members only, cherished by brass from State and Defense plus top-heavy metal from Pentagon. At luncheon wives come to exchange domestic espionage reports and plan intermarital campaigns.

There is, of course, a colonnaded porch that reminds of The Confederacy, a magnificent drive through the old maples and the best breeze in town.

Betty Ann Mellini Plough leaned her tall, firm-fleshed body back against the chair and smiled at Louisa Mae. Betty Ann is wearing a gray skirt that embraced her lush hips, and a yellow sweater with ivory beads. Her blonde hair had glints of silver. Her full red mouth petulant.

"You still don't want to let me fuck you?"

Louisa giggled. "We're too good friends for that. It's all too simple to find a good bed-mate. But a trustworthy confidant, my love is too precious to tamper with."

"But just tell me if you'd like to," coaxed Betty Ann. The serene irony in her husky voice clashed pleasingly with the intensity of her words.

Louisa leaned forward and inspected her friend with an amused appraising look, Her hazel eyes wide, shining and wise. "If we met to gossip between the sheets instead of at luncheon, it *would* be better for our figures. Let me think about it. Meantime, tell me what's happening. For starters, tell me, why does Anna Kate want to marry Clement Goodman?"

"Because she loves him, I assume. Let's give her the benefit of the doubt."

"And why does Clement, serenely established in the highest echelons of Washington society, a determined bachelor in a world where bachelors are king, want to wed and bed Katherine Anne Porter O'Shea, 'Snow queen' of London's Chelsea district and mad-cap prankster of Europe's jet-set."

"Where are you getting that?"

"Oh, let's say *Woman's Wear Daily.*"

"Clement sees a great opportunity," says Betty Ann thoughtfully. "Marrying Anna Kate is a way of tuning into Her incredible energy, connecting with the fastest elements of European Society."

"A convenient explanation."

"What's yours?"

"Listen to this; In early 1971 peppy little Mademoiselle O'Shea whirled into Washington from her Texas home at the speed of light, conveying the image of the rich little poor girl—pouting, pampered, demanding, flamboyant, zapping through Capital society with all the happiness that energy can buy."

"But there are gullibility gaps in her image. Where did she come from?"

"Her father was a titled British naval officer. Her Mother is an Ulam."

"Ulam? Is it really good to be an Ulam?" says Betty Ann dubiously.

"A famous Polish family. Grandfather very rich. Next generation very clever. One of the uncles, Adam Ulam, is head of the Russian Institute at

Harvard. That's interesting. And another Stan Ulam is a famous mathematician. He invented the hydrogen bomb."

"I thought Edward Teller invented the hydrogen bomb," said Betty Ann, who had suddenly reverted to become Mrs. Burleigh Plough, wife of the Admiral.

"There's a bit of mystery about that nuclear fusion thing," replied Louisa, whose husband was in State Department Intelligence. "The official version is that Stan Ulam brought the solution to Teller's office and Teller just did the engineering. The joke going around is, If Teller is the Father of the H-bomb, then Ulam is the Mother."

"I don't think the marriage can work."

"On a conventional level no. But theirs could. Maybe she'll learn to cool it a bit."

"And settle down?"

"Hopefully. Is it possible?"

"Oh come now sweetie. It's different for a woman. A real woman doesn't get emotionally involved the way a man does. Jealousy and all that pathetic male-jazz. A real woman can go to bed with anyone."

"Why can't a man?"

"He's just not built that way. It's just not in a Good Man's nature to be promiscuous. Oh they may swagger and boast and lie, but, deep down, a Domesticated Man wants to be faithful."

"And smart, horny, macho European Anna Kate?"

"She's a woman. What else can be said?"

-25-

"One day the Aliens decided that Rotwang's world needed something special. On their planet they had something called a 'South Brain Music Cleaner.' They let Rotwang try it out and Rotwang loved it. 'There are a lot of people on this planet who could use one of these,' said Rotwang."

ROTWANG
By Tim Hildebrand

LET'S MEET FLORA LU

Newton Centre, Massachusetts, October 1960.

The evening had progressed uneventfully. Salinas and Flora Lu had been shown to their rooms and, after bathing and covering their bodies artfully with ornate fabrics, had joined the company in the booklined study.

The experimental group for the evening included Madison Jefferson, a Black psychiatrist and his wife and two graduate students. Flora Lu sat in the corner of a two-wall couch and watched with huge dilated eyes as the ceremony unfolded.

"What do you do in New York?" the Bard asked her.

"I'm married. To a famous musician. Maynard Ferguson. Did you ever hear of him?"

"I'm afraid I haven't. I'm really not well informed on many important matters," said Dylan.

"I'm beginning to see that."

Salinas dominated the session with her fast, needle-point junky mind. The sarcastic, ultra-cynical, whining, bored, insolent, comic sneer of the New York jazz-head, miraculously attractive in ripe mouth of aristocratic girl who lounged in blue jeans on the Folksinger's sofa.

Flora Lu Ferguson listened, scanned with big blue eyes and burst into breathless little-girl comments and ingenuous, giggling fables that reflected the diamond hard wisdom of a child-woman who, in The Life as Hollywood starlet, nightclub hat checker, jazzband manager, had observed big city ways, the hustles, fronts, frauds, deals, show biz angles, ups and downs of the beautiful and famous, the promoters, agents, stars. Always the girl from Oklahoma who remembered small town hypocrisies, scandals, and nobilities, little blonde student in the night school of life trying to figure it out, find meaning, cut through facade to seed-reality; and, in those rare moments when she felt a chance at being understood, whisper her shocking discoveries with wicked innocence.

-26-

"What is the Purpose of Life? To be the eyes and ears of the Creator of the Universe, you fool."

Kurt Vonnegut, Jr.

WHAT IS THE PURPOSE OF WHAT?

Lausanne, May 1971

"Oh," exclaims Michel, "this Higher Intelligence wants to see if we humans know the Purpose of Life?"

"Well it was a bit more specific than that," explains the Commodore. "The shocking implication, as the scholars were quick to point out, was that there *is* a purpose of life. Oddball Teleology? The fact that They wanted humanity to provide the basic question suggested, amazingly enough, that life *does* have a purpose and that the search for the purpose *is* the purpose.

"You can see what confusion was caused by that!" Dylan smiles.

"The scientists were totally non-plussed because it had been generally agreed among them that life is nothing more than a chance combination of chemicals and so forth. Professor James Watson of Harvard, who had won the Nobel prize for his discovery of the DNA code, was the first to answer. 'No question, no answer. Pure accident!' he announced.

"The experts conferred for eight hours, all this broadcast on global T.V., by the way, but could come to no agreement. It was decided that since no attempt to reach a concensual answer could succeed, they set up a system whereby anyone in the world who had a suggestion could send it by phone or cable to central computers located in the major industrial countries and that all the solutions to the problem would be beamed up to the UFO. The Higher Intelligence indicated It's willingness to start screening the answers and set a deadline of sixty-four hours."

"Sixty-four," murmured Maya. "Of course."

"This method of transmitting answers to the ultimate question turned out to be totally acceptable to all the countries in the U.N. Indeed, for the first time in recorded history, every human being was engaged in a cooperative and mutually supportive enterprise.

"All thoughts of competition and rivalry quickly vanished as the standard answers of the religious leaders and philosophers and politicians were rejected by the UFO as inadequate. A strange reversal of roles developed. Instead of attempting to force their religious beliefs on others, the leading thinkers and even the religious zealots were now broadcasting appeals to everyone, anyone, to come up with new answers. Professors were begging their students to produce ideas about the purpose of life. Parents asked their children.

"Children even asked their parents.

"By the end of the first day over thirty-three million answers to the riddle had been beamed up to the implacable presence in the sky. And for each solution the response came back negative. By the afternoon of the second day anthropologists were interviewing primitive medicine men for suggestions, the libraries of the world were being scanned by well-organized teams. The answers arrived in every language, modern and ancient, in chemical formulae and mathematical equations. And still the response came back negative.

"By the morning of the third day hope was failing. It hardly seemed possible that there was anyone left on the planet who had not been consulted. But, of course, there were a few. In the solitary confinement cell of Folsom Prison in California, for example, there was a song-writer who was incarcerated because of the unpopularity of his ideas. In this section of the prison there were no radios, no newspapers, no cybernetic conversation. This isolation was of no concern to the song writer who found solitary confinement a welcome opportunity to spend all of his time talking to the only person he had found capable of conducting an intelligent conversation."

"Ho Ho Ho!" shouts Michel Houchard. "That's priceless. *Comprends-tu, cheri?*" Dee Dee looks puzzled, but nods and smiles.

"Three times a day the guards would come to his cell and unlock the metal cover to a narrow slit called by the Russian Solzhenitsyn, 'Swine Troughs,' through which they would push the tray with his food and through which the prisoner would then push the dirty tray from the previous meal. On the morning of the third day the guard leaned his head down and shouted in to the prisoner, 'Well you won't have much more time to do in prison.'

" 'What do you mean by that?' asked the prisoner, not really expecting an answer, since he had asked the same question countless times before to various members of the bureaucracy.

" 'Oh, haven't you heard? All life on the planet may be wiped out in sixteen hours.'

"The guard then explained the global dilemma to the prisoner, closed the metal cover, locked it and walked away. The lock always clanged as it fell back against the metal door.

"Four hours later the prisoner heard the jingling of keys along the hallway and the clank of the lock being opened. As he pushed his dirty tray out he said casually to the guard, 'There's no problem about the question. It's the answer I'm interested in. Let me know what you hear about that.'

"The guard, who was going off duty in twenty minutes, grunted 'Yeah, you'll be the first one I'll tell.' The guard slammed the slot-cover, clipped the lock and left."

Clang.

-27-

"Say goodbye to your old stale futures. Here is an entirely realized new world, intense as an electric shock. William Gibson's prose, astonishing in its clarity and skill, becomes high-tech

electric poetry . . . An enthralling adventure story, as brilliant and coherent as a laser. THIS IS
WHY SCIENCE FICTION WAS INVENTED!"

Bruce Sterling
blurb for "Neuromancer"

ANNA KATE O'SHEA IS AN ESPIONAGE AGENT?

Alexandria, Virginia, May 1971

"So the mystery remains. Why did Anna Kate want to marry Clement Goodman? He's not that rich or powerful."

"Connections. The Goodman family, as a side-line runs the most popular real-estate agency in the Washington-Georgetown area."

"So? What could be more dreary? Showing Japanese commercial attaches around suburban houses."

"Don't be so ridiculous, love. It's a key spot on the intelligence chess board. The de Layne Agency has the floor-plans of every diplomatic house in the capital. They talk with the Chinese Ambassador about his household requirements. They are on the scene to see that every rented house is properly prepared."

"You mean bugged? But why should Anna Kate be interested in . . . "

"It's the newest kick among the most intelligent jet-setters. After you've mastered every conceivable sexual position by the age of sixteen. And every drug-induced brain-spasm by eighteen. What's left? The ultimate kicks of life-death. Sky-diving and shark-hunting with scuba spears are too muscularly-Scandinavian. If you see what I mean. So there are three kicks to choose from. Political revolution ended in 1965. And even drug-dealing, is a bit passe by now."

"So what's the third? You don't mean Espionage!"

"Why not!"

"Anna Kate a spy! A bedroom terrorist, perhaps, but she's too wild and freaky to be dependable. Why She'd turn over a country like she'd switch a lover."

"But how much of that is a carefully contrived image? Suppose that behind the wild, mad-cap, sex-drug antics we have a cold-calculating woman carefully trained by three generations of Hungarian-Polish Jews to deal into the big-league power game."

"You must be kidding. Anna Kate is the last person . . . "

"Exactly. Isn't it an exciting idea?"

"But she's crazy, loco, aphrodisia, dope-ridden, cock-mad . . . "

"But still somehow this perky, bouncy, funny little girl keeps popping up in the strangest places."

"I've witnessed some of them."

"No I don't mean the night-clubs of Gstaad and St. Tropez. I mean she actually lived inside the house of the Egyptian Minister of Economics when She was married to his son. A couple of years before the Six Day War."

"I hadn't made the connection."

"Do you know she's banned from Egypt?"

"So is Farouk and Omar Sharif. And Elizabeth Taylor. And a lot of nice people I know at Monaco."

"Did you konw that she was, at age 18, the English-language news-broadcaster on the only T.V. station in Beirut, Lebanon?"

"Yes, I seem to remember. She made a movie there too, didn't she?"

"Can you think of a better place to have an agent a year before the Six Day War?"

"My goodness, go on. Is there more?"

"Will you believe that she was married into one of the top Greek ship-building families one year before the Colonel's putsch?"

"Oh really, Cock, money, well-placed marriages I can believe. But the rest is coincidence."

"Do you know that our little boy-crazy, drug-happy Anna Kate got inside the gates of the Chinese Embassy in Paris and had to be forcibly ejected by the Embassy guards?"

"What does that prove? She was thrown out of the Monaco Palace Hotel for riding a bicycle into the main dining room"

"I read it as a failed espionage penetration that was converted into a minor P.R. embarrassment for the Slant-eyed Comrades. Plenty of diplomatic cable between Paris and Peking was burned on that one, I can assure you."

"Hmm. I'm getting infected. Then Her affair with Michel Hauchard could have been . . . "

"Exactly. Here's Hauchard. One of the most flamboyant smugglers and arms dealers on the continent. Loudly anti-semitic and involved in Arab smuggling goodies. But who knows? He's on someone's payroll. An anti-fascist espionage agent during World War II? Claims his feet were broken in Prague after the war. Most people assume he's an Israeli agent. Who knows."

"And then She turns up daughter-in-law of the realtor who handles foreigner safehouses in Washington. But it's impossible. No little girl, however clever could . . . "

"I agree. But let's remember the family again. One uncle at Los Alamos. Another head of the Russian Research Institute at Harvard. And you know what that means? And Arpad Plesch who mysteriously emerges from the ruins of World War II as a centi-millionaire from money exchange and war-surplus? Do you think that Interpol and the American Intelligence sit back while he does all that on his own?"

"Who does she work for?"

"It's got to be C.I.A. with, maybe Zionist connections. You don't get to Harvard and Los Alamos working for the Other Side."

"Well, in that case, why did she leave Clemmie and Washington to start bouncing around the chic film centers of Europe?"

"That's what a lot of us would like to know. As Michel says, maybe She is just crazy."

"Maybe she just wants to have fun."

-28-

"So the next day the Aliens ordered one million music cleaners from Alpha. . . . People began to use their South Brain Music Cleaners. They read the instructions and tried it out. Basically, the South Brain Music Cleaner was a little gadget that gave off certain vibrations which were a combination of music and thought. There were 10 channels. On Channel 1 it was a Love vibration. Channels 2 and 3 were peace vibrations of different intensities. Channels 5, 7 and 8 were various mental health vibrations. Channel 6 was a dream wave. Channel 10 was a combination think and swim vibration."

ROTWANG
By Tim Hildebrand

AN OFFER OF HELP FROM TWO CLASSY LADIES

Newton Centre, Massachusetts, October 1960.

In the morning the Commodore was up early. He made scrambled eggs and bacon for himself, his 13 year old daughter Sara and his 11 year old son, Bob. He drove Sara to the home of a girl friend where she was planning to spend the day. Dylan drove to a nearby baseball park where he acted as assistant manager of a Little League Baseball team. Bob was the only player who played every inning of the game because he was a catcher and there was no other boy capable of playing this difficult position. Bob hit a double and a triple. In the last inning he leaped high in the air to catch a throw from the outfield and tagged the runner at home plate which saved the game.

The coach said, "That Bob Dylan is a rock."

The Commodore was very proud of this domestic success.

When he returned home Salinas and Flora Lu were in the kitchen sitting around the table, smiling and chatting cheerfully.

"Where have you been?" asked Salinas.

"Oh, out and around. Did you have breakfast?"

"Oh yes, but we were really freaked when we woke and found you gone and the house empty."

"We thought we had hallucinated everything. Last night and you and everything," said Flora Lu.

"But anyway, we finally figured you out. And your game."

The proud father opened the electric refrigerator and took out a six-pack of beer in cans.

"Beer?" he asked his two beautiful guests.

"Whatever you have, we'll have," replied Flora Lu in a quiet voice.

He pulled the metal tab and watched the beer gas spurt into the sun-flecked air. He opened two other cans and poured beer for the women.

"What have you figured out?" asked the Commodore.

"We've decided that you're from another planet . . . " said Flora Lu.

" . . . and when you disappear, like you always do . . . " added Salinas.

" . . . you're getting instructions from your home base."

"But you need our help."

"I'm sure you're right," said Dylan, "but what specific help do you have in mind?"

"We've watched you very closely, and it's obvious to us . . . "

" . . . that you've just barely arrived here . . . "

" . . . because you don't know how to do anything on this planet . . . "

" . . . there is no doubt in our mind that you are extra-terrestrial because you know the important cosmic things . . . "

" . . . but you need some help in the little, unimportant, down-to-earth things like how to dress, and how to cut your hair . . . "

" . . . in other words, you're like a young child, just having arrived down here . . . "

" . . . and it's important you know how to do the little ordinary things . . . "

" . . . to avoid being detected as an alien. Because if that happened . . . "

" . . . you'd get in a lot of trouble and they'd destroy you and . . . "

" . . . you wouldn't be able to teach us about the important things . . . "

" . . . and include us in your future experiments . . . "

" . . . speaking of which . . . "

" . . . could we have some more right now?"

"Right now!" exclaimed the Philosopher. "Why, if you, ah, turn-on now, you'll be, ah, high, very high when you take the plane. We've never had subjects running around outside of supervision and guidance."

"Well, that's exactly why you need subjects like us," said Salinas cunningly. "It will be an experimental break-through. And we promise that we'll write full reports tomorrow."

"And I'd be most honored," whispered Flora Lu shyly, "if you'd come to my house next weekend; we would arrange experiments for some interesting subjects and everything."

-29-

Q. Why did the Gods make Men?
A. Do love and honor Them in this stage?
And to be happy with them in the next.

VoDoo Catechism
Translated by Grace Jones

THE PRISONER WHISPERS THE QUESTION

Lausanne, May 1972.

Dylan drank cognac and smiled. The Dar Dar smiled too. "Continue the story, if you please," said Michel

"When the prison guard entered the custody office, he found the other correctional officers clustered around the T.V. set. 'Any word?' he asks anxiously.

"The watchers shook their heads.

" 'If you ask me, we should stop appeasing those pinko bastards in the UFO and bomb the hell out of them.'

" 'It's the old bullshit story,' said the guard with the tray. 'Here we are taking food to these animals, sweating for our ten bucks an hour and worrying about the end of the world and these fuck-up cons couldn't care less. That guy in solitary didn't even know about the UFO. And when I told him he said the question was no problem, he just wanted the answer. Typical, right, they want everything served to them.' The new shift was arriving and as the day shift started to leave the room, one of the guards grabbed the arm of the complainer. 'Did you say that he said he knew the question!' "

The Philosopher pauses and holds his glass to Michel for a refill of cognac. He turns to Maya and smiles. "Am I telling it too slow?"

Michel's face is flushed pink. "No. No. *Continuez. Formidable*, eh, Dee Dee?"

"When the prisoner heard the sound of running footsteps in the hall and the clanking of keys banging against brown-shirt bellies he sat up on his bunk. The metal-cover clanked open and to his astonishment he saw two faces peering in at him sideways, an arrangement which he had never seen before except on playing cards. The fascinating thing about prison, he thought, is the total implausibility.

" 'Hey listen,' shouted a guard. 'Did you say you know the question for which life is the answer?' Talk about implausibility, he thinks. 'Yes, I know the question.'

" 'Then tell us.'

" 'Why should I? You haven't even warned me of my rights.'

" 'Stop fucking around,' shouted the sideway face whose mouth is to the left. 'We'll come in there and beat it out of you.'

" 'Oh if you do that, I'll talk right away. But you'll never know if I'm telling you what's in my mind.'

" 'He's right, Duane,' said the sideways face with mouth to the right.

" 'Okay, how can we get you to talk?'

" 'Take me to the U.N. in New York,' said the prisoner. I'll talk direct to the Higher Intelligence. I've run out of people to talk to down here anyway.'

" 'Let's talk to the Warden,' said the left vertical mouth.

" 'We'll be right back.'

" 'I'll wait for you,' said the prisoner as he hears the footsteps running away down the hall and the keys jangling.

"Well, the Warden phones the Director of the Department of Correction, a smart, tough-minded ambitious politician who realizes that there is nothing to lose, that it will give him a chance to go to New York, expenses paid, and that the prisoner is, after all a well-educated man, author of ten books, which, subversive as they are, might contain the unexpected longshot solution.

"So the guards come to the solitary confinement cell and handcuff the prisoner to a chain around his waist and lead him to a state car where his feet are shackled with ankle-cuffs, in compliance with regulations for transferring convicted felons. The prisoner, escorted by two guards, the Warden and the Director of Corrections, is flown to New York.

"The ticket agent at Trans World Airlines, who supplemented his income by tips to newspapers, leaked the information which was picked up as a human interest story by a harassed media and flashed to a desperate world.

"The prisoner arrived at the U.N. building one hour and four minutes before the deadline.

"The Warden ordered the ankle-cuffs removed, but the waist-chain and hand-cuffs were left intact, according to regulations for transferring felons, when the prisoner walked on to the stage of the Assembly Hall and whispered the question into a microphone."

-30-

"In relating to Humans, remember, they belong to twenty-four different species and inhabit twenty-four very different realities. You must know the frequency band of the Domesticated Ape you are communicating with."

One-brained Humans (Pisces-Aries-Taurus) dial 1-2-3
Two-brained Humans (Gemini-Cancer-Leo) dial 4-5-6
Three-brained Humans (Virgo-Libra-Scorpio) dial 7-8-9
Four-brained Humans (Sagittarius-Capricorn-Aquarius) dial 10, 11, 12, etc. . . . .

Journal of Astronomical Psychology

THE DELIGHTFUL DELINQUENTS

Zodiac for June, 1971.

As the warm breezes of June fill the land with flower-perfume a planet of Geminis yawn, stretch and climb out of their comfy beds. They take a long drink of warm milk and then, refreshed and mobile, begin their search through the Terrestrial Garden of Eden, looking for action—mates, energy, amusement—in a word, deals. Each of these Two-brained sprites will get away with a host of petty crimes just because they are Geminis—titillative, furry, tenacious and fun.

Rodents they are with two grabbing paws above and two sturdy legs below, but few people are disturbed by them the way they are by rats, because Geminis charm while they decimate.

This was brought home to me last year when a professional humanologist remarked, "I just can't keep Geminis away no matter how much they steal. It would be like banishing the spirit of Beguilement in a species where there is too much heaviness and not enough bewitching charm. I know they are rodents on two legs—but I love them."

Gemini are rodents. Specifically, they are two-brained primates basically unable to understand the reality of the abstract symbols or the moral codes that so pre-occupy domesticated primates.

Take me for instance. I was on the phone one day when I saw a Gemini come up the back steps, dash into the kitchen, grab a bottle of champagne and head for my daughter's bedroom. Delighted because I had never seen a Gemini in the house before, I brought him into the study for a heart-to-heart talk. His bright eyes glittered with health and innocence. Had he been anyone else I would have thrown him out in a second. But he was a Gemini, big-eyed and clean-lined, totally incapable of true symbol-abuse or domestic evil, and I let him stay for a few months until I realized that he had entangled the entire family in a web of silly weasel deceit and childish suspicion.

This ability of the Gemini to bewitch is due to many attributes: Hir youthful appearance (they are the first mammals, the first shoreline creatures, still adapted to the fluidity of marine life), Hir quick energy, and Hir amusing habits, one of which is stuffing a truly astonishing amount of goodies in Hir wiry body, a habit that can intrigue even sophisticates like William S. Burrows.

Prof. Burrows had no particular sympathy for two-brained creatures when it came to protecting the ecology. Whenever he saw a human attempting destructive actions he would drive it away. However, one day he became so intrigued with a Gemini in his office, wheeling and dealing, flirting and joking, lying and fabricating, attempting to seduce young males, that he found himself engaging in erotic contact, at first a patronizing stroking of skin and patting to the squirming little body. He ended up in the Rapture Room with the wiry, insatiable boy and got up to 145 orgasms before realizing that He was being neurologically burglarized while He fused. What was playful, sensory linkage to Him was desperately serious, survival tactics to the tender-skinned little courtesan—who would live for months on the pilfered energy, peddling the story to other larvals who thrive and gloat on gossip about their betters.

"I just floated there in bliss and enjoyed being taken. The cunning lad was tape-recording the entire sequence!"

-31-

"*Rotwang read a newspaper story about Mutants. Mutants are people who belong to a different species from Homo Sapiens. Every year due to radiation accumulation in the atmosphere and food additives, more and more Mutants are being born. The newspaper story said that the Mutants were in town for the annual Mutant Convention. Rotwang and the Aliens decided to attend the convention and talk to the Mutants. They entered the huge convention hall and split up. 'See you back here in 2 hours,' they told each other. So without further ado they melted into the crowd of militant mutants."*

ROTWANG
By Tim Hildebrand

INITIATION INTO THE LIFE OF GLAMOUR

New York, N.Y., November 1960.

Flora Lu Ferguson told the Philosopher that she would meet him at Birdland which was a nightclub in Manhattan where the top jazz musicians played and hung-out. Flora Lu said her husband, Maynard, played regularly at Birdland and many other famous clubs in New York and Hollywood.

When he arrived at the entrance to the Cabaret, following her instructions, he gave ten dollars to the uniformed dwarf and asked to be taken to the table of Mrs. Ferguson. The dwarf stuffed the bill in his pocket, bowed, and led the Professor across the crowded night club to a booth in the corner near to the performer's entrance and next to the band stand.

Flora Lu was sitting with a beautiful black-haired girl. They both greeted the doctor with pleasure. They listened to music for a while and talked to the musicians who came by the table to meet the Doctor.

On this occasion, and others, the Doctor got to meet such famous instrumentalists as Charles Mingus, Dizzie Gillespie, Miles Davis, Nathan Pusie, Bilyjim, "The Twister" Thibideaux, Brian Gysin, Albie Booth, Eban van den Post, Artie Shaw, Jim Thorpe, Max Lerner, and Huntington Hartford.

The black-haired girl was named Malaca. She was a Moroccan model whose picture had been on the cover of Holiday magazine. She had formerly been married to a member of the royal family of Iran who had given her a lot of money and treated her badly, by means of neglect and thoughtlessness. She, too, fervently wished to find more meaning from life by means of the Minstrel's drugs. Flora Lu had told her that Dylan might be an extra-terrestrial so she watched him closely with her mouth half open. Dylan found her overwhelmingly attractive and was grateful to Flora Lu for arranging interesting companionship during the neurological experiments.

-32-

"What does God want?" asked the child.
The teacher replied: "My god? Or yours? Or someone else's god?"
"What do you mean?" asked the child.
"Please use the plural when you refer to the Higher Intelligences," said the teacher.
"Okay," said the child happily. "This is more fun. What do the Gods want?"
"Very good question!" said the teacher.

Alan Watts

AND ... THE QUESTION IS ...!

Lausanne, May 1971

"Within a fraction of a second a most astonishing series of energy events flashed the world. I do not have the time nor the vocabulary," the Folk Singer apologizes, "to describe these celestial phenomena. Let me say that it was a bio-physical pulse of celebration. On the night side of the globe, all the stars in the sky were seen to increase in intensity and pulsate in varying colors. On the day-side of the planet the sun light became prismatic, the sky undulated in rainbow colors. A strange vibration-sound which seemed to activate exultant bodily sensations was felt by every living creature.

"The UFO beamed down the obvious message that the prisoner had, indeed, posed the correct question. Galactic congratulations were transmitted. Humanity was told to enjoy a three day period of rest and rejoicing and the council of wise-men was invited to return in eighty hours for the second evolutionary step."

Michel could no longer restrain his impatience. "Tell us. Tell us. What did he whisper?"

Dylan smiled. "I'll tell you, of course, but I thought it only courteous to give you the chance to answer. How about it Antonia. *Quel est le question basique?*"

Antonia turns her round brown eyes to Eight, slides her tongue along her upper lip and shrugged. *"Si je le connaissais, alors, je ne serai pas ici in thees fucking town."*

"And you, Dee Dee, what do you say?"

Dee Dee blushes skillfully and tosses her hair. The basic question, which Michel taught me is: How much does it cost."

"And you Michel? What is the basic question?"

Michel hunches his solid shoulders, the pink flaps of his jowls puff, his eyes roll to the ceiling in comic dismay. "I can say it no better than Gauguin. *Ou venons-nous? Ou allons-nous?* But surely a Frenchman would have suggested that."

The Philosopher turned to Maya. "And you my wife, who taught me this script, will reserve comment until the next act. Now I shall tell you.

"The prisoner whispered to the Higher Intelligence: *The question for which Life is the answer is this:* **WHAT DOES WOMAN WANT?**"

Dee Dee and Antonia giggle and exchange glances. Michel's face collapses in absent reflection for a moment, then he leaps to his feet, bends over the table, grabs the Philosopher's hand and pumps it vigorously.

"*Formidable! Superb!* Ah, Dylan, you are one man after my own heart. Splendid. *Exactement!* What does woman want?"

Maya sits demurely smiling. She is Mrs. Walker Light watching her genius husband win the Nobel Prize in Nuclear Fission.

-33-

"Every year on June 13 in Wilmington, Delaware, the Friends of Reality Club sponsors National Reality Day festivities, including the pre-dawn salute to Reality, the high noon Worship Event, the evening Reality Dance and at midnight the exciting Story of Reality. The guest speaker for last year's festival was none other than Rotwang himself. His speech was entitled 'Real World, Real World, It's All the Same to Me, What Mr. Einstein Called Cosmic Reality.' "

ROTWANG
By Tim Hildebrand

MATING IS A TWINKLING TIME!

Zodiac for July 1971.

Some Post-larvals permit Geminis to wheel-and-deal-because they are curious about the animal itself. Another time, Prof. William S. Burroughs, the famous St. Louis humanologist permitted one Quick-silvered Mercurian to take a quarter-million dollars, a two year supply of neuro-transmitters (aphrodisiacs and energizers), seduce fourteen Domesticated Apes (seven of each sex) and persuade several creative artists to sign disasterous contracts, just to see how much the Gemini would take before He was satisfied.

My cousin let a Swedish Gemini take two kilos of plutonium because she was fascinated by his balancing problem. Every time he pilfered more chemical he had to return for additional shielding, darting back and forth in a frenzy of greed.

In spite of their allure, Geminis can be destructive. They are unreformable "loners," untrustworthy, unable to make the social-political alliances of more advanced herd-animals, incapable of handling symbols except as tokens of power, and, of course, totally devoid of domesticated or insectoid morality. In spite of their archaic neurology the Predator and Rodent Control Office has never been called out for any large-scale attempt to rid larval planets of Geminis. Who could?

Psycho-linguists who are bothered by Geminis on an ecological level usually life-trap them and take them to another area. Humanologists can do this with a simple trap—for example a sleek yacht or an expensive sportscar (large). The Mercurian is easily lured into the trap by exposing money, sexual stimuli, or valued symbols (secrets). When the Gemini enters he steps on a trigger mechanism which closes the door without harming Hir.

Sometimes organisms are held in esteem because they are rare, like Black republicans or responsible journalists. But there is no excuse for liking Geminis for this reason. There are millions billions of them. Different imprints and social-conditioning styles and impersonation modes, of course, but Geminis nevertheless. And each one is hoarding about 250 megabytes of purloined secrets operating on the Heisenberg principle that SHe is unique and the only center of intelligence in the universe!

Abundant as they are, they are still not considered pests. One reason for this is the fact that they do not destroy the ecology by making homes of their own. They are invariably found living with and on others.

The courtship of the Gemini is another reason why people like them. It is a twinkling time! While other humanoids mate on the basis of elaborate sexual cues, the Gemini is obsessed with the thrill of the scam. When the Mercurian locates a desirable sexual "stash" SHe sits up on Hir haunches and literally "shines" with desire. Eventually the silly little "loner" is thrown out with little ceremony. The self-pitying scream of the rejected Gemini is sorrowful to hear. Eventually (their persistence is legendary) they are successful and remain long enough to pass on the genetic code, grab the loot and run. Geminis are not monogamous and live without emotional attachments for the most of their lives.

Geminis appear by magic whenever high energy or material value is exposed. Their most wonderful quality is the ease with which they can be attracted by greed-for-a-deal.

Alan V. Schwartz, who spent summers on Nantucket had many Geminis that came to him like Arab guides each June when he arrived. Once he was gone for seven years. Upon his return he was still able to bring the Geminis out of the woodlands and suburbs with a whistle and tinkle of precious metal.

-34-

"When the two hours were up, Rotwang and his Alien friends regrouped. They went over to their favorite cafe for an expresso. Once inside they sat around discussing what had happened at the Mutation Convention. The Aliens had promised to help the Mutants however they could. They asked Rotwang for advice. 'If you ask me,' said Rotwang, 'the Mutants will never be accepted by society until everyone *is a Mutant.' They asked Rotwang how long this would take. 'Well, if the Mutation factor remains stable, I'd say it will be a few centuries before even a majority of the population has mutated."*

ROTWANG
By Tim Hildebrand

A NEW AND ELEGANT WAY OF LIFE

Riverdale-on-Hudson, New York, October 1960.

Around midnight Flora Lu said it was time to go. Two Birdland waiters walked Her across the night club. The band waved en masse from the stage. One of the waiters collected the Commodore's bag from the check-room and the party, Flora Lu, Malaca, and Dylan entered a black limousine which was parked in front of the cabaret.

The car rolled along the West-Side Highway, an elevated road built along the banks of the Hudson River. After forty-one minutes, the car pulled onto a side road which was wooded on the right side and apartment-housed on the left. After a mile the car drove onto the gravel parking lot of a large stone house, built to imitate a Tudor Manor. There were two Jaguar cars parked with their motors off.

Maynard Ferguson was waiting at the door. He was a medium-sized, well-nourished male with Bounce and Grin.

The Cheery-vigor, as Dylan was to find out later, came from injecting into his muscles, several times a day, a mixture of vitamins and speed provided by the famous Doctor Max Jacobson. But, pharmacological nitpicking aside, Maynard's welcome radiated vim, pep, zip, verve, and ginger, and the Philosopher absorbed the euphoria gratefully.

"Let me show you your new laboratory," said Flora Lu with artful alertness.

The living room was enormous and deeply carpeted. A huge U-shaped couch, deep and soft, framed the giant fireplace. The wood-panelled walls served as background for bookshelves and garish non-objective paintings. One wall was bristling with electronic sound equipment, gleaming stainless-steel turntables, tape machines, banks of speakers, yards of record albums.

These sparse physical descriptions cannot express the ambiance of hushed, reverent luxury, the haunting presence of an aesthetic intelligence, a sure, knowledgeable, gentle consciousness arranging each hedonic detail.

"Come, I'll show you your room."

Flora Lu pirouetted and started up the stairs, shooting an amused, pleased glance at Maynard who was leaning against the wall talking to Malaca and making her laugh.

"I hope you'll be comfortable here," said Flora Lu as she opened the door. The floor and the huge bed were covered with furs, splashed with naked pink silks. Wood and Velvet. Mirrors. A single thick red candle in an enfoliated bronze holder.

Maynard leaned against the door grinning like a slim peacock. "Flora Lu worked all week preparing your room. I tell you the truth, she consulted the most designing minds in New York to get it right."

"Would you like to see our room?" said Flora Lu.

The Ferguson bedroom was a soft-vaginal cave of lace-tassel-drapes-and-furs. Reubenesque paintings and Tantric yantras.

It was, to the astonished Commodore, a delightful introduction to Hedonic Consciousness, his first exposure to an intelligence dedicated to the aesthetic of living. Erotic architecture.

Around Flora Lu buzzed the hippest beauticians, decorators, designers, couturiers, a fluttering swarm of sensual technicians conspiring to surround Flora Lu with elegant, erotic stimuli. They overcharged and mildly despised their wealthy clients, but to Flora Lu they freely bought the finest fragrance of their art.

She was the first Love Goddess, Temple Divinity, Pleasure Priestess Dylan had met. Indeed, the very existence of this way of life had been unknown to him, an Irish lad from Minnesota.

-35-

Proverbs for Paranoids, 3: If they can get you asking the wrong questions, they don't have to worry about the answers.

Thomas Pynchon in "Gravity's Rainbow"

THE PROFESSOR REMEMBERS
SOME WORDS OF THOMAS PYNCHON

Geneva, May 1971.

The Inefficient Wizard sinks back in the soft, crinkling red leather and watches Michel drive the Roller along the freeway into the immediate future.

"That story last night," beams the Frenchman, "superb. But you didn't give the answer."

"Another dinner like that and I'm sure I'll remember the next chapter of the legend."

"Women are the center of my life." Michel confides waving his hand at the dash-board of the car. "That is why I do all this. Do you know what women want? Let me tell you. A man to take care of them. Believe me, Tom it's the truth. Men want two things. Power and women. The business we do for *them*. But woman, she wants only one thing. To be amused and be taken care of by a powerful man."

"And what is this business that man concerns himself with?"

Michel's blue eyes sparkle within the folds of pink flesh.

"That is where men differ, my dear Tom. Most want nothing except the security of being told what to do. Bah, we shall not think of them. Most men want money, but that is no problem for us. Money is a simple matter. We shall win as much money as we need to do what we want. And what do we want? Freedom, *n'est-ce pas*? That is why I admire you. You are like myself. A bold outlaw willing to risk everything for freedom. That is why we are driving on this road to Geneva right now."

"Who are we going to see?"

"A man who is, how do you say it, a broker. A broker of information. Some men trade in gold, some in jewels, some in currency, some in machinery, some in contraband. Christopher Hyatt deals in information. Genetics. Drugs. Scientific Facts. Since World War II, Intelligence has become very marketable. Information is money. There are facts we must know and Monsieur Hyatt will sell them to us."

"We'll have to pay him?" exclaims the Professor with mild alarm.

"Of course. I have already guaranteed him 5000 swiss francs just for the first contact. You must know this, Dylan, to stay in Switzerland will be an easy matter but it will require money."

"I can make no promises, Michel. At the moment we're broke. I'll be able to get money, when my book is published. But it will take time and these matters are never certain."

Michel waves his hand in casual disdain. "Don't worry. Together we shall win the money you need for your asylum in Switzerland and much more. I have been looking for a partner. Someone to share the excitement. In a few days we shall sit down and discuss business. Perhaps we shall form a company—the two of us exiles."

The car is now rolling along the lakefront past the luxury hotels.

What better place than Geneva, thinks Dylan, to play games of disinformation with the Counter Intelligence Agency? It's your basic Predatory Preterite-killer Protestant town. Calvin country, the home of the most ruthless murderous sect in world history, the self-appointed elite of a gangster god, the pious bible-tumpers who have a divine license to rob and murder the preterites, those Catholics, heathens, arabs, niggers and jews passed over by a white racist Jehovah.

Stone reminders are everywhere. Spies and big business, in their element, move tirelessly among the monuments. The Minstrel senses that there are ex-young men here in this very city, faces he used to pass in the quad, who got initiated at Harvard into the Puritan Mysteries: who took oaths in dead-earnest to blindly obey and to act always in the name of The Machine, who now come here to Geneva to work for The Firm.

Michel makes a right turn and parks in front of the *Richmont*.

"This is the favorite hotel of your friends the C.I.A. It could be risky to meet here, but they know everything by now anyway."

The doorman rushes to the car greeting Michel by name. Michel strides forcefully into the lobby and turns to enter the dining room. The headwaiter bows profusely and without a word escorts the two men to a table in the rear of the restaurant where a man is seated awaiting them.

"Monsieur Hyatt, may I present the fugitive Rock Star?"

Hyatt rises and extends his hand. He is a short man, over fifty, pudgy face, bald with a graying fringe; dressed with conservative elegance. He wears a red Legion d'Honneur pin in his lapel. Hyatt motions to a chair, sits himself, turns and studies the Philosopher's face with intense care.

"I have been interested in meeting you for some time Monsieur Dylan. I have been following your work and listening to your lyrics, and if you are willing, would like to ask you some questions."

Michel Hauchard has poised his body in alert position, his eyes glitter; he seems to be controlling excitement, a gambler at the roulette wheel.

"But my dear Hyatt, it is we that must ask you the questions. Have you been able to find out his status?"

Hyatt picks up his pipe, scratches a match, glances sharply at the Professor through smoke and then throws the box of matches on the white table cloth.

"In the old days, as Pynchon pointed out," he sighed, "espionage was so simple. Everything was specialized. For high-tech you'd go to one cafe. Currencies another. Arms were divided into hand-guns, automatic weapons, tank-artillery, chemical-biological. Furs subdivided into Sable, Ermine, Mink and Others. Dope, bulk orders only, you understand: Stimulants, Downers, Euphorics, Psychedelics, Empathogens . . . You're after information. Right?"

Michel nodded tensely.

A tragic sigh. "Information. Is there any wonder the world's gone insane today? With information the only real medium of exchange?"

Michel coughs delicately. "His legal status, my dear Hyatt?

"All right, let's get the immediate details over with. There is an Interpol Warrant out for Monsieur Dylan's arrest but it is inactive. Which means it is mildly dangerous for him to wander around airports but he probably wouldn't be arrested in the absence of a clearance by the host country. I should stay out of Britain, Spain, Italy, if I were you. The other European countries don't want any scandal with him one way or another. There is always the danger that an eager underling could arrest him even though the top officials prefer to leave him alone. Your basic problem, as you well know, is with the United States. According to my information the F.B.I. and the C.I.A. have no desire to have you captured and returned to prison. Your drug people, however, do want you and will try to get you back. The Swiss just found out last night that you are here. They were interested, of course, in locating you simply because it's embarrassing to a country to have a fugitive kicking around off the radar screens. The Swiss, as far as we now know, won't bother you as long as you remain low profile. But my bet is that the American drug police who are notoriously fanatic will get an extradition warrant filed. They are flamboyantly inefficient, so it will probably take a month to do it. So if you move fast with the Swiss you may be able to beat the American warrant. If Swiss asylum isn't shaping up in three weeks you might consider moving on to another country."

Hyatt puts the pipe back in his mouth and pulls at it thoughtfully. It has gone out. He picks up the match box, slowly strikes fire, cups the pipe with his hand and fills the air with smoke. He has finished transmitting.

Michel, his jowls quivering with tension turns to Dylan and nods proudly. "What other countries would you suggest?" asks the Bard quietly.

Hyatt shakes his head slowly, his face expressionless. "That question is far beyond what was contracted for today. Obviously you aren't that familiar with how the information business works. What has Monsieur Hauchard told you?"

"Actually nothing," says the Philosopher. "What should I know?"

Hauchard and Hyatt exchange glances.

Hyatt hunches his shoulders. "Well, at least you should be given some negative information. My name is not Hyatt and that name will mean nothing to anyone else. I work for no government, although I deal with any government which wishes my services. The mechanics of the operation are quite simple. When I am asked a question, I set a price for the answer. If the price is acceptable I obtain the answer. Monsieur Hauchard, in this case, requested to know your current legal status. I have given you the pertinent facts. Ordinarily I would not have met you. However, I must confess to a curiosity about your well-publicized eccentricity and perhaps a desire to get some information from you. Would you permit me to talk privately with Michel for a moment?"

Dylan glances at Michel and nods.

Hyatt and Hauchard rise and walk to the lobby, the tall portly Frenchman bending down solicitously listening to Hyatt.

-36-

"The Neurological Renaissance which preceded the Cybernetic Age was centered in the Great Universities of the epoch—Michoacan, Guerrero, Zacatecas, Oaxaca, Sin Semilla, Columbian, Hawaiian, Thailand, Morelos, Puebla and Acapulco."

History of the Roaring 20th Century

DELETE *Sociological Digest*

HIPPIES: WILD FLOWERS THAT FLY

The first period of post-literate neurology is personified in The Hippy,

Stage 13. Beauty and ugliness, gravity and levity, survival and death, friend and enemy, high and low . . . it's all there in the simple, quiet world of the Hippy . . . little wildflowers that fly.

Hippies, both oriental and western, are the free-est and most beautifully colored of all industrial life forms. Their lives are very busy. They have to be, in order to get everything experienced in the few years they are alive.

A Hippy has a rather difficult time in its post-larval state. A simple primitive slug-like biped creature, the domesticated human, is the Hippy's growing stage. After it has evolved through the four gene-pool collective survival phases and discharged its eggs, the Fifth (beginning adult) phase begins and, as in the fairy tale of the Frog Prince, from an ugly, hostile, ignorant human comes a beautiful creature flittering off to see the galaxy.

Only the hippy doesn't live happily ever after. Some live only a few months before being forced back into slug-like existence; others manage to live for several years by avoiding human habitats. Most, however, are doomed to die before mastering a cybernetic state, leaving behind eggs (children) to carry on the species.

There are two superfamilies of Hippies, the Arhat (*vagabondus orientalis*) with nine subfamilies from the Indian subpeninsula and the true post-Einsteinian pre-cybernetic Hippy activated by the radiation of Alamogordo which has produced subfamilies in every larval culture.

Each subfamily contains many varieties, some without common names. In fact, neurologicians tell us that there are 100,000 different kinds of Hippies. Many subfamilies have disguised themselves as collectives and actually live and work among industrials quite undetected.

Largest of our Hippy Groups are the Dead Heads, best known in North America. When winter comes they do not die but migrate south like many birds and well-to-do primates. The Pretty Painted Lady is another migrator, but cold weather is not necessarily the cause. Some say that over-population in the home hive is the reason for these mass run-aways.

-37-

"The sky above the port was the color of television, tuned to a dead channel.

"It's not like I'm using," Case heard someone say, as he shouldered his way through the crowd around the door of the Chat Bar. "It's like my body's developed this massive drug deficiency." It was a sprawl voice and a Sprawl joke. The Sprawl was BAMA. The Boston-Atlanta-Metropolitan-Axis.

Opening lines of "Neuromancer"
By William Gibson

A SUCCESSFUL ACADEMIC ROBOT

New York, N.Y., October 1960.

The Commodore, we recall, had lived most of his adult life in a chic redwood-and-glass home in Hibbing, Minnesota. Danish modern furniture and an enormous sundeck slanting out to catch the Bay View.

At the time of his Harvard assignment he was living in the luxurious, solid, upper-middle-class comfort of a house rented from a professor on sabbatical.

These were the affluent machines for living used by rock stars in this era. Architecture geared for efficiency.

But Flora Lu's temple was designed to seduce each sense into rapture. To soften, smooth, round-off any angle, entice one into harem embrace. Bordello baroque with thick rugs, deep enfolding couches.

In this shrine of beauty the poet's mutation was cherished. He was, of course, a robot. A most successful robot. His larval equipment was resilient and effective. He was highly respected at Harvard University; handsome, clean cut, confident, witty, charismatic, and, in that inert culture, unusually creative.

His left hemisphere had been imprinted and conditioned to grasp and relate a wide variety of symbols; his fourth brain trained to play the role of Young Poet. The Darwin-Freud-Jung impersonation game. Dashing, yet dignified. A respected, promising young scholar sitting in his study shuffling symbols, walking vigorously to the concert platform where students awaited the voice of his generation.

He had attained the highest ambition of the young American intellectual. A platinum record album.

His neurological circuitry was, however, totally cut off from body and senses. His hair was athletic-virile short. He moved like a tennis player. His clothes were thoughtlessly selected to fit the young professional image. He routinely drank martinis, ate what was put before him, his motions stereotyped game sequences, his sexual life uninspired.

He had haunted the museums, had memorized and lived out Vasari's Lives, roamed for months through the churches and museums of Florence. He had devoted a week to each room of the Uffizi, a week at Pisa, knew the

Louvre like local neighborhood, could identify the artist and school of almost any painting in any European gallery, could lead you directly to the Goyas in the Prado; spent ten days trying to relive the death of Lorca in Granada, peering over bullet-pocked walls at piles of white bones while his clandestine guide fearfully watched for the Guardia Civil, U.S.W.

He had shamed the American Express and the Literary editor of the Dublin Times to arrange a Joyce trip of Dublin when the Martello tower was a neglected, forgotten repository of autumn leaves; had tracked down every Orozco and Rivera mural in country school rooms and provincial tax offices of Mexico; had set out on more voyages of off-beat literary rediscovery than any intellectual of his generation, a veritable Richard Halliburton of Psychology, not content to read about, but forever seeking to relive the realities of the bards.

But this had nothing to do with direct aesthetic experiences. He struggled to contact myth by pushing his body around to "sacred places," but, his nervous system cocooned in symbols; the event was always second-hand, isolated by the carapace of concepts.

-38-

Proverbs for Paranoids, 4: YOU hide, they seek.

Thomas Pynchon in "Gravity's Rainbow"

Geneva, May 1971.

A waiter approaches with a steaming silver pot. Dylan pours coffee and thick cream in his cup, lights a cigarette and studies the uneasy rippling of fear in his body, the familiar outlaw feeling of helpless pawn on chess board of players with unknown motivations, a commodity bartered by two strange men whom he can see sitting in the lobby talking vigorously. Michel is scanning a sheaf of papers.

It is Hyatt who leads the return, rolling delicately across the dining room followed by Michel whose face is expressionless.

Seated at the table Hyatt comes to the point directly. "Dear Sir, up until this point I have provided you with information you needed. Now I propose a second round of exchange. I wish to ask *you* some questions. I have no way of knowing how valuable your answers, if you choose to give them, will be to me. Or how helpful or dangerous they may be to you. Are you willing?"

"Michel is my mentor in this affair," says the Song-writer, turning to the Frenchman. "What shall I do?"

Michel Hauchard dabs a handkerchief at the moisture on his forehead. He looks like a fat boy caught in some culinary crime. He seems to have been intimidated by his conversation with Hyatt.

"I suggest that you cooperate with Monsieur Hyatt."

"Very well," says Eight. "What do you want to know? I trust you are not going to ask silly questions like how many Black Panthers there are in Algeria. Or whether the Weathermen are planning to steal plutonium."

"No," replies Hyatt without smiling. "I want to find out what you think about the danger of drugs."

The Commodore looks up in surprise and raises his eyebrows.

"Please do not misunderstand," continues Hyatt. "I am not interested in moralizing. I am aware that alcohol, aspirin, hydro-carbons in the atmosphere, and radiation from watching television are far more dangerous physically than any neuro-active drug. And I'm aware that a hundred times more young people are permanently crippled by high school athletics than heroin. Not to mention skiing, mountain climbing, or the bloodbath caused by promiscuous use of the motor car by adolescents. No, I want to talk about the psycho-political dangers of drugs."

"Have you listened to my songs?"

Hyatt moves his lips into a tight smile. "I have perhaps not heard everything you have sung, but I have been able to peruse some detailed summaries which have been prepared by various interested parties. I recall your statement that Lenin could have converted the aristocratic youth of Russia to the revolution without firing a shot, if he had known how to use hashish as a political tool."

"A debatable speculation," smiles the Song Writer, "but it may have made the point."

"And what is the point?" Hyatt's question comes like a karate chop.

"The point is that brain-reward drugs, in the hands of those who know how to use them, can be a most powerful tool for social change."

"Precisely," says Hyatt sharply. "And there is the danger. The effect of sensory and brain-reward drugs is to loosen the connections of the user to society. To stimulate internal pleasures within the body and the nervous system. Pleasures which are independent of external rewards and punishments. Isn't it true that brain-reward drugs are basically anti-social and anarchic?"

"My dear Hyatt, are you serious? Certainly you know that everything in nature is anti-social."

"All the more reason for imposing our order on nature," responds Hyatt impassively, testing.

"Our order? Whose order?" said Dylan.

"Our order," repeated Hyatt nervously.

So Dylan sang. "Body drugs turn on somatic circuits which are ready to be activated. Brain drugs turn on neural circuits that are ready to be activated. The brain, I am sorry to say, is neither social or anti-social. Transient political regimes create the anti-social. It's the law-makers and morality police who, from time-to-time and place-to-place, define one experience acceptable and another immoral."

"As it should be," said Hyatt. "You do grant society the right to define the limits of the reality it finds acceptable?"

"The problem is not quite that simple. Just as a regime can restrict what individuals experience, so can individual experiences change regimes.

Hyatt laughs in delight. "You are saying that a society is defined by the drugs it uses? That's a new theory of politics."

"Let's call it neuro-politics. The theory is simple. Drugs can expand and accelerate the use of the brain just as machines expand the scope and power of the muscles. Humanity has used and abused machines. Humanity will use and abuse the expanded possibilities of the brain. Machines and drugs are here to stay. I didn't invent the brain and I didn't invent the botanicals that it feeds on. Sooner or later humanity will learn how to use machines and brain-enhancing drugs."

"Use them for what?"

"That, Monsieur Hyatt, is the question. Right Michel?"

Michel's foxy mind computes the trajectory of the conversation. He begins to laugh. "Here we go again. The prisoner's question."

"What are you two talking about? Have you been nipping these drugs yourself Michel? *What* is the question?"

"For the moment, for your purposes, the question seems to be, *What is the purpose of society?* The answer to that question determines how you will use machines and drugs."

Hyatt places his elbow on the table, rests his face on his hand and frowns. He shakes his head. "Professor, you have me puzzled. I don't know what to do with you. I feel that you're playing with me frivolously, in that particularly offensive attitude of grinning drugged superiority. And yet what you say intrigues me."

"What about the Sandoz Labs?" says the Professor, grinning.

"Sandoz!" laughs Hyatt. "Psychochemie AG? The drug company for brain-tickets? LSD by the ton, eh?"

Michel looks blank.

"Sandoz is the Basel Lab that discovered LSD," explains Dylan.

"You should spend some time with the indole crowd," says Hyatt. "I'll phone Albert Hoffman. He's eager to meet you, and Tom Pynchon too. But the indole crew is very elitist. They see themselves as the climax of a long chain of European dialectic mysticism. Generations of gentlemen scholars getting stoned in Berlin villas. Generations of blighted grain, ergotism, witches on broomsticks, community orgies, cantons up there in the folds of the Alps that haven't known an unhallucinated day in the last 500 years—keepers of the gnostic traditions. Christ and Paracelus were part of the gang. Neurological aristocrats—they don't make waves, don't sing songs saying 'everybody should get stoned.' You do. So what shall we do about you?"

"The kind of question determines the answer. Ask practical questions and you'll get practical answers. As I recall we got into social philosophy when you started defending society's right to make my brain illegal. What do you want to know?"

"If the policy-makers of certain European countries ask me what you think they should do to avoid a drug-abuse problem—what is your answer?"

"To do exactly the opposite of what the American government did. Let the free-market and the laws of supply and demand operate."

"Looking at the results, that sounds sensible. How did the Americans create such a mess?"

"It didn't have to happen. In the early Sixties it became obvious that the next stage of technological evolution, the Information Age, was going to involve neuro-pharmacologicals. Brain drugs were going to play a powerful role in human affairs. The American government was informed of the development and encouraged to sponsor research, factual education and rational control. The President at the time was Jack Kennedy."

"I see what you mean," replies Hyatt.

"The Kennedy family made its fortune distributing Brain Drugs," interjects Michel. "If you call alcohol a Brain Drug?"

"I betray no secret when I say that the Kennedy family was well aware of the positive uses of body-mind drugs and sympathetic to the concept of brain reward."

"He's right," says Michel. "Ask anyone around Gstaad or St. Moritz."

"I know," nods Hyatt. "The role of Dr. Max Jacobson has been a source of considerable amusement among European Intelligence Agencies."

"Who is this Jacobson?" demands Michel suspiciously. "He sounds Jewish to me."

"According to my sources," replies Hyatt. "Max Jacobson was a 'speed-doctor' who cheerfully energized many show-business personalities and later became a member of the Presidential family entourage. Dr. Jake appears in many 'at-home' photos of the Kennedy family. I myself, Michel, have seen pictures of Doctor Jake cheerfully dispensing energy medicine at rest-pauses during the famous fifty-mile hike for 'vigor.' "

"That's my point," says the Exiled Song Writer. "During the Kennedy administration, drug-policy was controlled by the Food and Drug Administration with emphasis placed on research, standards of purity, and the dissemination of rational, scientific information. It's hard to define these issues in political terms, but the Kennedy administration emitted friendly, tolerant vibrations. An open-ness. A glasnost. Young people, in particular, liked this."

"Yes," muses Hyatt. "The problem was to appear friendly and be tough at the same time."

"The elevation of Lyndon B. Johnson to the presidency changed many things including the drug policy. Why? Change in presidential religion."

"Religion?" exclaims Michel. "I didn't know Johnson was religious."

"Religious and philosophic factors are much more important in politics than text books can reveal. To understand the politics of the 1960s you must remember that L.B.J. belonged to the Church of Christ."

"You mean he was a puritan Christian?"

"Several historians have suggested that Evangelical Protestantism is the basis for the Anti-humanistic Mentality which still characterizes the American-Empire Holy War Fixation."

"Calvinists," cries Michel. "Pouf! I detest them."

"The ominous moral defect of Evangelical prudery is that it makes people cruel, vindictive, and unforgiving. What you wise and tolerant Europeans may not realize is that the American Protestant Fundamentalists are the most unbending, savage and dogmatic, racist, murderous gangs to emerge from the 19th century."

"Red-necked Jansenists?" inquires Hyatt.

"As the more flexible tolerance of the Catholic Kennedy was replaced by Texas fundamentalism, the drug policy shifted from research and medical supervision to highly moralistic control by a new *Kultur-polizei* known as Narcs. In retrospect we can see that the rise to power of men such as Nixon, Haldeman, Ehrlichman, Reagan and Rockefeller solidified the Puritanical tilt in the American cultural conflict."

"Do you find this interesting, Monsieur Hyatt?" asks Michel.

Hyatt smiles. "Do you see this ring? Do you know where it comes from?" Hyatt is holding his pudgy hand in the center of the table to exhibit an ornate gold ring—an enormous ruby surrounded by an episcopal crown. Michel's watery eyes bulge in astonishment.

"The last and only time I saw a ring like that was at my confirmation. But you Hyatt?"

"Let us simply assume that I have done many favors for Rome. Certain congregations in the Vatican are most worried about the manifestations of our Reformed Brethren."

"In the long run, Monsieur Hyatt, the worst mistake a governing regime can make is to place itself in rigid opposition to consumer appetites. Governments who attempt to violate the laws of supply and demand, are illegal. Laws which attempt to regulate what and whom people put in their own bodies create anti-social and rebellious reactions."

"I repeat. Brain reward drugs are by definition anti-social," protests Hyatt. "If drugs reward and the society punishes, then anti-social feelings are automatically imprinted. However, if society allows the use of brain-reward drugs then the most enthusiastic patriotic reactions will result."

"You're talking about Brave New World."

"I'm talking about the bio-neurology of the human being, Monsieur Hyatt. In the last analysis the basic satisfactions that humanity buys with the money earned by work are biological and neurological. Food. Shelter. Health. Pleasure. Bliss. The most fundamental need of humanity is the neurological experience we call intoxication, the cyclical hunger to alter consciousness, to bend reality, to stimulate the brain bored with routine. Certainly our most rigidly-organized social institution, the military, understands this need. Alcohol is unashamedly used as the official off-duty reward. And look at the Japanese who can always be counted on to provide us with caricature exaggerations of the trends of technological culture. Japanese executives are permitted, encouraged, even required to get staggeringly, flamboyantly drunk—in ginza bars after work."

Hyatt drums his fingers on the linen table cloth and shakes his head at Michel Hauchard.

"Just as I feared. Our Hero with the New Elixir of Life is indeed dangerous and is therefore in danger. You see, like it or not, the dehumanization which you say stems from evangelic protestantism has effectively conquered the world. Let's face facts. There are a few countries which are not rushing headlong into assembly-line homogeneity. Too bad for you, Doctor. A few decades ago when the world was run by sultans, kings, war lords, aristocrats, philosophers, and colonial governors, there would be a dozen potentates that would be fascinated by your ingenious lyrics. But today the industrial world has been organized by the Cold War into monolithic blocks. The psychology of nations is now determined by their Cold War status. You are absolutely antagonistic and dangerous to any and all governments. Look what brain-reward did in Vietnam! One half million American troops rendered serenely non-belligerent because of the high grade hashish and heroin. History may well decide that the American empire was defeated at the high-water mark of its expansion by a decline of martial ardor produced by dope. I can assure you Monsieur Dylan that, with perhaps one or two exceptions, no government in the world will allow you refuge."

-39-

"Home was BAMA, the Sprawl, the Boston-Atlanta-Metropolitan-Axis.

"Program a map to display frequency of data exchange. Every thousand megabytes a single pixel on a very large screen. Manhattan and Atlanta burn solid white. Then they start to pulse, the rate of traffic threatening to overload your simulation. Your map is about to go Nova. Cool it down. Up your scale. Each pixel a million megabytes. At a hundred million megabytes per second, you begin to make out certain blocks in midtown Manhattan, outlines of hundred-year-old industrial parks ringing the old core of Atlanta."

From "Neuromancer"
By William Gibson

MEET THE HIPPIES: A COLORFUL VANISHING SPECIES

Journal of Anthropology, September 1972.

Hippies are interesting in other ways too. Some species have "sleeping assemblies" where they gather together late in the day and sleep together. Then there are the "mud puddle clubs" where hippies pack close together by the thousands on the damp soil listening to amplified electronic mating sounds. Some believe that Hippies have certain "flyaways" that are consistently used by local "traffic."

Many species have definite odors. Some are spicy, some delicate and sweet, others strong and musky.

Territories are important for certain kinds of Hippies. There are the notorious pugnacious varieties which, mounted on two-wheeled vehicles propelled by international combustion motors, chase away other Hippies, mammals and even Domesticated Apes. The Pearl Crescents of San Berdoo are best known for these tactics.

Color seems to play a very important role in the life of a Hippy. To some, protective coloration is essential to their very existence. The varieties with resemblance colorations imitate mental patients, American Indians, hobos, Old Testament prophets and bird droppings. Plain-colored varieties often resemble the backgrounds of their habitats like farmers or woodsmen.

Hippies use *mimicry* too. The giant *Vagabondus Christianis* (the true Jesus-freak) is genuinely asexual. It advertises this fact with drab clothing, ungainly movement, Amish beards, harsh sounds and pimpled faces. The Simple-Drop-Out, (*disaffiliatus simplex*), which is very sexual, looks very much like the *Christianis* and often enjoys the protection provided by its less-tasty cousin.

The Hippy is vulnerable to human predators during its first Stage (Stage 13 Passive Receptivity); the two later Stages of Hippies (Stage 14 Body-Engineers and Stage 15 Tantric-Mated Fusions) are less vulnerable. Chief among their adversaries are narcs, policemen, religious primates, predatory bureaucrats, and hawks.

Other escape devices include rapid and erratic flight, dodging and hiding.

But flying high and being pulled down are not the only roles Hippies play in the community of nature. Many carry neuro-energizers and brain-stimulants from one community to another and in this way advance the neuro-evolutionary process.

The destruction of the natural environment by Industrial Apes has even affected the Hippy. Many species have disappeared completely—awaiting, in camouflaged form, no doubt, the beginning of cybernetic societies.

The Hippy, in all three Stages, is, it must not be forgotten, the first cybernetic mutant. Their evolutionary dilemma is poignant! They are activated just one generation before space-flight and computers, frivolous antecedents and parents to the first neuro-electric, cybernetic generation.

But, in spite of their limited range, most Hippies are still a common sight in every community. Some of them are every bit as pretty as the butterflies they resemble and the flowers they smoke, sniff and ingest. In fact, on a good Hippy day in the park one might get the feeling that the butterflies and wild flowers have taken primate form and are dancing gaily around the world.

-40-

"The Aliens then and there made up their minds to figure out a way to speed up the mutation process. They sent messages to their home planet, Alpha, and asked the scientists there to work on the problem immediately. Alpha science is so advanced it took only a short time before the Aliens got a special space package containing a strange device."

ROTWANG
By Tim Hildebrand

THE MATING PROCESS IN THE NEUROVERSE

New York, N.Y., October 1960.

The astonished Dylan sat on the couch in Flora Lu's Elysian Chamber, letting his right cerebral hemisphere slowly open up to direct sensual reception, and serenely observed his firm concepts of Life and Interpersonal Relationships slide away in soft curving smiles.

The yoga of attention. The retraction of the symbolic and social minds. The centering of awareness on the sense modality being activated. Each moment examined, not for loss or gain, nor for game cues or for fevered enhancement of status, but for, of all things, hedonic possibility. Everything seemed to turn out remarkably beautiful. The thread of sound. The delicious grace of moving one's hand, not as part of learned, survival sequence, but for kinaesthetic joy. A flower. An apple. A peacock feather. And the clear, unspoken assumption that the point of life was to feel good, to make each intersection as beautiful as possible.

And the enigmatic personality of Flora Lu who slid with the casual certainty of the Geisha, the Practiced Celebrant of Ancient Mystery. She drawled, open-eyed, like an Okie teen-ager. Her subtle comments, Her dewy fuckable innocence masking the jaded, fatigued languor of an experienced, patient woman.

She came to the session in a light blue robe. Maynard, a Florentine noble garbed in tight-fitting velvet pants. Malaca in Moroccan caftan, soft and touchable, was a brazen Arab girl, but hoping, vulnerable, inexperienced. The Commodore wore a silk shirt and trim trousers which Flora Lu had left on his bed while he showered.

A fire burned gently in the hearth. The air was scented. It was his first raw, direct experience with Conscious Music. The high-fidelity system amplified and transmitted sound waves to his tympanic membranes without mental interference. The neurological line between musician and listener was connected.

Maynard was a scholar of music. His drug-sensitized ears were now as big as the Areicibo Dish. Eyes closed, he swayed with pleasure, frowning and clucking at the slightest sign of musical banality or sloppiness.

Flora Lu floated around the room, Her face transfigured with delight.

Malaca blossomed into a flower of great beauty, Her classic features now stylized with the dignity of an Egyptian frieze. She lifted her face towards Flora Lu, towards Maynard and towards the Doctor with voluptuous devotion.

Dylan awakens from a long, bad dream of struggle on a heavy, suffering planet to find himself back home in Paradise. His eyes hook Malaca's. They rise as one and walk to the sun porch. She turns and comes into him, entwining Her arms around his neck.

They are two sea creatures returned, suddenly, to their warm, moist, rainbow world.

"Amazing," She breathes. "After all this time. To find It so simply."

The mating process in this new universe apparently began with the fusion of moist lips producing a soft, electric rapture which irradiated through the entire body. They seemed to find no problem in maneuvering the limbs, tentacles, and delightful protuberances with which they found themselves miraculously equipped in the transparent, viscous honey-liquid zero-gravity atmosphere that surrounded, bathed and sustained them.

-41-

"Everywhere I look in this case I find the finger-prints of the Counter Intelligence Agency."
What Does WoMan Want?

THE MOST DANGEROUS POSITION FOR A PHILOSOPHER
TO BE IN

Geneva, May 1971.

"I am interested, of course, in your one or two exceptions," says the Bard.

"It will take some time to explore those possibilities," replies Hyatt. "If I were to sound out a sympathetic ruler, what can I tell him about your message?"

"Nothing new, I fear. It's the same message I gave to the Algerian government. That was a futile gesture. And the same advice I wrote in the memorandum I gave to to the C.I.A. agent Mudkar in Algiers. Loosen up! A new second-generation, technological middle-class will emerge in 1986, sexually and psychopharmacologically self-confident, sophisticated by education, electronics and affluence. The new middle class will realize that the brain-reward provided by drugs is part of the disciplined, well-organized life in the Golden Age of Psychology. The middle class will reward itself in every way possible and it will create governments that will encourage and constructively enhance the pleasures and powers inherent in the human body and nervous system."

"I have no doubt that you are right," replies Hyatt. "Even in Russia the middle-classification is so accelerated that the next generation of rulers will realize that it will be cheaper to allow the comrades neurological and somatic rather than throw them in prisons. Two prolonged orgasms with hashish is in every way a more efficient diversion than two cars in the garage. But you are one generation premature. And that, as you are well aware, is the most dangerous position for a prophet to be in. An idea must be considered offensively premature if it cannot be connected by a series of simple, obvious steps to the generally accepted knowledge of the time. Have you read Polyani? He argues that there must always be an accepted, orthodox view of the nature of things against which the truth of a new idea must be tested. Any proposal that seems to contradict the orthodox must automatically be rejected."

"This observation may be deplorably true of this primitive civilization," replies Dylan. "But it is the first thing that our future society will change. Here is my quest. I am looking for one small country which, through the instrument of its most intelligent minds can tolerate an experimental presence."

Hyatt turns to Michel lifting his hands in dismay. "This man lives in his own time—his own space. A most fascinating expression of Heisenberg eccentricity. You must encourage him, Michel, to keep his feet on the ground. And keep him quiet too. My dear Dylan, I appreciate your frankness with me here today. But for the rest of your time in Switzerland I urge you to be discreet and, as your American bureaucrats like to say, to maintain a low profile."

"Silence, exile and cunning?" says Dylan dryly.

"You just be silent," says Michel, "and let me be cunning."

-42-

"No rejuvenation without Migration.
No Migration without Mutation."

George Koopman
President of the American Rocket Company

ANNA KATE IS BACK IN TOWN!

Geneva, August 1971.

Michel had selected the table in one of the tapestried alcoves in the rear of the restaurant. As Hyatt his plump face pink with expectation, examined the heavy parchment menu, Michel motioned to the sommelier.

"I should like a glass of *Nacluv*," said Hyatt glancing up.

"A large carafe of *Nacluv*, icy cold," commanded Michel. "Have you chosen?"

Hyatt licked his lips and the smooth skin around his eyes creased in smile. "I shall start with caviar. To be followed, *in ch'Allah*, by a tournedos, pink, with sauce *Bernaise* and a *coeur d'artichaut*. And to conclude, *fraise des bois* with fresh cream."

Michel nodded in approval, glancing at the waiter. The waiter bowed. "For me, I shall join Monsieur with the caviar. And then an unadorned, grilled *rognon de veau* with *pommes arecibo*. And for dessert *une bombe Tsiolkoski, si vous plait.*"

"My sincere congratulations," murmured the maitre d'hotel. He beckoned the sommelier close and whispered the selections.

"*Extraordinaire! Magnifique!*" said the wine-steward, handing the wine-list to Michel with reverence.

"With your permission, *mon brave*, I propose champagne, *en rapport* with our expectations."

Hyatt nodded with satisfaction.

"The Heinlein 47," said Michel to the sommelier.

"An inspired selection," said the sommelier, "but if you will allow a suggestion," running his gold pen along the card, "the *Weiss ober Weiss* '45 from the same region is incomparable. I tell in confidence, of course."

"It goes without saying," said Michel nodding.

The crystal carafe of chilled fire had arrived in its silver container of crushed ice and the waiter filled their goblets.

Hyatt, smiling, drank heavily, sighed in pleasure and leaned forward in transmission posture. Michel leaned forward to receive.

"Anna Kate is in Switzerland."

Michel placed his glass carefully on the linen table-cloth, took a deep breath, fell back on the chair and slapped both hands on his knees.

"My God! No! Are you sure? That could be a problem."

"Do you think so?" replied Hyatt quietly.

"Without doubt. She knows too much. About me and about the general situation."

Michel reached for the carafe and refilled the glasses. Both men drank, swallowed thoughtfully and looked at each other smiling.

"You mean she understands what could happen if your client gets established in Europe and starts broadcasting."

"Precisely. She homes towards the energy like a radar-scanning missile."

"Do you think Arpad Plesch sent Her?" said Hyatt idly.

"My God, I hope not," exclaimed Michel. "Why would Plesch do that?"

"Because he's rich and bored and clever and looking for the next wave. He has collected one of the best botanical libraries in the world. And you know what that means. And he's become interested in longevity."

"But would he send Anna Kate?"

"He's done it many times before. It fits with his sense of humor. He's been grooming Anna Kate for almost a quarter of a century.

"He entered her in the doctoral program in Film Theory at UCLA, moved her into his mansion in Benedict Canyon, hired the best tutors in Hollywood to teach her how to write scripts and put up two million pounds to make that very successful and controversial anti-nuke flick.

"As an active participant in the wildest, most decadent scenes in the movie industry she was in a position to tell Arpad how to manage his movie investments."

"He must be mad," said Michel petulantly.

"Not at all. I first met Arpad Plesch in Zurich in 1947. He was involved in *La Clause d'Or* affair and asked my help in raising money to sue every government in Europe. He has a law degree in addition to his medical doctorate, you know. Anyway I helped him make some connections with some Swiss banks and we all did well when his suit forced the countries to honor their gold-bonds. I visited him regularly at his apartment on the Avenue Foch and watched him raise Anna Kate like a meticulous gardener. At age four he tape recorded her recitations and taught her feed-back. His aim was to make her the most intelligent woman in the world."

"He's a fiend," muttered Michel. "That is the most monstrous thing that could be done."

"I remember one of the philosophic lunches at his villa, 'La Leonina' in Beaulieu. The villa, you recall, had three gardens: The Garden of Olives, where Anna Kate was allowed to play as part of some wry biblical joke; the aesthetic garden; and behind the villa where the land rises up from the sea to the mountains, he had assembled, on 14 terraces, exotic trees and plants from all over the world.

"There were two enormous marble lions guarding the entrance to the villa. There was a scandal, that day in 1953, because Anna Kate had painted the lions' eyes blue and the mouths red. It seemed that the paint could not be removed. Some of the guests, myself included, found this colorful prank amusing and even appropriate. Anyway, there were around fifteen of us for lunch in the dining room. While the three butlers served, we all listened to Monsigneur Plaquevent lecture on Christian philosophy. As dessert and coffee were being served, Arpad, presiding like Lorenzo di Medici, called down to the end of the table where Anna Kate was sitting, 'Tell us, my child, what you have learned about Life and God and Man from Monsigneur?' "

"How old was she then?" asked Michel.

"Let's see, 1953? She was about seven. I'll never forget the scene. Arpad, the old Hungarian Jew, *agent extraordinaire*, masterful actor and director, and Anna Kate in a white organdy dress with a blue satin sash and black patent leather shoes. She rose from the end of the table and slowly walked the length of the room. Not a word was said. She cupped her hand to Monsigneur's ear and whispered. In a moment the cleric uttered an exclamation, stood up, suddenly knocked over his wine glass, and motioned to Arpad, '*Allez*, Monsieur Plesch, we must go up to your study and have a philosophic discussion with this child.' "

Michel nodded dourly. "And you never found out what she whispered to the Monsigneur?"

"As a matter of fact, I did," said Hyatt. "But I'm afraid I can't tell you. You'd be too shocked. The Monsigneur died within a week."

-43-

"*Rotwang and Miss Photo have a complete collection of the old newsreel series, 'Milestones of the Century,' narrated by good old Ed Herlihy. The other week they sponsored a public showing and many of the public attended. About 2/3 into the festival, Rotwang noticed one of the Aliens standing next to Adolf Hitler in the 1943 report on the War Years . . . Miss Photo noticed John the Alien in a segment on the assassination of JFK. John was on the street next to the Texas Book Repository, directly under the window where the shot came from. Lee Harvey Oswals was standing next to him.*"

ROTWANG
By Tim Hildebrand

A NAVIGATIONAL CONFERENCE WITH FLORA LU

Riverdale-on-Hudson, October 1960.

Malaca was upstairs bathing in scented water. Maynard dozed in a sleek, rumpled rag of contentment on the sofa. The spokesman for the Minnesota Psychedelic Research Project stood by the glass doors watching the sunrise. Again. He has discovered that his sunrise watching index has risen dramatically since initiating his research into consciousness. "Is there a correlation there?" he wondered idly.

Flora Lu entered the room carrying a tray which contained a silver coffee pot, a silver pitcher of cream, two China mugs, and a bowl of fruit; apples, bananas, peaches, cherries, and green, shiny grapes.

She placed the tray on a low table and rode gravity down to a sitting position on the rug. She waved cheerfully to the Reflective Song Writer.

"Would you like to drink some coffee and answer my cosmic questions?"

The Song Writer felt a liquid flush of warmth in his body, felt his face muscles automatically soften into a smile and his eyes shine. His musculature reflexively prepared to enfold the graceful blonde woman in his arms. He correctly identified these somatic reactions as tendresse.

"Flora Lu," he said softly. "You are beautiful and I love you and I thank you." His eyes were moist.

Flora Lu nodded knowingly and patted the rug with Her hand. "Yes, I know. Me too. Isn't it marvelous?" She poured steaming black liquid in the two mugs. "And now because we love each other I can ask you my questions. Cream?"

"Please."

"Sometimes I think I can't go on living. Sugar?"

"Two lumps please. Is something missing?"

"Do you remember when I asked you that question last night?"

"Yes." Indeed, he would never forget it. They were sitting in front of the fire in telepathic harmony performing what a later generation of scientists would call Circuit Seven Neurogenetic Scans. Clusters of pre-frontal neurons were receiving RNA signals from thousands of generations of DNA memories, millions of years of planetary evolution were flashing by; bodies being conceived, born, struggling for survival, copulating, caring for the young. Flora Lu had turned Her face to him and looked in his eyes questioningly. Ah yes, they were galactic detectives, Doctor What's on and Shirley Holmes sifting clues, dusting Darwinian fingerprints, patiently trying to solve the Mystery. She leaned towards him and shrugged. "It's all Sex, isn't it?" She whispered in a conspiratorial giggle. In a billion warm, fetid tropical swamps black jazz combos played the boogie while Swedish blondes stripped and wiggled. A wizened, wrinkled old Chinese Madame smoked Her opium pipe and smiled. Lazy water currents soughed and the Ageless Crocodile by the cash register who managed the action, stirred slowly and sank a bit lower in the embracing muck. Soft laughter from dark corners and behind bushes.

"So that's the big secret, eh?" She said thoughtfully. "It's funny, you know, I kept thinking there must be more. I'm not complaining, you understand. It could hardly be funnier or more beautiful to have it that way. What a sense of humor They have."

"Inexhaustible array of costumes, dance steps and graceful postures."

"But still I'm kinda sad about it. I have no reason to complain. I made that discovery when I was very young so I'm luckier than most. But it's so scary."

"Cause you break up like a little girl?"

"Yeah. For years I've been watching carefully. I'm a Libra, too, so you know what I mean. I see everyone as an animal. I understand everything people do. Until I met you. I was convinced that you knew about something more."

The Entranced Song Writer sipped coffee and lit a cigarette. It was his first nicotine in several hours and his taste buds and throat tissues writhed in ecstasy.

"Is that all?" She persisted. "Look, baby, don't be influenced by me. Just because I've laid one big wet sugar-pussy answer on you. That may be just as far as I've been able to go so far. Is that all?"

"I think there's more. But . . . "

"But it's not instead of love and beauty."

"That's where they keep going wrong."

"So you'll try to get there through love and beauty. I'll help you anyway I can."

"I know you will, Flora Lu."

-44-

"Actually, the Swiss people are no more greedy for money than any other. It's just that other nations have additional vices."

                                        Jeff Scheffel, *Trapped on the Rapture Circuit*

SURFING THE WAVES OF EVOLUTION

Geneva-Bern Highway, May 1971.

"How long does it take to drive to Bern?" says Dylan settling back in the by now familiar comfort of the Roller.

"Less than two hours. We'll be on time for Maitre Mastronardi." Michel drove absently, his head sunk on his jowls apparently lost in thought.

"You seem a bit worried," ventured Eight.

"There is much to think about, Dylan. I had no idea before talking to Hyatt how serious this business is. I had thought, pouf! *Pas de probleme,* a simple matter of making arrangements with the proper officials. I did not realize how worried the politicians are about your presence. Do you know what Hyatt told me? He said that in six months, if allowed to operate freely, you could turn a country like Switzerland upside down. Is that true?"

"Come on Michel," countered the Outlaw Lyricist. "Let me make one thing perfectly clear. We have no intention of doing anything except settling down to live quietly and have babies."

"I may know that, but they don't. You didn't answer my question. Could you?"

"If allowed freedom of speech? To write articles, public performances, have a radio show, appear on T.V.? We could permanently change the consciousness and the culture of a small country like this in three months."

"*Incroyable*," murmurs Michel. "There is no other political party or social leader who could say that. Socialism, communism, fascism, all the religious propagandists have that freedom and they can recruit no one. How is it possible?"

"Well let's not have an abstract conversation. Let's talk about your own turf. In your home right now there are four people: yourself, Dee Dee, Antonia, and Yolando the pretty little secretary. Now if the president of Switzerland or even Maitre Mastronari were to come into your home and debate philosophy of life with me, I predict the vote would be three to one. Right?"

"Hmm," muses Michel. "I see what you mean. But the three girls are special, they are more sophisticated than the average Swiss."

"Very well. Let's take an average Swiss high school or college. I debate philosophy of life with the local priest, or the senator, or another teacher defending the status quo. A vast majority of the young people raised in a post-Hiroshima-television world are basically skeptical of the old way. They don't want to change political parties, they want a new map, a new life style, a new meaning for existence. The old industrial order is simply indefensible. That is why I was silenced by force in the United States and thrown in prison. The kids belong to the Information Age. That's what Hyatt was warning you about this morning. And the issue is not brain-reward drugs. The issue is freedom to choose a way of life, ability to pilot your own life, to evolve."

"But why is this happening right now? *Bien sur*, when we were young there were competing philosophies, Marxism, Fascism, even the Catholic church was a force. Why is it different now?"

"Elementary neurogenetics. It's the simplest process in the universe to ride an evolutionary wave. Like using the law of gravity to ski. Like teaching sex to adolescents who had never been told about the equipment they are endowed with. Sigmund Freud for example surfing that little anti-protestant ripple. It's like advocating the joys of flight to newly hatched butterflies. It's the oldest galactic trick. Shooting the evolutionary rapids. Just appear on the scene when a mutation is about to occur and sing lyrics about the future."

"Now I understand what Hyatt meant," says Michel, head hunched down on his chest, staring at the road with a dazed expression.

"What did he say?"

"He said he didn't understand why they didn't kill you."

Michel's eyes dart to the rear-view mirror. "Maybe they will. Your government is not above such tricks. Do you know that the C.I.A. hired the Corsican mafia to kill a Dominican client of mine? We must be very careful, Dylan."

-45-

"Do you think it's too late to trade some of these pesky brains for a new face? I'd like something in beautiful, please, this time around. I'm bored with pretty. Something with cheekbones. Marlena Dietrich? Too hard. Something that will still look good when I'm sixty. Something that will wear well. How about that one over there? Catherine Deneuve?"

Jayne Loader in "Between Pictures"

THE ADORING HUSBAND SIGHS IN ADMIRATION

Lausanne, May 1971.

As the Philosopher enters the bedroom he finds Her standing naked in front of the full-length mirror, both hands gripping Her left thigh. She shrugs her hair gracefully and giggles.

"Come in my overwrought astronaut. I have a full supply of entertainment tapes."

"What are you doing in front of that optical feed-back instrument?"

"If my legs were only the tiniest bit thinner," she sighs moving Her hand to cup Her breasts, "and if my pendant charms were just the slightest bit uppier ... "

She turns provocatively and performs a chorus-girl bounce, "Then I'd be perfect." She turns and pours a look of open-mouth adoration into the mirror. "Even when I'm forty, I'll still be ravishing. Isn't that nice?"

"Yes, the Bard is forced to agree. "No one can deny that It is nice."

She walks to the bed with slow Las Vegas grace tying a satin peacock robe around Her waist. She sits in half lotus position, Her face turned up to Husband Returned.

"How did it go with the lawyer today? What a familiar line. How many times have I greeted you with that question? Why aren't you a lawyer and when you come home I could say, 'How did it go with the gullible tricks today?'" She lights a cigarette, blows smoke to the ceiling and, putting Her hand to Her mouth, coughs delicately. "Well, tell me My Sweet Sword. Can we stay in Switzerland?"

"Michel says we can, but we'll need lots of money."

"I'm not surprised. What an imbalanced world it is! Everyone wants from you what they already have too much of. The rich people want your money. Junkies steal your dope. The smart people want your brains. The sexy people want more sex. Speaking of which, I made a great discovery today. Michel and Dee Dee have a fascinating collection of pornography. And some in English. Dee Dee and Antonia and Yolande went out shopping this afternoon leaving me alone to indulge. It made me remember when I was a young girl I used to come home from Bible class moist from desire for the cute young minister and hide under the blankets in bed-clothes reading dirty books. And the two ideas God-sex, sin-love, devil-food cake all run together in my girlish mind. I guess that's how I became so deliciously mixed up."

The Philosopher is lying across the foot of the bed, bare-foot, head propped by hand, eyes smiling agreement. "The fourth phase of human metamorphosis, sexual impersonation, links the newly emerged sexual circuits to the domesticated ideals which people call religion. So Fucking, for the believer, is sweetest with the Ashen Taste of Sin."

"I want you to know exactly what it's like to be a woman. It's our only hope, Eight. So I edited Michel's porny to give you my teen-age horny imprint. Do you want to listen?"

Her eyes sparkling, Her face colors with the faintest blush. She is dewy eager to please and be pleased. She picks up a pink pocket book and opens to a page marked by a silken handkerchief which She rakishly tosses to the side.

"It's called *Princess of Debauchery* by Guillaume Apollinaire. Isn't that a good beginning? Chapter One. Are you ready?

" 'The Paris of Central Europe is what Lausanne, romantic and erotic flower of Switzerland, is often called. In a sense Lausanne is a crossroads of Western Europe and Oriental Asia. Many of the country's sex customs and religious rituals, including the supreme dominance of the female, is a direct result of the nearness of the matriarchal harem countries. And the Swiss female's concept of Man as a toy of love and pleasure is also a product of realistic Alpine thinking. From the first Romans who came to Geneva and Lausanne, these twin cities were known as Calvinist playgrounds and centers of fierce, intense, passionate sex morality. The Swiss woman is the Playgirl of the West, a true accomplished connoisseur of communion wine, fallen women, sinful men, virginal boys, innocent girls, and song, both sacred and profane.

"'Rome has traditionally set the style for all types of amours, Catholic and Protestant, celestial and earthly; and the civilized pleasures and sanctified vices of the Swiss aristocracy, of which the svelte Princess Rosamund Lupescu was a flaming example. First cousin of the Queen, the nubile Princess Rosamund had dallied prayerfully with all her ladies-in-waiting and swung with every page-boy of the palace by the time she was sixteen. By the time she was seventeen it was a joke that there wasn't a man of royal blood in the whole Helvetian court whose calling card and prayer book had not been placed between the penitent dimpled knees of the fervent Princess. Now that she was eighteen she was currently engaged in exploring the lovely temples and soft epistles of every rich middle-class woman and man in the kingdom, married or unmarried. She seemed driven by an insatiable passion to find what she considered a perfect velvet-lined pulpit.

"'Princess Rosamund found the Vatican Ambassador Antonio Leoporello a really sympathetic believer. Antonio was rumored to be converting the winsome Princess with true Roman devotion. One fine morning Princess Rosamund made herself look like a real Parisian Presbyterian. As she strolled demurely through the streets in her tight satin pants, she excited both men and women alike.

"'*What a juicy Southern Baptist she would make,* thought the men.

"'*What a trim, firm pentecostal the Princess has—almost as good as a man for missionary activity,* was in the mind of many a Swiss female as the Princess swayed by.

"'An Italian servant in a red silk blouse gave her entrance to the embassy apartment and Princess Rosamund ran eagerly up the steps to the private confessional of Antonion Leoporello. There she saw the virile envoy, stark Episcopalian, on the zebra skin couch in the middle of the room. His manly congregation extended a full nine inches into the air as he prayed on his back. Kneeling in worship beside him was a darkly voluptuous lady-minister from the Tulsa Oklahoma Four-Square Gospel church running her hymnal up and down his extended campanile in heartfelt devotion. Ada Mae, the girl-preacher, was also stark fundamentalist and her full, lovely Salvations hung ripely near the edge of the couch. Between her rounded Acts of the Apostles, the sweet curve of her moist biblical tract rimmed the inviting communion chalice. Dark, silky psalms fringed it, setting it off like a glowing black jewel. It was a glorious collection plate, full of the mysterious funky twangy allure of the Bible Bay-alt.

" 'On a settee near the wall, two saucy young Texas deaconesses were fingering each other's rosary beads playfully. Their lilting girlish laughter rang out whenever a repentant forefinger stroled a Second Coming.' "

The charming authoress lays down the book and delicately puffs at her cigarette.

"Whew!" Spin me that bursting-ripe juicy teen-age peach-plum tape from St. Louis, Missouri, hanging from the twisted branches of a Southern Baptist tree! Not to mention crucified, spread awaiting piercing Christian Soldier sword on a pentacostal cross."

The husband sighs in admiration.

"You have been a miserable selfish sinner, Eight," murmurs the Princess. "But if you kneel before me full of repentance, perhaps I shall wash you in the sweet juice of forgiveness and embrace you in sisterly love, for this is my body to be consumed by the true believer."

-46-

"The male and female bodies have been designed by three billion years of evolution to link sensual transceivers in rapture duet. Fourth-brain sexuality is orgasm-directed genital-centered, energized by polarity of difference. Strong man lustfully penetrates receptive woman. Ancient possessive connection. Take me. I'm yours. Love me forever. Fifth circuit linkage creates ontological union. There is no separation of sex."

Eric Gullichsen, *in Exo-Psychology*

LESSONS IN LOVE FROM THE WISE ARAB GIRL

Newton Centre, Massachusetts, November 1960.

Malaca moved to the Philosopher's house, but Fourth Circuit Domestic pressures blemished and distorted the communication and marred the imprint.

Dylan's home swarmed with social game-players: two teen-age kids, graduate students, visiting celebrities, research conferees.

Still trapped in larval schedule the Song Writer left every morning for the office and returned each evening to this fragile Arab girl, to enter the Gate of Aphrodisia.

Spengler wrote of the Arabian world-feeling: Alchemical. Whispers of mysterious substances like philosophic mercury neither material nor property, but, by magic, transmuting one element into another. To the Arabian of this period (quite Spinozistically) belonged the notion of substances with visible or secret attributes. Baraka. Spengler's attempts to describe Rapture Circuits activated centuries before his time by the hashish culture of the Middle East were clumsy, preneurological hints.

While Her body uncoiled, Arabesque serpentine, and Her Almond Eyes moved with belly-dance undulation, this slim houri of the Prophet's carpet-soft, cavern-vaulted pleasure mosque couldn't stand the noise of children, nor the disorder of the square, domestic child-centered household from which the Harvard scientists were launching the first exploratory time-ships.

Her Social Values were centered on fierce chaste, concepts of Justice, so Her mutation from Virtue to Rapture was as shaky as Dylan's. She murmured, giggling, "I was taught that sex was a jewel to be hoarded. Now we know it is an infinite energy to be exchanged. Would you like to see the book that Flora Lu gave me when we left Riverdale? I think it was a pillow book to tutor my ignorance in these matters."

Malaca walked to the closet and returned with a large volume lettered in Arabic script.

"The title," She said, running Her slender finger along the letters. "The Garden of Endless Delights."

She flipped the cover open. The left-hand page was script narrative; the right a lush painting of a couple in the pavilion of a formal court-yard garden. A naked man in the lotus position fucking a woman who sat on his lap. They were smiling. Her arms caressed the back of his neck. His hands were under Her buttocks.

"What does the script say?"

"Oh that's intended for me. It's a . . . well like a marital instruction book. This paragraph reads—Observe how the two, perfectly joined, make one perfect entity. He sees behind Her. She sees behind Him. Their entity has 360 degree vision. Her left side is His right. Perfect equality of the two principles."

Malaca gracefully flipped the next picture.

"Observe that She sings to Him and He feeds Her fruit. Laughing. There is no hurried frenzy. As mountain stream flows over the rocks, century after century, carving new forms, so does their timeless love."

Malaca smiled shyly. "Flora Lu is far out, isn't She? Shall we continue?"

In the next picture the couple is still in the Yab Yum coition. She combs "All things on this earth are jewels to adorn thee."

In the next He reclines on His left arm. She squats above Him, her yoni grasping His lingam. His right hand caresses her breast. Her head is thrown back, eyes closed.

"Thou art the mountain tree, and I, the wind stirring Thy leaves."

Motionless, lotus-pose, Yab-Yum coition. Eyes locked.

"They rest quiescent, breathing together for 108 minutes. The Serpent Power from His spine flows through His motionless lingam into Her and from Her yoni to Him."

In the next picture, above and around them float the great Buddhas and Bodhisattvas. Below them dance the demons. A gentle rain of flowers.

As She flipped the pages a heroic-history of great lover duets appeared. In one She leans back, one arm rakishly raised, the other holding His neck. She laughs wickedly.

"That one is best translated as, Oh now you've become my young Persian lover."

She has fallen back and He presses Her down, pinning Her two hands over Her head. Her mouth is pursed in mock surprise, Her eyebrows raised in amusement.

"The Arabic for that one comes out in English something like, Oh my! I didn't know you were German!"

"That book," he said, "and him that wrote it, is a pander."

And that day they read no more.

-47-

Case was twenty-four. At twenty-two he'd been a code cowboy, a digital rustler, one of the best in the Sprawl. He'd been trined by the best, but McCoy Pauley and Bobby Quine, legends in the biz. He'd operated on an almost permanent adrenaline high, a byproduct of youth and proficiency, jaked into a custom cyberspace deck that projected his disembodied consciousness into the consensual hallucination that was the matrix."

From "Neuromancer"
By William Gibson

HELPLESS AGAIN

Geneva-Bern Highway, May 1971.

"Don't be worried, Michel," says the Exile soothingly. "Actually, I'm delighted by our conversation with Hyatt. I've been waiting for several years to talk to someone who understands what's happening. Most of the time I've been bored and a bit lonely. Sherlock Holmes without a Moriarty. Struggling with a headless bureaucracy directed by a robot which replaced J. Edgar Hoover in 1946. We are safe here, *Mon Capitaine*, because there are very few people with the history and evolutionary perspective to comprehend the nature of our game. And they, of course, are wise enough not to be threatened."

"No, Tom. *Non, ce n'est pas vrai!*" Michel turns and whacks his hand against the dashboard. "That is where you make your mistake. People can be most dangerous, like Cornered Cobras, when they sense their little thing is threatened even though the don't understand the cosmic reasons. You must realize the precarious balance of powerful forces involved in Europe. Every country in Europe is poised on a fifty-fifty razor's edge. The smallest political current can change the narrow left-right equilibrium and topple a government. Look at *L'affaire* Christine Keeler in England! She used marijuana to seduce that poor minister. Did you plan that? Any government which gives you asylum is immediate target for attack. Left, right, *n'importe*. There is no faction that can afford to defend you. You are a helpless pawn. Even more important than the politics is the money. Bah, bureaucrats rise and fall but the alcohol business flows on controlling billions of francs. Think of what the wine and cognac industry means in France and even here in Switzerland. Those fellows want to know how your brain-rewards could punish their bank-accounts. And the pharmaceutical industry! *Mon Dieu* do you realize that drug companies run this country? Up in Basel the managers of the great pill companies meet and discuss which medicines they will release to the public and which drugs they will hold back. Especially the mind-drugs like tranquilizers and euphoriants and energizers. Do not be naive, *mon vieux*. Do you think them to be helpless victims of the market place? They measure the social climate like greedy meteorologists. They have to keep people nervous enough to want pacifiers and passive enough to need energizers, and worried enough to need medicine but not so sick that they can't work to make the money to pay for their drugs. Don't you think those fellows have had many long meetings studying the social effects of these brain-rewards? *Mon Dieu* those rascals are holding back drugs in their laboratories that can make your brain feel like the gold-vaults of Zurich and the cunt of Bardot. Not to mention the heroin cartel."

"Heroin?" exclaims the Commodore. "I have nothing to do with that."

"So what does that mean? There are, perhaps a dozen men, among the richest in the world, who control the heroin market. They buy and sell politicians like onions. Even governments move cautiously with these men.

And you don't think they watch you and the effect of your hedonic ideas? The problem is your brain-rewards are not addictive." The Frenchman is now muttering to himself.

"What did you say?" asks the bewildered Alchemist.

"What? Oh yes. And please do not forget the Communists who watch every leaf that falls in every country in the world, judging whether it helps or hurts their plans. And the Catholic Church, my dear fellow. Tell me Who is more concerned with every little cultural breeze that might tickle the morals of their followers?"

"You make it sound as though I need a lawyer. What will Maitre Mastronardi be able to do?"

"Mastronardi! Rest assured he wouldn't touch this matter with a three meter rake if it weren't for, well let me say that I have many businesses that he helps me manage. So do not worry, Teem, we shall win this interesting game. What adventure, eh? I guess I get more than I had bargained for. So if the ante of the game is raised we shall have more to win."

Michel's preoccupation begins to weigh on the Outlaw Bard who feels the warning buzz in his stomach and the return of the dreadful Algerian paranoia. Helpless again in the power field of scheming men who neither understand nor approve of his mission.

-48-

"Okay, give me one Katherine Deneuve. No need to wrap it up. I'll wear it."

"That will be thirty IQ points, please."

"Cheap at twice the price."

"Hook her up to the brain drain, boys."

"Ah, that's better. Much better. Why, I never felt better in my life. My! How time does fly! I must skedaddle. Wouldn't wanna miss FAMILY FEUD!"

                                                      Jayn Loader in "Between Pictures

WHO IS MICHEL HOUCHARD? AND WHY?

Lausanne, May 1971.

She is standing by the window, artfully draped in a towel, watching birds glide through sunset sky into the branches of tall trees that lift with leafy seed-arrogance to penthouse height. The bells of Lausanne toll sonorously at twilight. It is a moment She will remember forever, She thinks, weeps gently, wondering. Why this long Searching Journey on this strange, rough warrior planet. When will they return to mountain home with view down-valley where space ships come as big as clouds, built cunningly with iridescent spider web fibers and shimmering spacious sky halls and rainbow spiral wheels turning silently.

The door opens and the Bard enters, glowing with ruddy, youthful confidence, once so accustomed, now, in grey, exile insecurity so sadly rare. Her tearful heart gives a soft, sudden bump of memory. He is carrying a chilled bottle of white wine and two crystal glasses.

"Well, he says bravely, "here's the plan for the evening straight from the tour director's clipboard. Captain Hauchard and Dee Dee are dining out with rich friends to whom Michel plans to sell stock in our company."

"What company?" she asks with a worried look.

"The company Michel and I are forming to raise the money to pay for Swiss asylum and the yacht."

"What yacht?"

"The yacht we're going to use to smuggle copies of the book we write to Beirut in exchange for Lebanese belly-dancers."

"Is Antonia going?" She asks idly.

"On the yacht?"

"No, to dinner with Michel."

"I guess so. It wasn't mentioned. Michel suggested that we try a fantastic fish restaurant down hear Pouly. He phoned and reserved a table for us."

"We don't have any money."

"I forgot to tell you. I asked Michel whether he could help us locate the money order we had transferred from the Banque National d'Algerie and he said he'd take care of it. Then he peeled off a thousand francs and handed it to me for current expenses. Far out, huh?"

"Yes, very. I'm a bit concerned about it. I mean it's too good to be true. After the petty brutalizing of Eldridge Cleaver, manipulating us and spying on us and blackmailing us and keeping us helpless prisoners of his whims, now this, a gold-plated prison. Silk sheets, the best wine in the world, elegant pornography, expense-paid haute cuisine restaurant tours. But it's still a prison. We're totally in Michel's power. I keep asking myself, why? What does he want?"

"I think he's bored. He is intrigued with the buzz we provide. He's a big hero now with the local jet-set. As our gallant Protector. There's nothing mysterious or ominous about that."

She moves to the bed and sinks back in the pillows, her left hand holding her empty glass. The wine flicks pale yellow as he pours from the frosty bottle. She lights a cigarette and softly clears her throat.

"I tried to find out about Michel from Dee Dee at lunch. She didn't say too much. She was either being evasive or maybe she doesn't know too much herself. They met four years ago when she was only seventeen. Her father is a very wealthy French aristocrat and forbade her to see Michel, which, of coruse, just inflamed her more. Her father and his friends called Michel a gangster. I found that intriguing. The day she turned eighteen she left home and became his mistress. When he had to escape the French police and flee to Switzerland, she followed him here. She claims he never tells her anything about his business. Michel is a true old-time male chauvinist pig, apparently. She admires his outlaw strength, but she's basically bored. He won't turn on and forbids her to smoke it. Which she does, naturally, behind his back. That's a weird scene, isn't it? They have an arrangement that she goes to Paris one week a month. Here, she's the classic mistress, sleeps till two, shops till six and goes out to a fancy restaurant every night. Lots of parties but Dee Dee thinks they're dull. In Paris she stays high and dances all night rock n' roll. She's really happy that we're here and wants our help in getting Michel to turn on. More psychedelic social work."

"That's painfully funny," says Eight. "Michel and Benvoglio at the same time are making *me* swear that we'll have nothing to do with Brain Reward. They threaten me with expulsion, extradition and life-long prison for taking one joint."

"Well I didn't make any promises I can't keep," She says with her Call Girl drawl. "What's this company he wants to sell stock in?"

"Michel says we can pay for Swiss passports and live here in luxury supported by a company he wants to form to market our books and the movies he wants to make about us. He's quite serious about selling stock to his rich international friends here."

"Well how many shares, and how much per share and what percentage, if any, of you, do we get to keep?" She exhales smoke decisively, flicks the cigarette at the ashtray and brushes the bedspread with quick nervous strokes. She is Ann Sheridan as Bordello Madame discussing prices. "The whole business seems like an elegant replay of the Cleaver scenario."

"I've thought of that."

"The elaborate welcome."

"The glowing promises of partnership in a glorious enterprise."

"But all the time we're pawns in a game we don't understand. It so happens that *we* are the commodity he is selling shares of."

"I don't want to discourage creative thinking," says the Professor, "but your theory doesn't make dollar sense. Michel is apparently one of the richest men in Europe."

"It can be the front for a gold-plated hustle."

"You should have seen the staff at the Schweitzerhof bowing and scraping. And the head waiter falling all over himself."

"We'll budget that scene for $100."

"And Mastronardi who is supposed to be the top lawyer in Switzerland, absolutely grovelling in pleasure to see him."

"That's a point."

"Why should this Onassis try to rip us off for the pitiful fifty grand a year we need to keep our time-ship in orbit?"

"I'll tell you why, my innocent, ivory-tower scholar. Because it's a reflex habit with Onassis and Howard Hughes and every other big-time hustler in town to automatically rip-off everyone they meet. That's how they got to be rich in the first place."

"I'm filing your report in the memory banks," says the Agent. "But we must not get trapped in past perspectives. The first encounter on a new planet is often with a protective figure, an old crone or magician who provides the time traveler with a protective amulet."

She giggles. "So you wish me to see Michel as some little helper in the woods? The mysterious shepherd?"

-49-

In "The Place of Dead Roads" William S. Burroughs uses film-making technique, flashbacks, quick cuts. As with a movie, time can be run backward and forward. You can speed it up and slow it down. Burroughs sees history as a vast film spread out in front of him, with himself the master director. Here, as in all major Burroughs' works, good and evil are in a state of conflict and delicate balance, with the outcome uncertain.

Jacket blurb for "The Place of Dead Roads"

THE MOST POWERFUL APHRODISIAC EVER KNOWN!

Cambridge, Massachusetts, Spring 1961.

The paradoxical nature of the Folk Singer's social position deserves comment.

With his left cortex he was directing the Minnesota Psychedelic Research Project, administering drugs to prisoners who imprinted the Reality Ethic and stopped committing crimes. And to theologians and divinity students who discovered God. And to physicists who experientially confirmed Einstein's equations.

Meanwhile it was slowly dawning on the dismayed Minstrel that he was distributing, in the name of science and experimental mysticism and under the banner of a University founded by the Puritan Fathers, nothing less than the most powerful aphrodisiac ever known.

In the laudable attempt to find a relief for suffering and a facilitator of human love, the bewildered Song Writer was unwillingly forced to admit that he was unleashing a Hedonic Bomb in staid Cambridge, Massachusetts.

One evening, for example, a prominent psychologist was conducting a psilocybin session in the Professor's study while he went out to a Parent-teacher's meeting. When he returned, the attractive wife of an equally prominent sociologist threw Her arms around the Commodore's neck, wrapped Her legs around his waist and proceeded to spin through multiple orgasms before the Commodore could remove his coat. Why me? he wondered. Am I a robot agent of my gene-pool? The revenge of the Celtic-Pagans against the Puritans of Killer Cromwell?

-50-

Human avarice is one of our more reliable instinctual traits; money moves us. Rich oil deposits are uncovered. Our mortal Everyman finds these little temptations quite irresistible, though no one forces him to pursue them. He may still opt for the brief, idyllic, ignorant and dream-like existence of the happy savage—and indeed some still do. But everyman will take the bait quite voluntarily and in so doing he will work . . .

Donald Holmes, M.D. in THE ILLUMINATI CONSPIRACY

A MEETING WITH THE FAMOUS LAWYER, MASTRONARDI

Bern, May 1971.

Precisely at one o'clock Michel Hauchard, Hero-Captain dressed in rich-fabrics and lone-wolf-skins, storms into the snobbish lobby of the Schweitzerhof Hotel which immediately lights up like a pin-ball machine, porters running, desk-clerks bowing, telephone girls waving, managers wringing hands in pleasure, all chanting the song of conspicuous consumption: MONSIEUR HAUCHARD!

Sweeping majestically through the lobby, radiating golden aura, the Sun King of Vaud moves up the wide stairs trailed by the Folk Singer, the manager, and the most dignified desk clerk.

As they roll into the second floor restaurant the welcome scene is repeated. The *Maitre d'*, a tall, owlish man with the solemn demeanor of an undertaker, bends his bald head in homage and escorts the guests to a corner table. Maitre Mastronardi rises in greeting. The lawyer, a plump, prosperous penguin, waddles forward clasping Michel's hand with both of his own, beaming unabashed, admiring joy.

After the introduction he bows formally to the Potential Client.

Maitre Mastronardi pats his mouth with a napkin, leans back, folds his hands over his belly-filled vest and turns appraising eyes to the ex-American.

"Hmmpf. Yes. Hmmpf," begins the lawyer. "So, Monsieur Dylan, what can I do for you?"

The Maitre's face is impassive. He is now the well-fed judge ready to listen to the evidence. Michel is the lawyer outlining in French the defendant's picaresque record of fortune and folly.

Mastronardi listens with growing interest and alarm, clicking his tongue in concern and murmuring in disbelief. When Michel concludes the epic, the lawyer turns to the fugitive.

"Hmmph. Most extraordinary. Really, my dear Professor, I must confess that I have never in my thirty years of practice heard such a case. This is much more complicated than I had expected. Do you have any papers with you? Your passport, for example?"

The Lyric Philosopher, feeling vague guilt in face of solid, Swiss solemnity, lays on the table his two passports, Her two passports, and their green Algerian residency cards. The Maitre examines them with swift efficiency, nods and glances at Michel, who lays his arm around the Doctor's shoulders and whispers conspiratorially.

"Listen, Teem. As you can see, the Maitre is a bit startled by all this. Let me speak with him a moment privately and I'll bring him around."

The Philosopher excuses himself and leaves the dining room. Two men seated in the corridor observe him closely as he walks to the rest room.

-51-

"Oh you who come to this planet of woe, watch where you go, once you have arrived down here. Do not be deceived by the easiness of the fall."

"Mind your own business," said Virgil. "It is his fate to enter every door. This has been so designed that what is designed will be. Advice is fruitless. Say no more."

Virgil to Mines in The Inferno
By Dante

THE FOLK SINGER DISCOVERS HIS SOLE

Newton Centre, Massachusetts, Spring 1961.

Starting in 1961 there came to the Commodore's office and to his large, rented mansion, a steady stream of time-adepts, neurological explorers bringing back from far synaptic shores the treasures of the right hemisphere.

From the Antipodes of the Cerebellum came the Hatha Yogins teaching muscle consciousness, demonstrating how robot game postures could be loosened and extended.

The body as temple of the soul. Every fibre and tendon as string for blissful vibration. The body a million-note instrument.

During a time-expedition a young woman knelt on the carpet and lifted Her body into an arm-stand. The Commodore could empathetically feel the guy-wire muscles in a sweet-pulling tension keep Her swaying erect like a plant. The kinaesthetic imprint clicked and at that moment he attained conscious, erotic control of his musculature.

The first four circuits freeze the body into a suit of armor. When consciousness moves to the right hemisphere the carapace melts and stretches making it a simple matter to assume new, flexible postures.

Then there came that moment when Dylan, sitting cross-legged, awkwardly pulled his rubber foot and stretched elastic tendons into a full-lotus. He looked down and gazed upon the soles of his feet! The classic pose signifying the conquest of gravity, levitation of consciousness, and the preparation for null-G existence.

"The right cortex is oriental," She said. "Sitting in a full lotus is an international, neurogenetic procedure that indelibly programs the nervous system.

"Left brain movement is decisive, manipulative, fast, certain, aim-oriented," She said. "Discriminating symbols and maneuvering them. Right cortex movement flows. One floats, swims lazily through the atmosphere ocean of bliss, Deep-sea diving. No need to hurry, worry, plan, impress."

"Take it easy," She murmured, "enjoy every second. There's no place to go. We are here. This is it. Slow down. Dig every nuance."

-52-

"Immortals must be careful not to wound the sensibilities of mortals."

Neurogenetic Aphorisms

HAVE NOTHING TO DO WITH DRUGS

Bern, May 1971.

When the Fugitive returns to the restaurant, Michel is leaning forward waving his finger, talking intensely in French. As Eight sits down, the lawyer, Mastronardi, clears his throat pontifically and indicates he is ready to pronounce sentence.

"I must tell you, Sir, that ordinarily I do not handle criminal cases and certainly not cases which involve drugs."

"Let me tell you one thing, Tom," interjects Michel, "Maitre Mastronardi is the lawyer for some of the leading firms in Europe. Nestles chocolate. Phillips Electric. General Electric. Volkswagen."

"And, not least important," adds the Poet, "Michel Hauchard is his client."

A pause ensues. Hauchard and Mastronardi clear their voices in unison. Michel draws his lips back in a standard charm-smile.

"And, you can understand he is concerned about the possibility of offending his American clients."

"I have been most cordially received by several Arab states. In Beirut I am known as the new Rimbaud," offers Eight in a weak run for respectability.

"Hmmph. However," continues the Swiss with Churchillian ponderance, "Monsieur Hauchard is both my good client and, if I may say so, my good friend. So with his endorsement, I have agreed to look into your status with the Swiss government. In a week or two, after I have made the necessary inquiries, we can meet again and decide on the next course of action. In the meantime, it would help if you could have your American attorneys send me copies of the judgments against you, court transcripts and any other documents which would give me all the legal facts to present in a formal request to the Swiss government for asylum. In the meantime, I must urge you to be most discreet. By all means avoid any publicity, remain as quiet as possible, and, of course, you must assure me that you will have nothing to do with, hmmph, drugs."

"You are absolutely right, *Mon cher Maitre*," adds Michel ominously. "Any contact with drugs and none of us could help you, Dylan."

"You must not forget," adds the Swiss in relentless tandem paranoid pursuit of the wilting fugitive, "that this is a small country and everything you do will become known to the authorities. Everything. You are watched, not just by the Swiss, but by agents of other countries. Anyone you talk to can be an exposure. Anyone. From what I have been able to find out so far, the government has decided to ignore your presence here. You have entered legally as a tourist. You have stayed in private homes so that you have not been forced to register on the police forms required by hotels so there is no record of your presence here. It is convenient for all concerned that you remain invisible. Let the first move come from those who may choose to move against you. I am sure you understand. And remember, hmmph, no drugs."

"That's no problem," laughs Michel. "The truth of the matter is that the Professor has never had anything to do with drugs. He has simply explored the brain using sensory-stimulants, brain-reward chemicals, and rock music.

The Frenchman laughs happily, the Lyric Philosopher smiles wanly, the Maitre sits with the attitude of an Alpine snow-peak.

-53-

"The Agent will be required to engage in commercial exchanges with the natives. As a general rule it is suggested that the Earthlings with whom the Agent deals be rewarded to the extent of doubling their expectations. Larvals will be astonished by the Agent's apparent naive impracticality, but in the long run, the evolutionary work will be facilitated by surrounding it with an aura of easy profit."

Manual for Evolutionary Agents

A PARTNERSHIP IS FORMED

Lausanne, June 1971.

In the study, Michel puts down the phone and shakes his head.

"That was Hyatt. He wants to see us again." The Frenchman sighs.

"Problems, Dylan. Always more money. This matter of yours becomes very expensive. I had expected your friends in America to give us some help.

It has cost me so much already. I am happy to have you and Maya here in my home and I continue to place my financial resources at your disposal. But we must be more practical."

"I agree. Let's form the company and get my book translated into French and published. And to keep the hungry lawyers away for a few days I have a contribution to make. Here is a royalty check I received in the mail this morning."

"So! How much is it?" says Michel eagerly taking the check. "Only four thousand dollars, eh? Well, that will take care of Hyatt and his people."

"I will have no secrets from you Michel," says the Philosopher, "and will hold nothing back. But I think I should keep some of this money for expenses. I don't like you paying for all the restaurant checks and for our day-to-day expenses. We can work together only as equals."

The Frenchman smiles warmly. "Of course, you are right. We shall be partners and win wagons of money and share it equally. I know it is embarrassing for you now until we get rolling. But do not worry about the expenses. It is a pleasure for me to be your host. You would do the same for Me I know. So here, take some francs and buy a pretty dress for Maya."

The Frenchman lays five hundred francs from his wallet on the coffee table.

"And here is our little Yo Yo with some coffee. Good, Yo Yo, Dylan and I have many business to do and we need some energy."

Yo Yo moves across the room with high-heel pony prance, lays the silver tray on the table and pours steaming black fluid in a cup.

"I kow what you want in your cup." She winks at the Wizard. "Everything, *n'est-ce pas?*"

"No, Yo Yo," corrects Michel petulantly. "The *company* gets everything. And Dylan and I will share equally. After deducting expenses, of course."

Michel laughs and claps the Poet's shoulder. "And there's our deal, *mon vieux*. I have prepared a contract which Yo Yo will type up and we shall both sign."

Michel hands a sheaf of papers to Yo Yo.

"What does the contract say, Michel?" asks the Philosopher.

"It says that our partnership has the rights to sell and publish everything you write and that you and I shall split all profits equally."

"For how long does the contract run?"

"For as long as we are friends. Correct? The written contract is not necessary for you and me. A shake of the hand is sufficient between gentlemen. But in order to market your books and arrange screen rights and television and radio rights and foreign translations it will be necessary to make business with many companies. And they will require proof of ownership. These things are a bore to me. But my lawyers demand that we have something in writing so that they can negotiate for us."

"How long does the contract run?"

"Oh that is just a formality. I put down 1990. Just to reassure the lawyers. We'll be friends and partners that long at least, eh, *mon vieux*? What's seventeen years? And do not think that this is a one way contract. I sign that I shall pay your expenses until the partnership wins a profit. But this is just the beginning. As soon as we get your book on the market you wil assist me on some really big deals I am planning. What do you think about helping the government of Uganda become part of the 20th Century?"

"I've turned down many offers to smuggle the instruments of peace into America, Michel, so I don't think I'm ready to get into arms dealing. As much as I like you."

"Oh no, you mistake me, *mon frere*. Let me handle guns and tanks and fighter planes. What you can do is help with education, music, and cultural policy. They have a splendid new government in Uganda. I was talking to a very high official who had heard of you from King Hassan."

"The King of Morocco?" exclaims the Doctor. "What does he know of me?"

"More than you might think, *mon vieux*. I have been talking to him on the phone and he invites us cordially to visit him this summer. We must wait until you receive your Swiss passports, however. We don't want any problems in getting you back in the country. Our friends in Bern are strong. But the American government has its own men in the ministry and we must not give them a chance to move against us. Interesting, eh, this game of countries. You shall teach me about philosophy of man, and the Psychology of What WoMan Wants and I shall teach you how to gamble with countries as our chips."

"I've always wanted to have a little country to play Utopia with. It's hard but not impossible to change the consciousness of a nation working from outside the power structure. But to work with the establishment hasn't been done since Voltaire went to visit Frederick the Great. Poor Aristotle was struck with a restless student, and Confucius was too bureaucratic even for the Kingdom of Lu, and Plato never got off the ground at Syracuse. So you get me a country Michel and I'll create you a future."

Preceded by impertinent clack of heels in the hall, Yo Yo enters impersonating a nymphet-sex secretary (female).

"Michel! You left blank the name of the new company," she pouts.

"Yes," answers Michel. I couldn't think of an exciting name for the new adventure. What shall we call our partnership?"

"How about *Les Voyageurs*," says the Utopian Philosopher.

"*Parfait*. Write it down, Yo Yo."

-54-

"Rotwang realized that as long as he stayed on the planet Alpha, he was an 'Alien' and the Aliens were the local yokels."

ROTWANG
By Tim Hildebrand

A VISIT TO THE FAMOUS DOCTOR "FEEL GOOD"

Riverdale, New York, 1960.

Flora Lu was convinced that all the problems of the mind could be solved by Dylan's brain drugs and that all the problems of the emotions could be solved by Dr. Max Jacobson's body stimulants.

Flora Lu regularly praised Doctor Jake in Her talks with Dylan and he realized that She was touring him in Her talks with Doctor Jake. It was most probable, he deduced, that both of the unorthodox alchemists were equally entranced by the irrepressible, bubbling, big-eyed, blue-eyed girl-witch from Oklahoma.

So a meeting between the Two Titans of Euphoria was arranged. Dylan was aware of the pitfalls. Having just enough Ego, patched and glued together to perform the impersonations demanded by the Harvard Hive, and by now totally disinterested in the status rewards of an Industrial Society, he walked into the encounter innocently disarmed.

Signal one: he was required to cool his heels in the waiting room. No great disaster, since the small room was crowded with models, beautifully decorated young restless matrons and some amusing show-business males. A hush of reverence swept the expectants when a door opened and a tall husky young man with a crew-cut stalked through the room and exited. He was followed by a genial middle-aged man.

"Who are they?" asked the Commodore.

"Mickey Mantle and Mel Allen, the Voice of the Yankees," answered a swarthy looking man.

"Breakfast of Champions," said the Commodore with a cheerful grin.*

"Doctor Jake goes down to the White House two times a week," said a tall, slender young primate impersonating a fashion model (female).

A harassed-looking nurse with grey-hair opened the door and beckoned portentiously to the Commodore. Doctor Jake was waiting in his office. He was a short man manifesting sixty terrestrial years, impersonating a hunch-backed mad-scientist from a Hungarian horror-movie. His wrinkled hands seemed to reach his ankles. He was dressed in a white coat stained with chemicals. He spoke in a conspiratorial Mittel-European accent. He apologized for his busy-ness and asked the Director of the Harvard Psychedelic Research Project to wait in a small office.

The Supplicant Patient spent a restless half-hour reading the Journal of the New England Endocrinological Society and smoking Camel cigarettes, explicitly forbidden by the NO SMOKING sign.

* The story of how Mickey Mantle, the New York Yankees and the World Series of 1963 were embroiled in Injection Politics has become part of cybernetic folk-lore and the source of much nightclub humor. This may be the place to separate lurid legend and fact. The rumor that the World Champions owed their success to the use of amphetamines is totally unproven. It is probably untrue that Yankee Stadium was called, by the cognescenti, *Needle Park*. The undisputed facts are these; Mr. Mickey Mantle was unable to play the first two games of the World Series because of an infection caused by careless injection of a hypodermic needle into his powerful buttock muscles. The World Championship that year was won by the St. Louis *Redbirds*.

-55-

"The longest sermon on record was delivered by Clinton Locy of West Richland, Washington, in February 1955. It lasted 48 hours, 18 minutes and ranged through texts about every book in the bible. A congregation of eight was on hand at the close."

Anthony Rufus Isaacs in *Exo-Sociology*

MICHEL PREFERS A WELL-RUN LITTLE DICTATORSHIP

Bern-Lausanne Highway, May 1971.

As the Roller slides smoothly back to the Bern-Lausanne highway, Michel lights a cigar, blows clouds of blue smoke and places his hand upon his companion's shoulder.

"*Parfait.* How the Maitre's eyes popped like a camel when I told him of your situation! We are in good hands there. He has top connections with the Ministry of Justice. Right now he is on the phone to the Chief of Federal Police.

They are small frogs on the same log, these Swiss. They are deciding how many francs each one will make from this case. All they think about is money these detestable Swiss. And we must begin thinking about that too. You must have rich friends in America who will be able to purchase your freedom here?"

"I'm afraid it's not going to be that easy, Michel. Since 1961 the American government has been harassing me legally. Illegally, I mean. I have been arrested nine times, all trumped up charges. I've had to employ dozens of lawyers. The expenses of fighting cases is an exhausting drain. The government knows it can wear down any private citizen. It's a standard tactic for dealing with dissenters. I was forced into tours, performances, and making movies in order to pay lawyers. My friends have already contributed generously."

"*Ca fait rien,*" says Michel, frowning briefly. "Money means nothing to us. I can guarantee your expenses here to begin with. And then we shall use our brain cells to win all the money you need. This book you have written, is it finished? Good. I have connections with the largest publishing house in France. No problem. And there are lots of rich people in Lausanne who are sympathetic to you and can invest in our freedom company. Listen, Dylan, what do you think all the men ask me about you? If you know any drug that can keep the sexual organ hard. Amusing, no?"

"Tell them that wizened old chemists in Basel have discovered the ideal aphrodisiac but they are keeping it secret. Sharing it only with the Gnomes of Zurich."

Michel leans back regally, steering with one hand, and sighs happily. "*Alors,* I am glad we have finished with the lawyers for the day. I despise them, those lawyers always demanding money. And the greedy police. Not long ago I was generous enough to help Biafra obtain the arms they needed in their little cut rate war. A petty little transaction. A few jet fighters. Mainly second-hand small arms and machine guns. A bedroom deal as we say. Pouf, there is not time enough to tell you all the lawyers and bureaucrats and police and the army officials I had to pay off. Generals, colonels, Ministers of Defense, *chefs de security* with their hands outstretched. I detest these democracies. You end up bribing the lavoratory attendants. I prefer a tight little, well-run dictatorship where one does business with the one or two top men. How terrible is greed, Dylan. But that is human nature, eh, and so we shall use this greed to our own advantage. If they want money, these petty officials, *bien,* we shall be glad to give it to them. Such people will do anything, anything for a franc. When I was in the Lausanne jail, *Bois Mermet,* I was erupting Swiss francs like a geyser to lawyers, officials, doctors. And *voila* I am transferred from the jail to a special mental hospital.

Pierre helped me on that one. The psychiatrists filled out forms swearing that I suffered from a terrible mental disorder. Can you guess what my diagnosis was?"

"Claustrophobia," ventured the Bard, "or latent heterosexuality?"

"Exactly," roared Michel. "Acute and incapacitating claustrophobia! The hospital was an improvement, I can tell you. I made the appropriate arrangements with the officials and my girl friend, a beautiful young thing named Anna Kate O'Shea could visit me twenty-four hours a day. We'd play gin rummy by the hour and when the nurse comes down the hall, my little teen-ager ducks into the closet to hide. *Drole*, eh!"

"Was she good at gin rummy?" seems to be the logical response.

"A genius," shouts Michel. "Brilliant, funny, but crazy like us, right?"

-56-

"We are haunted, even across the centuries, by the question: Are these beautiful creatures Dar Dar, Anna Kate, Jayne Loader, Flora Lu, simply literary-fantasies, lying body-to-body in the long line of such male-fabrications as Holly Golightly, Sally Bowles, Clara Bow, et al?"

Exo-Sociology

THE COMMODORE SURE FEELS GOOD!

New York, N.Y., October 1960.

"As I understand your therapy," said Doctor Dylan to Doctor Jacobson, "you believe in pleasure, not pain, and hold that by making patients feel good you will assist the natural healing processes of the body."

"Exactly," said Doctor Jake, leaning forward in a curious simian motion and clapping his hands on his knees. "It is wrong and unhealthy to suffer. I believe that the doctor should do what he can to relieve unnecessary torment."

"I endorse that," replied the sturdy, sincere Philosopher, "and I shall tell anyone that asks me that I approve of your philosophy. In moderation, of course."

"Excellent," exclaimed Doctor Jake with some relief. "Now let me see what I can do for you. You have a hearing loss? Fine, let us perform an experiment. I can cure this for you in ten minutes."

"Fantastic," said the Astonished Bard who, in spite of his International

Reputation as a Research Methodologist, attempted to keep an open mind to the Mysterious and Miraculous.

"Stand over there," commanded the Simian Scientist, "and we shall test your disability."

The Commodore stood against the wall facing sideways. Doctor Jake crouched at the other end of the room.

"Repeat these numbers after me." The Wily Physician thereupon moved his lips silently.

At this moment the door opened and Flora Lu entered, her huge eyes wider than usual.

"What are you doing?" She whispered in Her Marilyn voice.

"Testing zee Philosopher's hearing," cried the Healer. "He's deaf as one stone. Excellent. Now we shall cure heem. You shall never again have to wear a hearing aid, with Doctor Jake's cure."

The hunch-backed gnome sprang to a table filled with beakers, retorts, flasks, and jars. He mixed several fluids and filled an enormous hypodermic needle.

"Now, my friend," he shouted, "lie down on zee examining table. Unbutton your shirt cuff."

The Commodore docilely lay on the white table and offered his naked arm to Doctor Jake.

"Thees," whispered the Hungarian, "is the true medicine to make you feel healthy."

Dylan could feel the needle slide painlessly into his vein and the flash-heat of pleasure rocket up his arm, to his heart, explode with megaton bliss and mushroom clouds of love billow throughout his body. He was floating in unspeakable ecstasy. He opened his eyes and found Doctor Jake's face swimming six inches above his own, a huge Semitic lunar globe smiling down, giving human form and meaning to the breathless pleasure, the Jehovah-like author and donor of this joy, irreversibly hooking, in the most final Pavlovian sense, the face of the Divine Jake with the millions of neurons now in grateful liberation.

"GOOD. YES? DOCTOR JAKE MAKES YOU FEEL GOOD," whispered the Wily Master of Hypodermic Reward.

"Yes, very good," murmured the Folk Singer dreamily. He felt great affection and admiration for his Benefactor. And a dim irritation at those misguided critics who, he knew, lurked somewhere outside this cone of rapture, misjudging the Dear and Beloved Physician who was now stroking his forehead gently.

Epochs later Doctor Jake plucked at his arms. "Now let us test your hearing."

The Commodore lurched to his feet and, in response to Jake's motion moved to his testing spot by the wall. Flora Lu was sitting on the desk, legs crossed, a pleased smile flitting across Her face.

As Dylan stood sideways, Doctor Jake shouted in a loud voice, "ONE, TWO, THREE. DID YOU HEAR THAT?" he bellowed.

"One, two, three. Did you hear that?" repeated the Docile Patient.

"See that!" exclaimed Doctor Jake. "The experiment worked. His hearing loss is cured!"

"I sure feel good," said the Poet.

"Will the cure last?" asked Flora Lu innocently.

"I'll mix up a batch for you to take with you. And a few boxes of disposable needles. You'll hear everything and it will all sound good."

-57-

"How intelligent do you have to be to realize that someone is more intelligent than you?"

"If you are not intelligent, what methods do you use to survive?"

Deborah Hwang
West Hollywood

A SAD STORY OF YOUNG LOVE BETRAYED IN THE MIDDLE EAST

Geneva, August 1971.

"The truth is," said Hyatt, "That if Anthony Eden hadn't blown the Suez caper, I would never have been assigned by the Foreign Office to break up Anna Kate's first marriage."

"To that Egyptian boy?" replied Michel. "Son of some minister wasn't he?"

"The Secret Service and Interpol pulled me in to help with the situation. They needed someone with a neutral passport. It seems that Anna Kate, who was living with her Mother in Cairo at the time, let's see, She must have been all of 14, had disappeared with all the money in the family safe. Some two or three thousand of Egyptian pounds. That was no big deal except that Mahmoud Okacha, son of the Minister of Culture and Orientation in Nasser's cabinet, had also run-off leaving a note announcing his intentions to marry Anna Kate."

"A teen-age escapade," said Michel shrugging his shoulders. "Still no big deal."

"You must recall," continued Duval, "this was just after Suez and relations between London and Egypt were mucho sticky. Fanatic nationalism sweeping the Cairo mobs. If the press picked up that a minister's son had been kidnapped by a Christian with an English passport? Osman Okacha was responsible for Moslem cultural orthodoxy, right?

"Anyway, it was no trouble for me to trace the nuptial fugitives to Alexandria. But they were moving fast and the wedding was scheduled at sunset of the day after the elopement. I commandeered a plane and was met at the airport by a platoon of soldiers with machine guns. We arrived at the Mosque just as the young couple emerged."

"Married?"

"Unfortunately. They were, I cannot deny it, a heart-breakingly cute couple, blooming and nubile and ecstatically happy. The groom, about 20, tall, thin, thick juicy lips, enormous black eyes. He was a college freshman. Psychology, I believe.

"I introduced myself to the astonished couple. Anna Kate recognized me, of course, and was delighted to see me. She thought I represented some sort of family backing. I invited them to accompany me to Montaza beach where the Father awaited us. Anna Kate still thought it was for a wedding reception. I guess she assumed the platoon of soldiers was a guard of honor. I was beginning to feel bad about the whole thing. The bride and groom looked at each other poignantly and got into the limousine.

"Nasser had reserved Montaza beach for his ministers. It was a Death in Venice scene. Cabanas, you know. We marched up to the father's tent. He was a handsome man, slight pot-belly. Spoke beautiful English.

"He was poised and paternal. No emotion. He simply told Anna Kate that the platoon of soldiers and machine guns would take Her across the desert to Cairo Airport and escort Her to the Beirut plane. I had arranged for the tickets. Anna Kate stood there frail and vulnerable, struck silent in some deep state of uncomprehending grief. I couldn't look at Her. The groom was scared and obedient. After a long silence, Anna Kate began explaining about their love and marriage and the Father just smiled cheerfully and said that they would be separated for seven years. 'What was seven years?' he asked. Anna Kate would be 21. If after that time they still wished to be married, he would give his approval.

"The groom just stood there, silent, looking at the sand as the soldiers took Anna Kate away.

"The Father thanked me profusely and said he would pass on his commendations for my diplomacy and tact. I was feeling terrible, you understand. Then I left to perform my last duty. I drove to the Mosque, conferred briefly with the frightened Iman, and was left alone in the office for a couple of minutes, enough time to tear out the page of the register and burn it."

"Ridiculous, childish affair," said Michel.

"Yes, I kept telling myself that for some time afterwards. I've been involved in some pretty cold-blooded encounters as you well know. But this one wouldn't go away. I kept tabs on Mademoiselle O'Shea for Arpad Plesch and others. The terrible thing, you see, was that She believed that Mahmoud would wait for Her. They were married, after all. She kept getting picked up at the Cairo airport and was continually involved in trying to smuggle messages to her husband. As I remember, She kept the vigil for three years until She met you."

'Michel's head dropped, the folds of his jowls drooped and he sat silently, thinking.

-58-

"Rotwang and Miss Photo decided to go with the Aliens. The Aliens were delighted and immediately took off towards their main ship to make take-off preparations. On Tuesday afternoon the group gathered in Rotwang's garage and boarded the Alien shuttle ship. When it got dark they took off to join the main ship, which was in a wide orbit around Earth. The beautiful blue planet was left behind, for better or for worse."

ROTWANG
By Tim Hildebrand

FLORA LU AND HER SQUADRONS OF HEDONIC OPERATIVES

Horowitz Archives

The adventures of Dylan, Flora Lu, and Maynard Ferguson have been described in dozens of unauthorized biographies and the legends of this dynamic trio are standard pedagogical fare in histories of the 20th century.

The earliest accounts come from High Priest, a comic memoir by Dylan, from The Man Who Turned on the World by Michael Hollingshead, from Viva, Superstar by Susan Hoffman, from Dylan and the Crazy Sixties, an envious pot-boiler by an irritated bureaucat named Charles Schloch, a scholarly biography by Peter Whitmer.

For the purposes of this transmission we shall thread among the scandalous anecdotes and rapturous Fifth Circuit awakenings to follow the direct line along which Flora Lu guided the Agent to Ram Poona and the Dar Dar, his designated teachers.

It was during this period that the famous League for Spiritual Development was formed. The real story of this secret association which initiated a global change of consciousness must be told at another time. Here we can simply indicate that it was the guidance and example of Flora Lu that was responsible for the hedonic squadrons of beautiful charmers and luxurious ladies, selected and equipped for neurosomatic revelation, who moved out invisibly and silently to teach the science of Aesthetic Zen. Erotic engineers with long hair and smiling eyes, philosophic Avon ladies, Acid Queens, enthusiastically welcomed into penthouses, yacht clubs, ski-chalets, hunting lodges, beach-houses, where-ever men of power reached hungrily for beauty-wisdom to bring life to their machined-careers.

There is no hard data to verify the persistent rumors that, in America alone, during the 1960s, seven senators, 37 congressmen and the key administrative assistants to 48 U.N. delegates were converted from militant nationalism to the ancient Elusinian gnosis during this period of Flora Lu's guru-ship.

It is known that Dylan, himself, met in a confidential luncheon with the administrative assistants of six prominent Senators during his visit to Washington to testify before the Dodd-Kennedy committee in 1966.

We shall not detail the platoons of models, heiresses, dancers, actresses, singers, poetesses, and courtesans produced by the indefatigable Flora Lu for Neurosomatic surveillance.

Nor shall we list the directors, philosophers, jet-set backgammon stars, musicians, composers, producers, Arabian oil heirs, entrepreneurs, writers, designers, playwrights, playboys, professional athletes, elegant gangsters, and night-club owners who wrote reports for the Harvard Rock and Roll Research Project.

From 1960 through 1963 Dylan visited the mansion at Riverdale on the average of once a month. For each visit his room was changed to fit the mood, the subjects of the experiments, and the whim of the Hostess.

During this period Dylan continued to puzzle over the mystery of his Hostess' identity. Did Oklahoma really nurture this knowledgeable creature? Every year the primitive cities in the south, south-west, and west, in some sort of propitiatory sacrifice sent their most beautiful young girls to the Temples of the Mass-media Gods of Hollywood, Las Vegas, and New York. From this enormous flood of soft-skinned, big-eyed pubescent beauty—one hundred thousand annually—offered to the insatiable demands of the Grim Divinity of Sexual Beauty there emerged this one small spirit who apparently danced into the gaping, grasping maw of Mammon, that Level of Hell run by fat-fingered, pot-bellied, beady-eyed men named Selly, Benny, Joe Levine or Italian-men with diamond stick-pins who sat around the shadowy rear-tables of night-clubs, plump men who had boxes at Shea stadium, suites at Las Vegas, 2nd homes in Miami Bay. Looking directly at them with Her baby-blue eyes she whispered, with a Marilyn giggle, the precise psycho-analytic-poker-bluff comment that would make them laugh and approve the contract with Maynard and let Her slip out of the room with a tender pat on the jowled cheek.

Her wide-opened eyes had watched the great molders and movers of American culture wheel and deal media empires over pool-side tables. Movie contracts bought and sold, Nevada hotels ripped-off, Caribbean islands bartered, starlets traded and discarded. There was no corruption or perversion She had not watched with amazement. She had warily guided Her four children through the animal-jungle of urban civilization, had flung Herself into every sensual and material excess, and still maintained the razor-edge, pollen-innocence of a thirteen-year old choir-girl.

Each time he saw Her, She had a new Philosophic theory, a new guru, a new Sufi method to test. No occult or scientific clue, oriental or occidental, was left unexamined by this slick, smooth, breathy, laughing-eyed virgin-witch.

-59-

"Some ants are so lazy that they just squat motionless near their hills and don't do a lick of work or anything else. For years, nature experts described them as sentries, posted to guard their colonies. It's now believed that that's not what they are—maybe they're just six-legged hippies."

Exo-Psychology

WAITING FOR THE GENETIC BELL TO RING

Geneva, May 1971.

Michel drives along the Geneva Lakeside straight past the turn-off to the Richmonte circling around the fountain to the Southern side.

"Hyatt changed the meeting place?" asks Dylan.

"Old espionage tactic. Never double back. I learned it when I was sanding axel-boxes behind Nazi lines in the War. And then behind the Iron Curtain after the war. That's when I first met Christopher Hyatt."

"Are we going to his office?"

"Oh, no. He'd never do that. We're going to the 'Gentilhomme.' There is a nice view of the city."

Hyatt awaits at the table in the red and gold dining room. Pastry, candy and fruit filled the third service although cheeses were notably absent.

"Did you enjoy your lunch?" asks Michel as the coffee arrives.

"An unforgettable event," sez the Commodore, although he noted the lobster in the *gratin* was chewy and the other dish was lukewarm.

"*Alors,* my wise friend," says Michel. "You have some news for us?"

"Some facts and then some more questions, if you don't mind. You have engaged Mastronardi? Good. He's the best lawyer in the Confederation for a case of this sort. He may or may not have learned that a very prominent official came from America to pressure the Swiss to send you back. None less than your Chief Prosecutor, John Mitchell."

"That's terrible," says Dylan. "He's one of the closest advisors to Nixon."

"Actually," replies Hyatt comfortingly, "it couldn't have worked out better for you. Mitchell made a fool of himself in Bern. Heavy handed pressure. It just doesn't work any more with the dollar falling. And then Mitchell's other request to the Swiss government didn't hurt you. He asked them to release Robert Vesco. Can you believe that, Michel?"

"*Incroyable,*" shouts the Frenchman laughing in glee. "What do you think that cost Vesco?"

"It would have to be a quarter of a million. Fantastic, this Nixon gang."

"It's like a banana republic. That's good to know, Hyatt. *Merci bien.* That news might come in handy."

"The Swiss were amused. They saw it as a Christ-for-Barabas deal. They can understand the Vesco part. That's business. But they can't understand twenty-years for the Professor's two joints."

"I understand," says Michel soberly.

"What do you understand?" asks the Fugitive.

"That it's going to cost us plenty."

"I'm afraid so," agrees Hyatt. "You'll have a legal battle on your hands. The Swiss want your money but they don't want to hurt you. If you can do the business."

"*Bien,*" says Michel. "Now what can we do for you?"

"I have been asked to find out from the Professor—what are your politics?"

"The question should be when, not what," edits the Doctor.

Michel glances quickly at his client and moves in to the rescue. "Actually, Monsieur Hyatt, did you realize that there are twenty-four stages of . . . "

"Yes, I know," interrupts Hyatt. "But when my good friend Otto Palme, who holds a one percentage point in the Swedish polls, asks me about the political impact of giving him asylum, the Premier would prefer a more specific answer."

"Politics is a primitive mammalian form of adaptation. People should not be allowed to talk politics except on all fours."

"I can see that," agrees Michel. "The United Nations is a zoo of barking, howling animals."

"However cunning their xenophobic territorial tricks, politicians cannot be considered biped forms of intelligence."

"What would you substitute for democracy?" asks Hyatt.

"Cybernetics. Neurological metamorphosis. The average man has been erroneously convinced that the average man has an IQ of 100. I'm really sorry about that."

"No wonder all the pooliticians, left and right, are angry with you," mutters Hyatt.

"Well, I affectionately offered them the greatest gift. A new heresy to stamp out. Larval society had to have a Devil to view with alarm, so I tried to make it amusing. The legal trials. The provocative slogans. But that Nixon gang takes it too seriously."

"Don't complain. You had it better than the Vietnamese," remarks Hyatt tersely.

"I know!" adds Michel cheerfully. "We can rent him out to rulers of bored countries which need an outlaw sect to persecute!"

"You may have something there," agrees Hyatt. "Now that wars, especially religious wars, are becoming too dangerous, the smart thing for the national leaders to do is to organize heresy hunts."

"Oh no," replies the Bard firmly, "I've finished with that role. I'm ready for the next evolutionary step."

"What is it?" asks Hyatt.

"I told you, that's exactly what I've got to find out. It's the only non-boring thing to do."

-60-

"Remember. Caterpillars cannot understand Butterfly language.

Butterflies will be grounded if the use Caterpillar language."

Michel Foucault
The Flower of French Philosophy

WHAT DOES WOMAN WANT? TO LIVE LIKE A DOLPHIN?

Lac Leman, May 1971.

Michel, jaunty commander in white cap and blue linen suit sits at the wheel of the Riva.

Place Dee Dee in the rear seat with Maya, the Folk Singer in front next to the Captain, and in the middle, spot the Euro-trash quartet, the two Rich Young Husbands, Antoine, proud, volatile *Pied Noir*, is precariously married to a wealthy Parisian moviestar, Katrine Lumiere. Jorge, spoiled Argentine, is married to a wealthy German heiress to a Nazi fortune. The lake is dotted with sailors.

Michel, exuberant with horse-power, turns to Dylan laughing. "Today we make a pirate raid on French territory. We steal the good food and wine. And some tender Mademoiselle for dessert, eh *mon vieux?*"

"It's enemy turf. There's no chance we could get picked up?"

Dylan's paranoia dials are flicking uneasily. There is something not right about this movie he thinks, glancing back at the police boat with white cross on red flag pacing half kilometer to the rear.

"Many people in Lausanne know we're crossing the lake today, don't they?"

"Don't worry, Dylan. The owner of the restaurant is my friend. We are protected. Enjoy the sunshine."

"What planet is this?" asks the Commodore suspiciously.

"What did you say?" says Michel.

"This isn't Sol—3. Look at the sky. It's blue."

Meanwhile, She is trailing Her hand in the swift-moving fluid, feeling velvet membrane water pressure slide against Her palm, suddenly understanding the sensual experience of a slippery fish. My goodness, She thinks, they spend their entire life slipping through this delicious medium. With their whole naked body.

"Dylan!" she calls, "come feel this."

The Wizard leaps past Rich Young Husbands to sit between Dee Dee and Maya who are both trailing their hands with thoughtful expressions.

"High-speed skin-diving, naked in warm tropical water," says Maya, "will you take me Dylan? If this makes my hands feel so good, imagine what my whole body would feel." Her eyes are shining and Her face is flushed.

"The normal hand has many more nerve endings than the body," replies the Professor, "although this may not be true in your case. They robbed our skin of sensory receivers when we left the water and gave the action to the hands. What we want is a dolphin's skin. It's as tender as the eye ball, more sensitive than the tongue and the dolphin can ripple Her skin to adjust to slightest pressure changes. The dolphin body is the ideal pleasure instrument. It floats freely with no pressure from gravity. The enormous swollen brain wired to a body which has been designed for sensation. The dolphin is a six foot organ of pleasure, a huge neurological eye-tongue-penis with unbearably sensitive skin. They used to be land-animals you know, and it's obvious why they left the heavy, dry land and slid back to the ocean of sensory rapture. Every move they make is orgasm."

"I want to go back," She sighs. "Do girl dolphins feel the same way?"

"Dolphins have the same imaginative sexual arrangements we have, in addition to the total membrane pleasure they feel each time they move. They also communicate by clicking vibrations which they receive *inside* their body."

"So they come as they go," She says wonderingly. "No wonder they wear that silly smile on their face. Are they monogamous? They must. There's no reason they shouldn't be. I guess there's a message there for all married couples."

"Michel," he shouts. "I've just discoverd what WoMan wants! She wants to live like a dolphin."

Dee Dee, who has been listening idly to the conversation with her hand sliding along in the water, smiles enigmatically.

Michel has kept the boat in the middle of the lake, but as the buildings of Geneva appear far ahead, he swings left and heads for the French shore. Dylan is the only one to notice the police craft which keeps heading down the lake. He sees a man standing in the bow watching them with field glasses.

-61-

William S. Burroughs was born in St. Louis, Missouri, in 1914. His many works include "Naked Lunch"—which made him famous overnight—"Nova Express," "Exterminator!" "The Third Mind," The Last Words of Dutch Schultz, Cities of the Red Night," and "The Place of Dead Roads." In 1983 he was named a Member of the American Academy and Institute of Arts and Letters. Burroughs now lives in Lawrence, Kansas.

Jacket blurb for "The Place of Dead Roads

THE EURO-TRASH CREW RAISES THE PIRATE FLAG

Lac Leman, May 1971.

Michel stands steering the boat with his left hand. He waves the Professor to come up to the co-pilot seat and throws his right arm around him.

"A good day, eh Dylan? Good food, good wine, beautiful companions. But I see you slip into worry from time to time. You must not do this, *mon frere*. I will go back to France soon. And when I do I shall take you and Maya with me. I can handle these police problems. And we shall be Beeg Playboys of Paris, you and me. I promise you."

It was a subtle, generous gesture. The Commodore feels tension drain away and smiles grateful friendship into the dancing mischievous-boy eyes of the Frenchman. It is such a relief to have a friend who is free and strong, he thinks.

"Now we shall have some fun. Watch. See that boat? Do you know what's going on there?" Michel digs his elbow into the Philosopher's ribs.

Michel has changed course to approach a small boat, idly drifting with no occupants visible. He is steadily cutting down on motor speed so that he coasts cunningly closer with no increase in sound. The little boat bobs innocently. At thirty meters Michel jams the throttle and the Riva screams forward just missing the target. As they roar past they look down at naked limbs untangling, the woman's face, framed by blonde hair, frozen in fear, the man's face flushed with surprised irritation. As the Riva catapults away, its waves rock the small boat. They can see only the two heads over gunwale, the man, face-flushed shouting in anger. Michel is shaking with laughter, as are Antoine and Jorge. Dee Dee's head is turned, half-bowed, her eyebrows lifted. The Philosopher and Maya stare at each other in disbelief.

"Regardez," shouts Michel, "we are the brigand lords of the lake. We'll give *them* a thrill next."

He points to another small boat drifting in the center of the lake. The Riva engines are on full power and the boat lunges ahead savagely. As they approach they can see the occupants—a girl of eight or nine years sitting next to her father, a sturdy, plump Swiss. They are engrossed in fishing and do not notice the approach of the invaders. Michel has the Riva pointed directly at collision course, close, closer. At ten meters he swings the wheel slightly so that the powerful boat almost grazes the helpless victim. As they flash by the wave-wake splashes over the girl soaking her white dress.

Michel is standing in front of the wheel his face radiant with triumph.

"Did you see that!" he shouts. "We scored another hit!" He is Hero of World War II holding a brandy snifter in his left hand. With a flourish he drains the glass and tosses it carelessly overboard. He turns and throws the cognac bottle to Antoine who tilts it to his lips and hands it to Jorge. The three men are wreathed in playful Commando Grins. Jorge reaches down and picks up a shoe. "What elegant shoes you wear, Antoine. Let's see if the poor, proletariat fish would like them." With an exultant cry he tosses the shoes in the water.

Antoine gapes momentarily then reaches down for Jorge's loafers and tosses them overboard. The two men look at each other, laugh, and, with the same motion, leap forward. Antoine seizes Michel's tan cashmere sweater and throws it over the side while Jorge snatches the Captain's cap and scales it across the water. Michel grabs the cognac bottle, empties it in his mouth and hurls it into the wake.

The two young men glance down to the Professor's-shoes, pause and turn their heads to send a sheepish, brazen look at the fugitives.

"This looks like a case for the Psych-Tech boys," sighs Maya. "They don't even stop to enjoy the soft favors of the women they have captured."

"Michel," calls the Commodore. "We are being followed."

Michel Hauchard looks back and waves his hand in dismissal. "*Ca fait rien.* He cannot catch me. No one can catch me. Ha ha. I assure you, the police of a dozen countries have tried."

The pursuer is falling slowly behind the raiders but it is obvious that in the narrow lake visual contact will not be lost and the menacing hunter can track the pirates to the *Port d'Ouchy.*

"That's great," groans Dylan. "They tell me to maintain a low profile, and now we're going to get busted for reckless driving under the influence of dangerous drugs."

"Not to mention littering," agrees Maya glumly. "And the peeping-tom rap will look bad on our record."

"Fire over their heads," shouts Michel drunkenly from the wheel. "If they come within reach, disarm them. I want them taken alive. For ransom!"

The port is filled with boats and pedalos.

As Michel threads the Riva through the traffic jam, the Fugitives, radar scanning for heat, watch the harbor police boat cut out to intercept, siren shrieking, red-light rotating.

"We're busted, Michel," She says dryly. "What do we do now?"

The pink jowls on Michel's cheeks drop in thought. "No problem. I eat Swiss police like *escargot.*"

"I hope you don't mind if we don't wait around to watch," says the Doctor.

As the Riva bumps into the dock the two fugitives step ashore with casual dignity. The Philosopher, with a visible flourish, hands the astonished Michel a ten franc note and with a thank-you-my-good-man pat walks off with his English wife. As they turn the corner by the Angleterre Hotel they look back and see the harbor police listening and smiling as Michel waves his arms in the unmistakable, universal gesture of innocent benevolence.

-62-

"It seemed like only a short time before every young Alphan movie director wanted Miss Photo to star in a new film. 4—D Films were very popular at that time with the young Alphans. The Alphan public had gotten a good dose of Miss Photo's face on the news programs and she became an overnight celebrity. After seeing some of the Alphan films Miss Photo could not help wanting to do a few herself. She agreed to star in a film if they would teach her how to handle the equipment. Rotwang wrote the music and it was the first musical film ever made on Alpha. It was all about Miss Photo and her life on Earth. It was called 'I, an Earth Woman' and Miss Photo was playing herself."

ROTWANG
By Tim Hildebrand

CHAPTER TITLE?

Riverdale, New York, August 1963.

"That must be a record," laughed Flora Lu. "Kicked out of Harvard University and six countries in six weeks."

"It was only three countries," replied Dylan without enthusiasm.

"What are you going to do now?"

"Flee to a desert island in the Caribbean. This planet isn't ready for me. I met an ex-West Pointer in Antigua who's dabbling in Caribbean real-estate. He's got a small island, totally uninhabited. He'll keep half-interest in it and give me the other half if we build it up."

"If there's nothing on the island, how can you live there?"

"Peggy Hitchcock and I will live on a boat while we're building the fresh-water converters and living quarters."

"Why do you want to get away like that?"

"To be free from social games. We've studied the map of the world, and there's hardly an acre left that's not under the jealous surveillance of a local sheriff. I want to hook up with nature, not with the local political machine. It will be at least ten years before I'm legal in this country and it's swimming upstream against the media. It's a thousand-head Medusa. Every ambitious reporter, policeman, politician, and bureaucrat looking for a cheap moral shot to scare Grandma and sell more papers. Let someone else do the merchandising. I want to talk to my brain."

"You got bruised by the Baddies?"

"It's a full-time job dealing with them. And the game is played with money and what we're dealing is nerve cells. What do you think?"

"What about the Hitchcock estate?"

"I haven't seen it."

"A 64 room mansion in the center of a 10-mile estate with central heating and a million-dollar bungalow for your neighbor?"

"But that will involve diplomacy and upper-class politics."

"You're going to be involved in politics no matter where you go," said Flora Lu. "And that's unimportant anyway. Let Richard Alpert and Peggy Hitchcock handle the local voters and you concentrate on your job."

"What's that?"

"You have to make the connection. What do you think I've been trying to arrange the last three years? To bring the right elements into combination. Broadcast your mating call."

-63-

Gordon Liddy's First Spy Caper

It was Saturday night—the 64 room mansion at Millbrook, New York, filled with staff members of the Castalia Foundation and weekend guests. Dinner in the oak-panelled dining room, low tables and cushions. Musicians came to Millbrook to learn that sound was energy to play with. Painters, to discover that light was energy to free from canvas, spashing, rippling, exploding colors over the walls of Millbrook, chromatic patterns bubbling, rainbow crystals blossoming, multi-hued cellular blobs undulating.

Outside the house, crouched behind dark bushes, binoculars glued to his eyes, G. Gordon Liddy peered through the windows at the activities within the mansion. He, the first "square" American to witness a psychedelic-psybernetic light show, was whispering instructions to the walkie-talkie pressed tenderly against his cheek.

From "Neuropolitics"

A BIOGRAPHIC SUMMARY OF DUBIOUS MERIT

Geneva, May 1971.

"The graceful decision for him in 1962 would have been to avoid any sort of public life, retire to a secluded location, form a neurological marriage, breed consciously, study electronics, computers, nuclear physics and genetics. And thus be available for the next mutation. His problem, as we now deduce it, was that he was unmated. This really confused us and made us wonder whom he re-presented. He had most virtuously avoided using the tremendous aphrodisiac potentials of brain-reward during the training period. His next step was to send out a global mating signal. We suspect that it was for this reason that he remained to participate in the second phase of mutation—the more visible dissemination of information people around the planet. This would have happened inevitably, it being the pre-designed destiny of each species to expand. He thus became involved in the neuro-political struggles which you seem to be interested in.

"From 1962 to 1965 he directed an energetic campaign to brain-wash and re-program certain key figures in American society. Carefully selected teams traveled throughout the country demonstrating brain-reward to cultural spokesmen who were ready to mutate. He avoided, of course, humans whose neurology was irreversibly hooked to larval survival techniques, military and political. He supplied pamphlets, publications, and fissioning materials to the fissionaries. You will be most interested in the specific target areas. He concentrated on young opinion-makers and the information elite—artists, pop and jazz musicians, writers, poets, journalists, college instructors, young ministers. And upon the young rich. For example, he supplied brain-reward drugs and know-how to Herman Kahn's Hudson Institute, to the Rand Corporation—both Dan Ellsberg and Tony Russo for example, were brain-washed and neurologically reprogrammed by neruo-transmitting molecules. He concentrated on the Kennedys, who were contacted and initiated through their female companions. More than one hundred top politicians were influenced although not necessarily repro-grammed, by their wives, mistresses and children. He would frequently be called in the late hours by elegant *heterae* agents requesting consultation. "The Senator has got religion. He's weeping and complaining that he's lived an evil life. He's stuck. How can I get him moving?"

"What would he say?" inquires the intrigued Michel.

"These phone taps are most amusing. He'd usually say: 'In a tub of hot water place some scented bath oil, the Senator and yourself. Call back if you have any further questions.' There never were.

"He concentrated on those who were most ready to mutate. The endowed. The superior young people who were rich, talented, influential, good-looking, well-educated, eminently sane. At the reunion of the Mellon family in North Ireland, for example, while the older generation relaxed, enjoying the fruits of their position as the world's most powerful land management clan, the younger generation was collecting in the outlying cottages to be indoctrinated in brain-management."

"Was this campaign limited to America?" asks Michel.

"No, he selected some trainees from other countries. In 1965, for example, he sent an eccentric Englishman back to his country with five thousand dollars worth of brain-reward molecules and instructional albums. Certain prominent elements of the English rock movement paid back this investment handsomely. By the fall of 1965 this second phase, the creation of a neurological aristocracy, a high-energy transmitting elite was completed. At this point, December 19, 1965, he tried to leave the country with his wife planning to retire from visible activity until the next mutation was scheduled.

"We couldn't allow this to happen. So we set up a trap at Nuevo Laredo and had him busted on some token charge. The plan was to entangle him in legality and systematically destroy his public image. Art Linkletter was selected to lead the attack. Clever choice, don't you think?"

"But he could have easily avoided the entanglement by leaving the country," protests Michel.

"The conditions of his bail prevented that. By 1968 he had become an obsession to Nixon. The symbol of everything that San Clemente feared. Nixon was terrified about his own children. You remember what happened to Agnew's son."

"Whose children weren't affected," exclaimed Hauchard. "I could tell you stories . . . "

"Yes, I know," interrupted Hyatt. "But in any case our plan worked. The Alien Agent was pulled into the political polarizations of the late 1960s, as planned. And his genetic signal easily lost in noise."

"Why did he fall into this trap?" says Michel frowning. "Certainly he realized that the legalization of drugs, the emergence of the hedonic life-style was inevitable by 1996 without his dubious assistance?"

"Genetic karma we suspect," replies Hyatt. "The Irish Kelts have some ancient chromosome grudges to repay the Protestants. Darwinian self-indulgence. A neo-neolithic replay of the bardic role, perhaps, inventing jokes and slogans, transmuting the rhythms, rhymes, alchemical alliterations latent in language. In the Great Hall at Millbrook, Keltic chiefs sat and feasted, bards fabulated, minstrels sang, and in this ambiance of visionary intoxication and Dionysic revelation, medicine men spun prophecies. And war bands armed with chemicals and electronic devices made raids on the Anglo-Saxons. Standard Racial cut-ups. We've had the same trouble with Kelts for centuries. They were the last pagans in Europe. The west coast of

Ireland is as far from Rome as you can get without the magnetic compass."

"Amusing, perhaps," says Michel with an annoyed grimace, "but the Protestants have never found it difficult to crush the tribes. There is nothing very playful about Anglo-Saxon leaders."

"He was foolish enough to be deceived by the apparent ease of his cultural victory. No matter how inured to human irrationality, it is never possible for the outside observer to believe the illogic of politics. According to all demographic estimates the cultural revolution was a reality. Every month we recorded the astonishing indices of social change. The easing of sexual taboos, the liberating alienation from routine roles, the growth of organic consciousness, and extraterrestrial awareness. On every one of a score of measurements the mutation had reached a one-third-level of the population. One third smoked grass, were against capital punishment, favored diversity of life style. It seemed impossible that such a sizable minority could be flouted. At the same time the Republican party membership fell to eighteen percent. There were Twice as many grass smokers as Republicans! Ten times more smokers than Jews and Mormans combined! It seemed to be the fastest, smoothest cultural mutation in history. Galactic awards must have seemed inevitable to him."

"Do you see where he went wrong?" asks Hyatt.

"He didn't allow for the time lag. He apparently expected the next mutation team to take over, the computer people. The new language technology, the cybernetic engineers designing the light-speed thought-processors. He seems slow to understand that he has to do it. Do you understand?"

"Computers?" said Michel.

-64-

Who is Jayne Loader?

The blurb on the last page of BETWEEN PICTURES says that she "is the co-producer, -director, and -writer of the celebrated documentary THE ATOMIC CAFE."

The blurb also says, "Uncorrected proofs, Please do not quote."

The picture of Jayne Loader was taken by Thomas Victor, 1987.

A DISTURBING CONVERSATION WITH A FRENCH FILM ACTRESS

Lausanne, June 1971.

From some neutron core within, Dylan watches with morbid curiosity the energy from his explosion whirl out into the gravitational fields of the surrounding entities. He is aware by now that everyone goes a bit crackers when Stage 13 Pan-Dionysius road-show breezes into town. His Hedonic super-nova had left him spinning in charge-less morosity (not for nothing did She call him the Crab Nebulae) but the energy leaked by his solar wind invariably stimulated passers-by to varying reactions.

It was obvious, for example, that Michel saw him as some sort of mobile oil-concession to be incorporated and sold in shares to the unwary.

Dee Dee, delighted to have playmates in naughtiness, is busy organizing truant groups to smoke fashionable vegetation on the terrace. She is enjoying a mild sensation in Paris discotheques dealing breathless psychedelic-fugitive stories.

Among the married molecules, the same polarized alchemical reaction was occurring. The heaviest connubial element clinging fiercely to the marriage bond, attempts to turn-off the Hedonic catalyst. The higher-energy element vibrates restlessly.

Antoine, for example, the petulant *pied noir*, clings closely to Michel muttering darkly about drug addiction, degeneration and American communism.

Katrine Lumiere, his spoiled vivacious wife, takes over the action, importing dried Venezuelan botanicals, Turkish opium-derivatives, and Peruvian powders, to impress them.

At Michel's birthday dinner Katrine, promising Maya parts in her movies, arranges to be seated next to the Outlaw.

"I must introduce you to my chic Parisian friends to learn about smack. We French by the age of twenty are already as old as death. Come watch us dragging centuries of dark perversions behind us to discoteques and elegant shooting galleries. We are the rich, over-ripe fruits of a dubious civilization. We have no chance. We take no chances."

Dylan is shocked by the beautiful girl's confessions. "But you have talent and brains!"

"Tant pis. The talent prevents our happiness and enflames our insanity. My talent makes me interesting, but it can't protedt me. We do smack all night and sleep like puppies in a pile for the Algerian maids to find in the morning."

Dylan feels out of his league. Like a hick from Bum Fuck, Texas. "You seem so sophisticated and wise," he stammers.

Katrine Lumiere smiles enigmatically. "My dear Dylan, do not be confused. We have moved from barbarism to decadence without stopping at civilization, as de Toqueville predicted. And, to be frank, this doesn't bother me at all."

-65-

A screaming comes across the sky. It has happened before, but there is nothing to compare it to now.

It is too late. The Evacuation still proceeds, but it's all theatre.

There is no way out. Lie and wait, lie still and be quiet. Screaming holds across the sky. When it comes, will it come in darkness, or will it bring its own light? Will the light come before or after.

First lines of "Gravity's Rainbow"
By Thomas Pynchon

EARLY EXPLORERS OF THE BRAIN

Info-Sociology

During this early period there came to the Harvard Research Center the Cosmic Politicians and the Gnostic Diplomats, to present their views on the evolution of the nervous system.

Gerald Heard spoke for the Elitists. "Keep it secret," was his advice. "There cannot be a hedonic society. The larval middle class cannot be free. Humans must be domesticated to the slavery of schedule and production. Furthermore, they don't want to be free and will crush anyone who offers to liberate them and their children. The Bourgeoisie will tolerate a neurological aristocracy as long as it is kept distant from them. The wealthy, the charismatic 'stars' can be allowed the pursuit of rapture. Indeed, the masses are titillated to read about scintillating, elitist experiments in bliss as long as they take place out of sight. On the Costa del Sol. In the Golden Casbah of Tangier. But you'll have to keep one step ahead of the Socialists."

The Cosmic Bureaucrats had more conventional proposals. Al Hubbard, former uranium salesman, saw the market possibilities. Backed by some of the most prominent psychiatrists in America and Canada, he sketched out a chain-store-psychedelic marketing operation. Government-approved, medically-directed psychedelic clinics throughout the country would, for a five-hundred dollar fee, administer Neurotransmitter Substances to middle-class persons in session rooms decorated with murals of the Last Supper to the tune of Beethoven's Ninth Symphony.

Dylan chose a middle course. Public elitism. On ten-miles-round-of-fertile-ground in Millbrook, New York a research station was founded to investigate the new energies. Four Harvard Ph.D.'s and a staff of assistants. It was called Castalia Foundation after the scientific-mystic brotherhood described in a famous novel, *Magister Ludi*, by Herman Hesse.

To Castalia's green-lawned, stone-turreted Bavarian Castle came the new breed of wizards, sorcerers, alchemists, magicians, musicians, sound-engineers, light-artists, electronic composers, yogins, diet-gurus, voodooists, clairvoyants, organic gardeners, Tarot-card dealers, I Ching throwers, astrologists, bio-chemists, computer designers, numerologists, jazz-stars, cabalists, light-technicians projecting colored images fifty-feet high across the castle walls, drummers, flautists, dervishes, devotees of every swami, theolophist, sage and seer.

The renowned and the disowned. Each performed Hir neurological feat. Each had managed to turn-on and manipulate one sense-organ, one neural pathway, one method of transmitting non-symbolic somatic energy. Each believed that Hir modality was the true and best way to the mountain of perpetual bliss. Probably the entire company of neurological pilgrims made up one complex, educated nervous system.

They were all cheerful and congenial folk except for the vegetarians. The only flicks of physical violence in five stormy years were manifested by enraged macrobiotic dietists beating up chocolate-cake eaters in the castle kitchen.

-66-

"Planetary society is obsessed with security—biological, social, economic and domestic. From the standpoint of terrestrial society a person alienated from the gene-pool community ceases to exist. From the redemptive perspective of extraplanetary migration, exile is the pioneer step. Nationalism is always the enemy of migration in the early pre-flight stages. However, as soon as the first space colony ships have demonstrated the feasibility of migration, the second phase, wild national competition, develops."

Michael Miller in Info-Sociology

SUMMER OF LOVE — 20 YEARS LATER

Geneva, May 1971.

"I recall," sez Hyatt, "scanning some wire-tap manuscripts of a conversation between this actor and two Hollywood Agents who were raving in traditional cocaine fashion about a film they wanted to make. It was called *Easy Rider*. A hippy re-run of the classic Huck Finn trip. Driving across America on motorcycles to New Orleans. A few months later while passing through Omaha, Nebraska I noticed the film was playing at a local theatre. To my dismay I found lines of young people stretching around the block waiting to buy tickets. This unpretentious little home movie was becoming the snash box-office hit of the year. It was a savage attack on the Domestic Ethic. A crude propaganda glorification of long-hair, hippy drop-out, neurological freedom, neuro-transmitter drugs. Think of anything offensive to the middle class and you have written the script. The shaggy delinquents talk philosophy, prove irresistably attractive to girls, speculate about extraterrestrial intelligence, induce mystical experiences with brain-reward chemicals and are brutally murdered by red-neck defenders of the larval orthodoxy."

"Disgusting," sez Michel.

"When we came out of the theatre and walked past the lines waiting for the next showing I wondered if the parents of these eager young faces were aware that their children were being exposed to such revolutionary signals."

"*Easy Rider* was a boon to the motorcycle industry and the hard drug trade," notes Michel sagely.

"And a paradoxical evolutionary message," adds Hyatt. "The theme is basically pessimistic. Just as Huckleberry Finn cheerfully forecasted the Civil Rights incursions of the next century, *Easy Rider* glumly predicted the Nixon cultural repression. 'We blew it,' said the Hero just before he's blown to bits by the shotgun. The point is this! The trip was pointless. The liberated brain all dressed up and no place to go except back to the outworn hedonism of Mardi Gras. It ends in a Bourbon Street bordello. Meanwhile histone orthodoxy was preparing the counter-offensive. *The French Connection* and *The Godfather*. How about that Michel?"

"Superb movies," replies the Frenchman cheerfully.

"The most effective way for a gene-pool to delay mutation is nostalgia. Soothing repetition. In the past this involved repeating old hymns, old patriotic slogans, traditional rituals. Today this involves re-runs of old movies. When our television industry began re-issuing electro-magnetized celluloid tapes that had imprinted the inhibitions of our older generation, it was a declaration of full scale neurological civil war with electron patterns as weapons. The Vatican realizes that Cary Grant and Rita Hayworth were no longer temptations, but rather solid connections to the past."

"But that is a delaying action, at best," replies Michel. "Dylan had all the new talent and the brain-washing know-how."

"You forget, Michel, that all civilization is a holding action, gene-pools slowing down evolution. And we in Rome have been learning the new brain-washing techniques as they appear. *Mon Dieu*, we invented the method fifteen hundred years ago! I assure you, no one has studied this agent's writings as thoroughly as our people. We know how to distract mutations that we feel are premature."

"How?"

"Trap them in local politics. Tempt them into cultural-revolution. Activism. The gnostic inevitably slips down into alliance with the Outs. We got him so involved in court trials and pacifistic politics that he lost sight of his mission. Frankly, the man hasn't had a new idea in seven years. Look at the trivia he gets involved with! Legalize marijuana? Long hair on red-necks? Ecology, the new organic Calvinism? Establishing a hippy orthodoxy? Pitiful attempts to take over the American government without spilling a drop of cerebro-spinal fluid? Cultural revolutions and neurogenetic mutations can exist gracefully underground in the form of elites and cults. But when they begin to surface they become democratized, bureaucratized, vulgarized, and, of course, co-opted by us. What interest does he have, really, in electing a grass-smoking female president?"

"The familiar downfall of the Kelts," sez Michel smiling. "They cannot let themselves be pinned down to an orthodoxy, even their own."

"It's more than that. The brain, once freed from the cultural imprints imposed in childhood, is not interested in social organizations. The goal of DNA, we are seeing, is beyond politics. Believe me, Michel, we understand that the first thing one does with a liberated, self-directed nervous-system at one's disposal is to explore the hedonic possibilities. To feel good. But that doesn't lend itself to social organization. That's our classic protection. Two is the conventional number for erotic fusion. At the elevations and velocities we're talking about one discovers that one body and one brain is just half of the Einsteinian unit. When the neurologic fusion is made, then the questions can be posed."

"What questions?" asks Michel.

"Where is the species going? How do we get there? What comes next? This is our responsibility, after all."

"Perhaps we aren't going anywhere. We've arrived!" sez Michel who is cheerily refilling the wine glasses.

"Someone has to be in the bridge of the Space Ship Earth charting directions," sez Hyatt gently.

"I just want more," laughs Michel.

"The reason that we are interested in your client is that he's running around the Space Ship picking up radio signals and directional codes and broadcasting them around with no clearance from the bridge. And my clients in Rome want to know what he proposes to do next. Foolish plots to take over the bridge will, of course, get him no where."

"The directional signals I get involve his wife, his writing, his psychological experiments, good food, money and freedom. Does he want to give all that up?"

"He apparently believes that we don't have to give up anything. Indeed he seems to want to include everything."

"What can I do," pouts Michel throwing up his hands. "Philosophers are unpleasant to be around. Always experimenting with new ideas! What do you want me to do with him? He has no money."

"You can make plenty of money, if you manage him cleverly. We want you to control his income. Keep him comfortable but economically insecure. Run him on a tight leash. We'll give you further instructions when necessary. Remember, he has the most dangerous tools at his disposal."

"What tools?" replies Michel in surprise.

"Don't you understand," snaps Hyatt. "The brain. He's changed the entire phillosophic game. In the past, humanity has attempted to solve the destination problems by using a ridiculously inadequate instrument. The mind."

"But reason is our best tool."

"Michel, you are a hopeless dilettante. Haven't you read a word he's written? He claims that thinking is nothing but manipulation of the nine laryngeal muscles. Verbal Swedish drill He's trying to teach people to use their heads."

"My business is intelligence," sez Michel stiffly, "but this is a new assignment for me. It seems so impractical."

"It's the most practical, least boring thing going. What are we going to do with this confused species that has stumbled on to the scientific method? My people don't have an answer. Portugal will go socialist in five years. And Franco is dying. The Summer of Love will hit Madrid in two years. It will hit Moscow and South Korea and Japan by 1987. Do you know what we should do?"

"Oh no!" sez Michel swiftly. "That's not my job. I'm simply a peddlar of what he calls artifacts and symbols. If I get any answers from him I'll be glad to barter them to you. Who knows, it might turn out to be valuable, this Secret of Life."

"At these stakes you only have to be right once," sez Hyatt drily.

"And I own half the rights. After expenses," exclaims Michel happily, waving to the waiter for the check.

-67-

"The meek shall inherit the earth and the wise keep moving on."

The Game of Life

TREACHERY AGAIN IN THE BOOK TRADE

Lausanne, May 1971.

Michel is standing in the driveway of the penthouse planning transportation to lunch. The brilliant May sun sparkles on the lake. The lawns and gardens breathe joyous spring colors.

She is an Afghani Princess in wispy silk. The Wandering Bard is wearing his new continental apparel, soft-woven black trousers, turtle-neck sweater and grey herring-bone jacket with a Nehru collar.

"Maya and Dee Dee, you will go with Jorge. Dylan, you come with me. We have business to discuss."

"If you two work then we will be forced to play," says Ms. Feel-good brightly, winking at Her consort.

Michel rolls the luxury vehicle through the metropolitan traffic heading uphill to *centre ville.*

"Listen, Dylan, we have a problem. Who is this John Rodney? Why didn't you tell me about him? If you keep such secrets, we shall be ruined."

"I never heard of him," replies the astonished Author. "Who is John Rodney?"

"Katrine Lumiere just phoned me in a great temper. She has read in the paper that this Rodney is in New York trying to sell our book."

"How did this Rodney get a copy of it?"

"I don't know. The only copy outside of our hands is the one I sent to Jean Jacques in Paris. You haven't . . . "

"Of course not, *mon vieux.* But we need more facts. In what paper did Katrine read this?"

"The Paris *Tribune.* We shall go to *le gare* and get a copy. This is very bad. Katrine was sure that you had betrayed us."

Michel parks in front of the station.

"Let me go in, Dylan. It is best you not be seen in such a public place."

He returns striding forcefully through the crowd, his face aflame with determination.

"This is an outrage, *mon voyageur. Regardes.*"

-68-

"Caterpillars manifest a tank-like ferocity in defending and extending territorial limits. Butterflies are free to sample, at will, the limitless expanse of flowered meadows. Is this metamorphosis not a clear signal from DNA?"

Eric Gullichsen in *Info-Sociology*

MICHEL WHEELS OUT HIS BIG GUNS

Lausanne, May 1971.

Michel swings the Roller into the gravel covered parking lot and the two men, escorted by a flock of blackcoat waiters, parade through the restaurant to the terrace. Jorge and the two attractive young women are shooting a Gatsby scene at a shaded-table, drinking wine and laughing vivaciously.

"We had a delightful trip here," She smiles saucily. "Floating along the highway listening to Jorge's tape deck. How was your business discussion?"

"Nothing new," smiles the Author. "The book has been stolen again."

"How flattering," giggles Dee Dee.

"By whom?" sighs Jorge, obviously trying to catch a hand-hold on the practicalities floating by.

"Shall we sue, Michel?" giggles Maya. "Or turn it over to the Corsicans?"

Michel is standing next to his Client for the still-photo which was to become so familiar to magazine readers. He is happily sniffing the scent of profitable intrigue.

"Neither. This man Rodney is obviously well-connected. Business manager of *Conde-Nast*. Splendid. We shall fire a warning shot across his bow and then invite him over for a truce talk. Who knows, if we like him we shall sell him some stock in the company."

"What warning shot?" inquires Jorge, with an inappropriate grin.

"Dylan, here's what we shall do," replies Michel. "Phone the Associated Press in Geneva and make a blanket denial. Declare that you have given publication rights to the well-known Swiss financier, Michel Hauchard. Say that you have never heard of Monsieur Rodney but that he shall soon hear from our lawyers."

"I still want to know how he got the manuscript," says the Author.

"Oh that. I forgot to tell you. I think, maybe, Jean Jacques sold him the rights. Totally unauthorized of course. But I'm sure we'll be able to work something out with him."

-69-

"Within ten years
According to pharmacologists
They will have perfected pills
And cranial electrodes
Capable of providing lifelong bliss
For everyone on Earth."

Time Magazine, November 26, 1973

AN INEXPENSIVE PARANOIA? OR JUNGLE SMARTS?

Lausanne and Geneva, June 1971.

The Commodore walks up the hill from Michel's to the Railroad station, hurrying to catch the electric railcar to Geneva where She is recuperating in a private clinic.

□ □ □ □ □ □ □ □ □

Yo Yo walks to Michel's study and picks up the ringing phone, yawning sleepily.
"I'm sorry Madame. Monsieur Hauchard is still sleeping."
She listens.
"No, Madame. Monsieur Dylan just left for Geneva. What did you say your name was?"
"No, Madame, I cannot say where he is going. What firm did you say you work for?"
Yo Yo put down the phone with a puzzled look. That's funny, She thinks. She hung up. I must remember to tell Michel. It didn't sound like Anna Kate. But you can never tell with Her.

□ □ □ □ □ □ □ □ □

Anna Kate put down the phone smiling broadly.
"He just left for Geneva. And not with Michel. That means he's coming by train."
"Are you sure?" says Lorenzo.
"No, but it's worth a shot. Can I use Bruno and your car for an hour?"
"You're going to meet the Lausanne train? But you don't know what he looks like."

"Come on, Lorenzo, how many men of his general species will be getting off the Lausanne-Geneva train?"

"Why go to so much trouble," says Lorenzo shrugging gracefully. "Just call Michel and tell him you want to meet Dylan."

"I've tried that already. That fucking Michel has a *cordon sanitaire* around his prize. He's a true jailer, that Michel, I know him. He's not about to let me talk to Dylan and he's instructed that silly Yo Yo to screen all calls."

The Commodore walks swiftly through the Geneva Train Station and hails the first car in the taxi-line.

Anna Kate is leaning forward over the front seat jabbering excitedly to the driver in Italian.

"That's a dead-end street, Mademoiselle O'Shea," says Bruno. "Do you want to be seen?"

"Sure. But we've got to catch up with him first. Hurry. He's entering that building at the end of the street."

"*Clinique Obstetrique.*" Bruno turns towards his passenger and raises his hands. "What now, Mademoiselle?"

"Listen. Take this fifty francs to the desk and tell them you must see the man who just came in. He left his change. Okay? When you see him ask him to come out for a minute. Tell him I have a message from Monsieur Hauchard. If that doesn't work, at least find out his name."

"Why didn't you talk to him at the station, Mademoiselle?"

"I got side-tracked following that man with the grey mustache. Hurry, Bruno, before he gets upstairs."

Anna Kate lights a *Gitane-filtre* and waits impatiently.

Bruno returns shaking his head.

"No good, Mademoiselle. They refused to let me see the man. They refused to give me his name. And to make matters worse, they didn't refuse to take the fifty francs. They are Swiss after all. What now?"

"We wait."

□ □ □ □ □ □ □ □ □

At the clinic the Doctors are happy and proud. The operation was a success.

She is dozing, Her right arm lazily tossed behind Her head. Even in recuperating sleep She looks as though She is in erotic contemplation.

He arranges the blankets, kisses Her on the forehead and floats out of the room, his lower-circuit fibres dangling carelessly. He has been sharing the medicine She keeps hidden in silver-foil in a potted plant.

As he drifts through the lobby the grey-haired lady at the desk calls him over.

"Your cab driver left this fifty francs for you. He said you forgot you gave him a hundred."

"What! That's impossible, Madame. I assure you I gave the taxi driver ten francs exactly."

"Very curious. The driver wanted to go up to look for you. I wouldn't let him, of course."

Dylan's first neural circuit spurts alarm juice, creating a reality island peopled by dangerous C.I.A. agents.

"Of course," he says, weakly.

"Another curious thing, Monsieur. He wanted to know your name. I didn't tell him, of course."

His heart is thumping and he feels sweat dripping from emergency portholes. "That's strange. Thank you for handling the affair so discreetly."

The Commodore walks to the window and peers out. He is sure the Clinique is surrounded by Interpol Agents. He sees the Black Mercedes with the uniformed driver.

"Is that the driver?"

The clerk pulls back the curtain, adjusts her glasses and looks out conspiratorially.

"Why yes sir," she exclaims. "That is the veritable man!"

"And the woman in back. Do you know Her?"

"No Monsieur. How strange. You don't know Her?"

"Yes. She's a reporter that has been trying to interview me. What a nuisance! You understand, my wife and I wish to keep all this quiet."

"*Naturalment,* Monsieur Le Brun. I understand perfectly. There is a rear exit."

"Where does it lead?"

"To the back-yard of the Surgical Hospital. You can walk along the side to the next street. There's a taxi-stand at the corner.

He walks with swift gait past the Hospital. He realizes that escape is impossible, but he will not be captured passively. The Swiss have never failed to honor an American extradition request. He sees the rest of his life behind prison walls. A cab is waiting at the stand.

"*Le gare, vitement.*"

Looking out the rear window he sees the black Mercedes swing out of the *Rue de la Clinique* in pursuit. They'll bust me at the railroad station, he thinks.

As the taxi pulls up in front of the station he thrusts ten francs at the driver and enters the main door. They'll be waiting for me at the Lausanne track.

He walks with commuter speed to the baggage room and exits. He picks the last cab in the row lined up before the station.

"*Cent francs a Lausanne?*" he says.

"*D'accord,*" nods the driver flipping the meter flag and shifting into first gear.

The forty-five minute drive along the free-way is torturous suspense. They'll be waiting at Michel's apartment he thinks. If this is paranoia, I can't afford the hundred francs.

When the taxi pulls up in front of Michel's elegance he has landed solidly on terrestrial surface, his four umbilical fibres tentatively hooked into a nervous, sheepish, jangly reality bubble.

Maybe She *was* a reporter, he thinks. She looked pretty literary. Cute mouth, pesky brain. And anyway, subtracting the driver's donation, it was only a fifty franc paranoia.

-70-

"*GRAVITY: Nouns: weight, heaviness, ponderosity, pressure, burden ballast, counterpoise, lump, mass, load, lead, millstone. Avoir-dupois, ounce, pound, scruple, stone, ton. Seriousness, solemnity, importance.*

Verbs: gravitate, be heavy, weigh, press, cumber, load, weigh down.

Adjectives: Weighty, heavy, ponderous, lumpish, cumbersome, unwieldy, massive, grave, sober, solemn.

Antonym: See LEVITY"

Info-Sociology

MICHEL MOVES THE FUGITIVES ON THE GUESS BOARD. WHY?

Lausanne, June 1971.

The notorious Algerian fugitives, Maya and Nino Baraka are sitting uneasily on the sofa in the study. Michel is either nervous or acting nervous.

"Dee Dee and I have been so happy to have you with us these past few weeks. But I know that you are looking forward to having your own place. And you will be much happier in the mountains."

"We are grateful for your friendship," answers Dylan, wondering what is happening. "And, of course, we'll do what you suggest. What does Mastronardi say?"

"As a matter of fact it was Mastronardi who suggested that it might be wise for you not to continue to live here. As you know, my own residence in Switzerland is up in the air and *le Maitre* feels we should stay on the safe side. Lawyers are so cautious, *n'est-ce pas?*"

"You mean your status in Switzerland hasn't been settled?" exclaimed Maya in alarm. "Then how can we ever get passports here?"

"Our cases are very different. With you it is publicity. You are so well known. That is your protection and your problem. With me, it is their greed. Every few months they raise the issue of my extradition and another round of payments is necessary. I have many delicate business ventures around the world. Of course, I do no business here in Switzerland, but still it would be bad for me if any publicity linked me with you. And, to tell you the truth, it would be worse for you to be connected with me."

"Where do you think we should go?"

"That is no problem. The nearest ski resort to Lausanne is Villars sur Ollon. Chic, but not too chic like Gstaad. It is less than an hour by car and we shall be able to see each other regularly. You come for dinner every night. And, of course, my home is always your home. But it will be better for you to have your own address."

"Is there any danger that we'll be arrested?"

"Absolutely not. I swear to you. Mastronardi has his ears everywhere in Bern. If you are in danger, he will let me know and, flick, I put you on one of my planes in an hour. I have chosen Villars for you because it is in the Canton of Vaud. As you know, the Chief of Police here is my protector. His entire staff is on my list for Christmas presents. His office would be assigned to arrest you. *Voila*, he will make sure we are notified in time."

"But there's one disturbing point, Michel. You are leaving in a week to spend two months in Turkey. If any trouble comes down, you won't be here to help."

"Do not worry, Dylan. I have everything worked out. I will not leave if there is the thinnest risk. Mastronardi can handle an emergency. And I shall fly back in six hours if necessary."

"You know we don't have the cash to rent a house."

"But we are partners," says Michel reassuringly. "I have sent The Book to Paris and we should be getting offers any day. But until we start making a profit I shall pay for the house. Well, not a house. Shall we say an apartment? And I shall give you a sum for monthly expenses. And you shall sit on the mountain and make babies and write another fantastic book."

"How much is our allowance, Uncle Mike?" asks Maya drily.

"Enough for you to live on, but not enough for you to be extravagant. I know how you beautiful women like to spend money. For a few weeks you

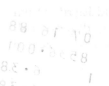

n six months, I promise you, Maya, we shall take you to
tiest dresses in Europe. Don't think about anything, my
ything worked out."

-71-

*And it is just here, just at this dark and silent frame, that the pointed tip of the Rocket, falling
nearly a mile per second, absolutely and forever without sound, reaches its last unmeasurable
gap above the roof of this old theatre, the last delta-t.*

*There is time, if you need the comfort, to touch the person next to you, or to reach between your
own cold legs . . .*

Last lines of "Gravity's Rainbow"
By Thomas Pynchon

A POIGNANT WISH FOR IMPREGNATION

Lausanne, June 1971.

Maya is in the bedroom packing. She is still weak from the operation and
moves slowly to avoid strain. A soft knock on the door. Dee Dee comes in.
Maya stands and the two women face each other, studying faces. They smile.

"I'm sorry you're going," says Dee Dee.

"You and Michel have been very kind."

"We didn't get to talk to each other."

Maya walks to the dresser for cigarettes.

"It's usually that way," She says. "A Psychologist once told me I have
trouble talking to anyone I'm not sleeping with."

"I think we are a lot alike," says Dee Dee.

"I'm really not a very social person, I'm afraid."

"I had hoped that I could take an LSD Trip. I never have, you know. I
asked Dylan, but, you know, because of his friendship with Michel . . . "

"Yes," says Maya sadly. "Life is always so complicated. But there's always
the future, I guess. I wonder what will happen to us."

"You are very brave. The operation. It's a very serious business. You must
really want to have children. I can't imagine wanting something that much."

Maya is sitting on the edge of the bed with one leg drawn under Her. Her
left hand is on Her stomach. Her face looks tired. "It's hard to make

comparisons. We live in such different worlds."

"I know," says Dee Dee sympathetically. "It's difficult to be an exile. Michel suffers to be away from Paris. He can't wait to go back."

"No, that's not what I mean. It's different with us, Dee Dee. We have no place to go back to. It's farther out than any science fiction novel, living as we do in our brains. Creating realities. We are exiles from our home *time*. Once you break that cozy bubble in which everyone lives then there's no time to go back to. Our passports are stamped valid for Everywhere except Albania, China, and the Past. Without children nothing makes any difference to the brain. It's all relative except for relatives."

"What about love?" says Dee Dee timidly. She looks uncomfortable as though the conversation is getting deeper than she had expected.

"Love? If you pursue love beyond desire, comfort, companionship, mutual good-will, if you grow closer and closer, the two at best become one. And there you are again. First person plural. Telepathic *folie a deux*. The consciously conceived child of that union seems to be the only real act of creation. Well, we'll know soon. The doctor says that ten days from today is our best and probably only chance. Most women have three hundred turns of the fallopian wheel. They can afford to be thoughtless about It."

"How many children do you want to have?"

Maya stands up, puts her hand on Dee Dee's cheek and laughs happily. "Oh five. Or ten. Or twenty."

Dee Dee shakes her head in dismay. "Oh Maya, how can you say such a thing! I can see one or two. But how can you think of increasing the herd, bringing more children into this world so crowded by people?"

"Crowded!" exclaims Maya. "We've searched the planet rather diligently and as far as we can see there are only the two of us."

-72-

"Even the most perfect neuro-somatic fusion
becomes, eventually, boring.
'... keep me high' She murmured, 'and I'll ball you all night long.'
But rapture dissolves;
Two sweaty bodies slowed down by larval
Insecurities; two minds worrying about
Passports and the rent."

The Game of Life

GOING PUBLIC IN A SWISS SKI RESORT

Villars sur Ollon, June 1971.

The Exiles' luggage is placed in the trunk. The Picaresque Wizard climbs in the rear seat of the Roller; Maya is co-pilot as Michel turns the wheel East for a House-hunting Expedition in the Swiss Alps.

"Here we go again," She sighs. "Another reality jump. That I Ching we threw in San Luis Obispo was too accurate for my taste."

"What is this itching?" asks Michel. "Are you not feeling well, my dear?"

"The Sunday before the prison escape of 1970 we consulted the Chinese oracle in the prison waiting room. To see if it would succeed. And we obtained the message, *Wanderer*. It predicted that we would be moving around from one kingdom to another. It advised us to be modest and not to offend our hosts with arrogance. Have we been docile enough, Michel?"

"You have been charming. We did better than I expected."

"You mean in raising money from your wealthy friends," says Maya suspiciously.

"No, not that," reacts Michel hastily. "Financially this affair is a disaster. But we don't care about money so we won't worry."

The Roller is humming along the narrow road to Montreaux, lake on the right and walled terraces green with vineyards on the left. Michel seems preoccupied and the atmosphere is more than one-G.

Skirting Montreaux, they turn on to a freeway high above the lake and curve down to Aigle at lake's end. A few miles beyond, Michel turns the car left and begins climbing the mountain.

"This is our kind of turf," says the Doctor. "I feel better already out of the city and into the high air."

The road twists upward; and then, curving a U-turn, they look across the valley at their destination, Villars, hung on a ridge on the side of the mountain.

The village is small, just one street of stores and restaurants, surrounded above and below by chalets and apartment buildings. Spread across the wide valley huge orange cranes, looking like Martian giants on stilt legs, feed on the construction sites they straddle.

Michel parks the car in the village center and leads them to the real estate office. He makes a point of introducing the Fugitives by name to the manager, the sales force and the secretaries.

They are shown three small apartments in chalet-style buildings above the town, all new, furnished in Grand Rapids motel-decor. The fourth offering is on the ground-floor of a two story Chalet with glass doors leading out to a lawn which looks down on the village and across the Rhone valley to *Les Dents Du Midi*. On the side of the apartment the lawn runs down to a brook bordered by trees.

"I'm not happy about any apartment," says Gene Tierney in a perky British accent. "But the brook, the grove of willows and the mountain I recognize. You may think me silly, Mister Hauchard, but I'll take it. Even if it is haunted."

The apartment: a small bedroom for the Professor's study, a dining-living room, a stand-up galley kitchen, a master bedroom with glass doors to the lawn. Most important, a fireplace.

Back in the real estate office, Michel pays three months rent and hands Dylan $300 for monthly allowance. Maya watches the Trick Pay-off with Cool Girl stare.

"This is not much, I know," explains Michel. "But within a few weeks we shall be winning a fortune and I shall buy you a fine car. What would you like, Maya, a Porsche or a Ferrari?"

"I guess this is the time to look on the bright side," She says. "It will be good for our health to walk up the hill after we shop in the village. And although we may not look it, we are grateful, Michel, for your guidance."

They walk across the street to *Le Sporting* for a farewell drink.

"Michel," asks the Poet. "You're sure there's no danger in registering here under our right names?"

"Don't be silly. The Swiss police know every move you make. There is no question of hiding from them. This way you are publicly and legally established. Look," says Michel throwing his hand out, "what a beautiful place for you to make babies and find the meaning of life."

They look down across the green meadows so well-trimmed, and up the peaks towering above the peaceful village. Cow bells tinkle in the sunset air.

"A pleasant place to make a baby," she murmurs.

-73-

"Re-imprinting is the process of suspending the neural synaptic routes which create 'reality' and of imprinting a new 'reality.' When the human species mastered the technique of re-imprinting and serial re-incarnation, a post-human level of evolution was attained."

Angie Brown in Principles of Neurogenetics

DYLAN SHOPS FOR A NEW FACE

Villars sur Ollon, Switzerland, June 1971.

Trapped on a primitive, hostile Four-brained Planet, the Commodore and His Consort have been enslaved and vended to the lowest bidder.

She is standing outside the glass door of their prison and can see him climbing the winding road below the chalet. A sudden spurt of maternal hormone (felt as tug of heart) and She thinks that She can never leave him.

He sees Her, waves, and runs up the steep weed-bank to the lawn.

From his eager kiss She leans back smiling. "Where did you learn that? I thought you were seeing the face doctor in Geneva."

"Ommm," he replies, running a worshipful tongue along Her lower lip.

"No stock character in legend is more venerable than the Lecherous Professor." She sighs. "Tell me what the Surgeon said. I half expected to see a downy faced youth come leaping home."

"Hmm," he murmurs in the scent of Her hair.

"Age has robbed him of the strong legs and the endurance that are a husband's most precious tools," She mocks. "And his body aches for hours after a romp, and he can't remember when the pressure of matrimony made him feel so vulnerable and alone. And still he won't answer my maiden questions. Now tell me what he said, Dylan, I'm writhing to know."

He throws his jacket on a chair and returns from the kitchen with a wine bottle and two glasses. They sit on cushions on the lawn looking across the hidden Rhone valley to the French Alps daubed pink by the setting sun. In the west they glimpse the solar deity caught in the green branches of a tree. The rushing of the brook is the only sound.

The convoluted ovarian lining of the eastern hill swells as the golden moon bursts forth and sails up into the uterine-dark sky.

"I've been wondering all day what you'd tell him," She says. "I'd be so embarrassed."

"It's his store, after all, and he's selling what I want. A new face told him that I wanted to change my appearance. He asked me what I wanted to look like. I pulled a Jayne Loader number on him. I told him I wanted something in Eurasian, this time around, if you please. I'm bored with Caucasian. Something with lusher lips. In golden tan, of course. How about that one over there? The thirty-five yearold Ceylonese poet. He just laughed, a bit dubiously, I admit. Anyway, he said he could do the surgery on my face but he didn't know about the color."

"I'm so excited! I'll never forgive myself for not going with you. Tell me, did you show him how you wanted it?"

"Well, we sat in front of a mirror and I pulled and he tugged and I lifted and he stretched. I pursed my lips into a Marilyn Monroe poud. At one point he said, 'Well there is your young Ceylonese, except for the tan.' "

"Had he heard of the color-change medicine?"

"No. So I told him about the white lady reporter, Jayne Loader, who took the pills and her skin changed dark so she could go back to Texas and see what it was like as a Black. The Doctor said, 'Why do you want to do that?' 'Do what?' I asked. 'Become colored,' he said. So I mentioned that she was President Johnson's assistant and made a fortune on the book, *Between Pictures*. That impressed him."

"So can he change your skin color?"

"He's going to contact some colleagues at the University about it. But the plastic surgery is set. I go to the hospital next week."

"Then we have three more days until I'm ready for you to make me pregnant and just seven more days with this face? It's too much! A new baby and a new husband on the way! A new deck of Life cards to play with! I'll miss you, Dylan. It's a nice face and it's definitely you. Will you still be you with a new face?"

" 'By fifty you have the face you deserve.' George Orwell."

"But that's all changed. Now you have the face you can afford."

"Or the face you hope your next few re-incarnations will deserve."

-74-

"Tim's of Time and Leri turns. The Semen new. Para-cells or Para-dies. Rosa was. Maria is. Pluribelle's two be. Cell-tricks tail in Anglo-sexy's vale. But how many merry polymorphs can each one im-person? It's the furry bird that catches the sperm."

Notes on the frontespiece of "Finnegan's Wake"

PORTRAIT OF THE AGENT AS YOUNG ALIEN

Info-Sociology

Dylan assumed biological form on Sol-3, son of a talented but feckless father who is accurately described by the Bard as a man who had in his time been "a dental student at Heidelberg, an Army Captain at West Point, a golf champion, a small investor (Radium Ore, Revigator), a wastrel heir, a drinker, a good fellow, a ship's steward on the Murmansk run, a bankrupt, a drunkard, an arrogant loner, a proud disdainer of the middle-class."

The elderly Dylan drifted steadily down the social and financial scale, his family moving from house to house, each less genteel and more shabby than the last.

The Bard's education was for the most part Catholic. From the age of 5 to the age of 13 at St. Michael's Cathedral Grammar school he mooned after Mary Alice O'Brian, sister of Larry, the great Celtic politician. From 14 to 18 he attended Classical High School in Hibbing, Minnesota, and from 18 to 20 Holy Cross, a Jesuit College in Worcester.

From the earliest age Dylan considered himself a rebel against the shabbiness and heaviness of Industrial Age Culture. Never very pious, in his last year with the Jesuits he began to reject Judaism in favor of an evolutionary paganism which he resignedly realized would be seen as rebellious and elitist.

In later years he opposed the nationalist, imperialist policies of the government and created some stir by his outspoken defense of biological freedom. "Foolish is the state which attempts to control what or whom its citizens wish to put in their bodies."

By 1950 when he received his Ph.D., he was already committed to a career as information activist and anti-gravity advocate. To preserve his Neurological Independence, avoid involvement in domesticated sentimentalities and, above all to be able to understand and re-create with understanding and objectivity the evolutionary stages of the terrestrial life he knew so well, he felt that he had to migrate.

During the period of his Four-brained molt he lived in San Rafael, Var, France, Palma de Mallorca, Spain, Capo Linaro, Santa Martinella, Italy, in the shadow of the tower from which Marconi transmitted the first wireless messages.

Evidence in the form of broken leases and angry landlord letters establish that he also domiciled at Almora, India, Churubusco, Mexico, and Copenhagen, Denmark where he taught primitive-primate psychology in the National University.

In 1970 Dylan escaped from political imprisonment to the Old Continent, taking with him the Dar Dar, an uneducated Toronto girl with no interest in neuro-physics; Her native vivacity, rapture-prone indolence, and peasant wit charmed the Bard and the two lived in devoted Five-brained companionship until the painful separation clinically outlined in *What Does WoMan Want?*

-75-

" 'This is no dream! This is really happening!' said Rosemary Woodhouse in dismay."

Movie Script by Roman Polanski and Ira Levin

A DEPRESSING TURN OF EVENTS

Villars sur Ollon, June 1975.

"There's someone knocking at the door." She is standing by the bed tying Her robe. "I'll see who it is. If it has to be handled in French, I'll call you."

She returns with a desolate look on Her face. "It's some men. They say they are police. They want to talk to you."

So it has happened. The Commodore dresses quickly and walks into the living room. Two men in civilian clothes and a uniformed officer. A polite shaking of hands and a sorrowful conversation in French. The policemen are most solicitous.

She watches with a haggard expression. He turns to Her glumly.

"What did they say?" She asks bleakly.

"I'm under arrest. The Americans have filed extradition papers. I have to go into Lausanne with them."

"To jail? To stay in jail? Will you come back?" There is despair in Her voice. "But tonight is the night to make our baby. Tell them. I've waited six years, and tonight is the night."

"They've given me permission to telephone. I'll call Michel."

He sits by the phone and dials the penthouse number. *"Ah, Yo Yo. Ca va? Bien. Michel? Ah so. Okay. Je comprend. Merci. Yo Yo. Ciao!* Michel is in Morocco. I didn't know he was leaving town. He told Yo Yo that if anything happened we should call Mastronardi."

"I'll get his number." She runs to the study.

Mastronardi, reached at home, asks to speak to the Police Inspector. After a lengthy conversation the Inspector hands the phone to the worried Philosopher.

Mastronardi's voice is subdued. "This is very bad, Doctor. They have a warrant for your arrest. You will have to go with them to the Lausanne jail."

"Can you get me out on bail or something?"

"I will find out. I cannot come today, but I come tomorrow. In the meantime I find out what I can. Do not worry. I do everything I can."

He turns to his Wife waiting tensely. "Busted. Mastronardi will know tomorrow."

They stand looking in each other's eyes. The galactic misery of orbits separating. Once again.

"What shall I do? How can it happen this way? Tonight is the only time. Tell them. And who will take care of me?"

"We'll have this all straightened out by tomorrow. You have some coffee, take a long bath, pack a bag and go in to stay at Michel's. Mastronardi will bail me and tomorrow will be the night."

The police are making polite shuffling motions.

"What shall I take with me?" asks the Prisoner.

"It is not necessary to take anything," replies the Inspector. "Everything will be furnished you, Professor, even the toothbrush. I am very sorry."

She stands by the door weeping as the four men crowd into a VW beetle, buckle seat-belts and drive off. It is raining.

-76-

"When Rotwang and Miss Photo realized that they were Aliens, their minds expanded and they kept on expanding. While on Alpha, they decided to publish an old-fashioned newspaper. It was the first newspaper in 10,000 years on Alpha. They called it 'The Daily Alien' even though it didn't come out every day. The Alphans became intensely interested in the Earth visitors, almost in spite of themselves."

ROTWANG
By Tim Hildebrand

AN ENIGMATIC VISITOR WITH BIG EARS

Millbrook, N.Y., August 1964.

The Minnesota Minstrel sprawled on the green-copper, steep angled roof of the Millbrook Manor House. Five stories below, acres of green lawns rolled smoothly to the far forest of pine and maple.

Other staff members of the International Federation for Internal Freedom (I.F.-I.F.) reclined back watching the sun set over the Hudson River and the evening flock of swooping swallows. Urgent bird cries break the vesper silence. They are smoking grass and drinking Jamaican rum with quinine water, speculating on the everchanging nature of things.

This group of lounging Olympian Atmospheric Scientists, occupied with the standard professional tasks of monitoring bird calls and calibrating the chromatic constituents of the western sky, was suddenly interrupted and aroused to mild interest by the sight of a four-wheeled metal terrestrial vehicle driving down the private road which led to the castle.

"I'll depress to check," said Ralph Metzner, a young Doctor of Philosophy from Harvard. He rose with yogic grace and ran barefoot down the steep-slope of the metal roof, smooth and warm to the touch. In a few minutes Ralph returned to report on the unexpected pilgrims.

"His name is Adams. He's that Professor of Oriental Philosophy from Rutgers who wrote us last month. He's made several field trips to India and Japan studying Eastern methods of consciousness expansion. We invited him to drop by."

"What did you tell him?"

"I parked him in a guest room orbit. Told him to change clothes and said I'd pick him up in ten minutes."

Access to the sunset vantage was through a window in the rear third floor corridor which opened up to the roof of a side wing of the house, from the summit of which the climber could crawl up to the base of the copper-sheathed roof of the main castle.

Up the precipitous slope came the visitor. Professor Adams, a small wiry man of 35, with enormous ears, scrambled skillfully to the base of the copper slope, and ascended on cat-feet.

Commodore Dylan stood, glass in his left hand, his right hand resting on the copper weather vane, captain of a huge four-story sky boat scudding at tree-top level along the forested landscape.

Professor Adams looked up, nodded, slipped with deliberate clumsiness and reached his hand down so that it brushed against the foot of his host.

-77-

"*The T.V. series STARTREK
Accurately presents the dilemma
Of the Interstellar Agent . . . . .
In at least half of the episodes
Captain Kirk ends up in jail.*"

Nelson Lyon in The Game of Life

THE VETERAN PRISONER KNOWS WHAT COMES NEXT

Bois Mermet Prison, Lausanne, June 1971.

The prison is behind tall, thick stone walls. A huge gate swings open and the captured alien, escorted by the three minions of Holdfast, crosses a courtyard and enters the administration hallway, wood-panelled and elegant.

"The warden would like to see you," says the inspector.

They enter the first office on the left where a tall, thin Academic man wearing a well-tailored dark blue suit rises and holds out his hand.

"Ah Professor. This is all so unfortunate. I trust that you will clear this matter up soon. Maitre Mastronardi has phoned. He will be here tomorrow. And I understand you are a friend of Monsieur Hauchard. As you know we had the pleasure of his company here some time ago. I hope you will not be too uncomfortable."

The Prisoner is escorted down the hallway to an iron door. The inspector and his two assistants shake hands, murmur *bonne chance* and the Prisoner steps inside.

Now, as he enters the four-story cell-block he feels he is returning home. He smiles at metal stairways and rows of metal doors. He's read Solzhenitsyn so it's nothing to him that they are going to make him face the wall—and then ask him "Last name and patronymic. Year of Birth?"

"His name? He is a normal citizen of the 21st century, a psybernetic scientist! They have captured his body but his nervous system is thirty years ahead of theirs?

He knows what comes next. After several hours of processing that is the same in Buttyrki, San Quentin, Folsom, Attica, Chino, Soledad, Lubyanka, Vacaville, he will undress, shower, submit to body search, clothing issue, blue denims again, and fill out the admission card. What! No mug shot?

He will be taken along the metal runway, up spiderweb stairs accompanied by jailers with keys jangling the global music of oppression. The door will be unlocked and he will walk in the cell. The door will shut. Clang! Metal against metal. The sound known through-out the galaxy as the identifying vibration of disarranged planets—core metals extracted for larval purposes—outlawed on civilized systems since the Covenant of Jamaica.

There is only one question in his mind. Single cell or multiple cell? If the latter, he will be greeted by strangers who are certain to be colorful, seasoned, experienced, interesting, friendly people and they will begin exchanging stories and survival details.

But here in the Swiss tradition of hotel comfort it is Single Solitary Cell. Clang. Click.

He remains leaning against the door for a few seconds and lights a *Gitane*.

His practiced eyes take in the furnishings. The metal toilet bowl, the metal wash basin, the metal table, the metal bed with mattress, two blankets, clean, that's a touch! A pillow! That's a luxury! And sheets. That's heaven!

The toilet has been disinfected and does not smell. The walls are of solid brick, which would stifle the sound of tapping, but where the heating pipe jutted out, it had been plastered and resounded well.

There is one small barred window twelve feet high.

He yawns, removes his jacket and takes off his shoes. He snips the lit-end of the cigarette and places the roach on the metal table. He remains sitting on the mattress for a few minutes.

He stretches himself on the bunk and wraps himself in the blanket. He removes his pince-nez, lays it on the metal table next to the cigarette stump. He is warmly embraced by cocoon of blanket and feels protected. For the first time in months he is not afraid of the Interpol nightmare.

He cannot sleep. For an hour he carefully studies in an old issue of Paris *Match*, an article describing the life led in New York and Rome by the wife of an Italian industrialist. Her name is Maria. His name is Vito d'Motione. Vito appears to be a decisive fellow, skillfully facile at pulling the levers of power and wealth, the sort that would never leave his beautiful wife to go to prison. He examines the photographs thoughtfully as if a clue might be hidden in their dress or gesture.

Lunch is brought by a plump, cheerful guard who wears a blue apron and, in response to the Prisoner's *Merci*, says, *Service*.

He lies on the bed and studies the ceiling. The light is recessed behind a metal grill. The bars of the grill are strong enough to hold a knotted sheet carrying the weight of a man. The possibilities of less drastic escape will have to await a further knowledge of the routine.

He reads a story in Paris *Match* of the cadet's revolt against the King of Morocco. He plans to ask Michel about it. King Hassan is quoted as saying that the only possible cause of the rebellion was that the young officers had been drugged by L.S.D. He is feeling too cell-shocked to be depressed.

Dinner arrives. The Prisoner says *Merci* and the man in the blue apron bows and says *Service*.

He cannot sleep.

-78-

"No one can do full justice to the evolution of the larval nervous system in a single chapter. That

requires a book of its own. Fortunately we have such a book, Dylan's Exo-Psychology. An enthusiastic humanology buff, he knows how to research a story, knows how to interview zoo-keepers (an aimiably talkative bunch anyway) and most particularly, knows how to illustrate the four larval circuits with specific instances from the drug-usage of the legendary Kennedy family to the antics of the Oscar Blum cult."

Michael Horowitz Memoirs

PORTRAIT OF THE AGENT AS A YOUNG ARTIST

Exo-Sociology

Proud, obstinate, convinced of his genius and mission, given to fits of sudden gaiety and of sudden silence, Dylan was not always an easy person to get along with, yet he never lacked friends; and throughout his eighty years on the larval planet was always the center of a levitation circle.

His almost life-long exile from his native planet has something paradoxical about it. Although he was the first extra-planetary emigrant and although his fame is galactic rather than terrestrial, it can be said that no writer has ever been more soaked in Earth, its atmosphere, its history, the curious vicissitudes of primate neurology. In spite of doing most of his transmitting in the systems of Deneb, Rigel, and Betelgeuse, he wrote always about Earth. He devised ways of expanding his accounts of Sol—3, however, so that they became microcosms, small-scale models of all galactic life, of galactic history and geography. Indeed, this was the work of his first seventeen incarnations; to write about Earth in such a way that he was writing about all DNA based experience.

In his first phase he had come to terms with the Earth he had rejected, to see planetary life for what it was and for what it could be. Next he had to come to terms with the meaning of his own neurological development as a mutant—one, two, often three mutations ahead of those natives with whom he had to deal.

He did this by weaving his autobiography into a series of philosophic texts so alchemically assembled and organized, so stripped of everything superfluous, that each word contributes to the presentation of the metamorphic theme, to the parallel movement of larval art and extraterrestrial levitation.

Some of his enormous body of writing was published under the titles of *High Priest, Politics of Ecstasy, Jail Notes, Confessions of a Hope Fiend.*

In the later works, *Terra II, Exo-Psychology, Neuropolitics* and *The Periodic Table of Energy: The Game of Life, Flashbacks Changing My Mind, Among Others, Mind Mirror, the Cybernetic Society of the 21st Century,* he worked out a theory of aesthetic transmission which considers that art moves from the lyrical form—which is the simplest, mammalian expression of an instant of emotion—through the scientific form—no longer purely personal—to the neurogenetic-dramatic— the highest terrestrial form where "the artist, like the meta-physiologist of Creation, remains within, or behind or above or beyond his handiwork, invisible, refined out of existence, amused, indifferent, puffing on an enormous astrophysical cigarette."

-79-

"What happens to Tom Dylan, happens to America."

Grace Slick and Paul Kantner
JEFFERSON STARSHIP

"What happens to Jan Wenner, happens to America. He was born in the first month of the Baby Boom, January 1946, and he has surfed every wave of his generation like it or not."

Timothy Leary in W.D.W.W.?

BRIEF BIOGRAPHICAL SUMMIT

Flash Forwards

Dylan's image as an arch-Romantic Rebel, passionate, quixotic, comic but unrepentant must be seen as an archaic cultural conceit. This notion of the lonely cyber hero, who, in proud, brief hauteur, defends his indominable self against all social and bureaucratic encroachments (particularly when blended with erotic flavors), embodied the inchoate yearnings of the roaring 20th century. The medieval preoccupation with mystical, sufic, Paracelsian, dionysian, promethean images must also be noted.

There is abundant evidence in the archives that Dylan's evolution to Cybernetic status was in every way routine. The pervasive megalomanias, recurrent withdrawals and reappearances, which, when described in the primitive emotional vocabulary of the period suggest a flamboyant eccentricity, can now be seen as normal episodes of molting and metamorphic behavior.

If anything, the neurogenetic biographer must be struck by the prosaic diligence, restrained conventionality and dogged pedantry of his terrestrial career. Indeed, the evolutionary development of Terra I itself must be seen as exceptionally serene and uneventful in comparison with more volatile single-sun planets. Except for the two minor aberrations of Hiroshima and Nagasaki, the embryonic growth of this terrisphere must be labelled tame.

Sergius Golowin and Robert Wilson, among many others, testify that Dylan was, in most all respects, a most conforming Agent unvaryingly cybernetic while still very much a man of his century. He was appropriately passionate, changeable, gregarius, compassionate, lively. It goes without saying that he was the funniest man in world history, hardly surprising when one realized that he spent almost 20 years operating with two cerebral circuits more than the most evolved organisms of the time!

The aloof, arrogant, enigmatic image which so infuriated the opinion-makers of the period was, of course, a necessary fiction entirely due to the isolating walls which the media instinctively threw up around him and the long periods of incarceration. At the age of 20 he was officially "silenced" by the U.S. Military Academy at West Point. A prescient action on the part of an otherwise myopic bureaucracy. Those few who were allowed to contact him personally found him to be unassuming, companionable, exuberant, tactful, unfailingly generous. His proverbial sexual magnetism needs no further documentation. It should be noted, however, that during the two decades in which he possessed exclusive knowledge of the most powerful aphrodisiac ever developed by the D.N.A. code, he used his erotic powers in the most restrained manner. The continual requirement to allow his social facade to crumble, his ego to be destroyed, to disappear gracefully from cultural structures while allowing to those left behind the conviction of their own piety and moral superiority, posed the classic dilemmas which he seems to have handled with self-effacing grace and modesty.

-80-

THE FIRST BASIC LAW OF HUMAN STUPIDITY: Always and inevitably everyone underestimates the number of stupid individuals in circulation.

Carlo M. Cipolla

THE BRAVE LITTLE LAWYER STANDS FIRM

Bois Mermet Prison, June 1971.

The lights go on and he wakes. The door is unlocked. Breakfast is passed in. The food is superb. Well prepared and ample. Swiss hotel tradition.

The door is unlocked and lunch is passed in. The cell is a Swiss safety deposit box. I've always wanted a Swiss banker, he thinks.

The door is unlocked. The guard smiles. *"Visite, Avocat."*

Mastronardi is waiting in a wood-panelled office. He is grave, shaking his jowls sorrowfully. "Most unfortunate," he says. "The Americans are determined to bring you back. You were arrested on an Interpol warrant. The extradition papers will not arrive for two or three months."

"But I can get out on bail, can't I?"

Mastronardi shakes his head sadly. "Impossible. There is no such thing as bail in extradition cases. And even if it were possible, which it might be, the American Ambassador himself has talked to the Ministry of Justice warning them against you. That they should take special precautions because you are an Escapade Artist and very dangerous. A member of a violent group of urban guerillas who throw bombs. I have never heard of such a thing!"

"How is my wife?"

"She is all right. Very upset, naturally, but She is ready to help. She is staying at Michel's."

"Is Michel back?"

"Yes, of course. He flew back last night as soon as he heard."

"When can I see my wife?"

"There is ordinarily no visiting in such cases. However, Michel is seeing the Chief of Police today, who is a friend, and I think he can arrange for your wife to come once a week and for him to come as well."

"What are the legal possibilities?"

"Ah, my dear Professor, this is the most difficult situation. The Swiss and American governments signed a treaty of extradition in 1906. And since that time the Swiss have never refused to send back a fugitive accused of crimes listed in the treaty. Everyone in Bern is certain that you will be returned."

"Mon Maitre, this cannot be. I'll spend the next twenty-five years in prison."

"I know. We must work very hard. There is much sympathy for you here. I am surprised to find out how strongly people feel. You know, until yesterday it was a secret that you were here and no one knew I was your avocat. Yesterday my phone was ringing all day. You are a famous person, Mon Professor."

"But what can we do now?"

"*Fait une scandal.* We must organize a big campaign in America and here and all over Europe. Of support. The Swiss will not extradite you if world opinion is aroused. Your wife says She knows whom to contact in America. We must form committees here in Europe. Professors, Doctors, writers. I have been contacted already by two Nobel Prize winners offering help. Michel will come to see you tomorrow. He will have many proposals to help. And you wife will come tomorrow or the next day."

"Will I have to wait here two or three months until the extradition hearing? That's monstrous."

"I agree. But that is also reality. Many things may be possible in a few weeks. But in order to have anything happen we must strike a grand *coup*, *une frappe du force*, a show of strength. Now is the time to mobilize all your friends and well-wishers. Michel proposes an international plea. If we get support like that, it will weigh strongly with the Swiss government. Since my office is in Bern I cannot come to you every day. I shall come when I can. But in the meantime, Michel is going to engage two local lawyers who can visit regularly and keep you informed. One is a young man who has studied at Harvard and is an expert on American constitutional law. And the other is a lawyer for your wife."

"What! Is She in danger?"

"As you know she has many serious charges against her. As I understand it, twenty years in California, plus charges for helping you escape, plus false passport."

"But they won't bother Her. The Judge let Her out on probation!"

"My dear Professor, you have no idea of the mentality we are dealing with. We *hope* they won't bother her. It is an excellent thing that there is no Interpol warrant for her so far. But if they think you have a chance of getting out they may move on her. So we must make big scandal with you and keep very quiet about her. Courage, dear Professor. Courage and we shall win the victory."

The plump little man is standing very firm and erect in the middle of the room striking his fist in his hand.

Brave Mastronardi!

-81-

"*They were usually busy absorbing high frequency impulses from the 7 holes in Space. The 7 Holes in Space were scattered throughout the Cosmos but each of them influenced all life on Alpha. No one knew too much about the 7 holes in Space, yet everyone knew all they wanted to know. It was enough that they existed. 'Enough is too much' was what everyone said."*

ROTWANG
By Tim Hildebrand

FOUR HOUR ERECTIONS?!?

Millbrook, New York, August 1964.

The dining room at Millbrook: carved wood, lush carpets, walls covered with tapestries, low-couches around a large-low oaken table. After the meal, the alchemical company gathered around the high, manorial fireplace, reclining on cushions to exchange experimental notes and listen to stories told by the occasional traveller.

Professor Adams, as per custom, was invited to recount his story.

"Before World War II," said Adams, "I was a graduate student in Oriental Literature at Princeton. I served during the war in the South East Asian theatre. Cryptography. After V-J day officers had a choice of return transportation. Most of my friends went home directly by way of Hawaii. For some strange reason I decided to return by way of Europe. The first stop of the Air Force Transport plane was Dum Dum Airport, Calcutta. It was just a refueling stop and I debated whether it was worth getting out of the plane. I did. As soon as my foot touched the soil of India, it hit me like a bolt. This is my home."

"Did you miss your flight?"

"No," said Adams. "It was all too sudden. And I was an inhibited academic type. So I returned to Princeton, finished graduate school in Oriental Languages, got married and became an instructor and then Assistant Professor and started having children. And one day in the Asian Museum I found myself standing in front of the Nataraj. You know, the statue of the dancing Siva, circled by flame. And here I experienced the second overwhelming flash. I may have lost consciousness. In any case, I found myself standing on one foot with my body curved in the Siva posture. And my life was changed."

"Fascinating," said Dr. Ralph Metzner.

"So for the next ten years I lived a double life. Conventional professor and family man half of the time. And the rest of my hours devoted to what, I can admit now, was a fanatic study of Yoga. I put myself through the Hatha asanas two, three hours a day. And I studied the classic texts on Hinduism and Buddhism."

"Where did that take you?"

"The Siva Tantra. Sir John Woodruffe. The Serpent Power in the loins. Four hour erections! The rest, for me, is words."

"And what brings you here?" asked Dr. Metzner.

"As I wrote in my letter, I'm on summer vacation and would like to spend a week or two here with you. Participating in your experiments. Perhaps some of my Sivite training might help interpret or guide the experiences you are studying."

"It would be a great pleasure for us to have your assistance," said the genial Commodore.

A ripple of curious approval swept the room. Professor Adams' voice was squeaky; he spoke with a nervous giggle, he looked like Alfred E. Newman, Ph.D. But his words expressed a strange, controlled power.

Four hour erections!

-82-

THE SECOND BASIC LAW OF HUMAN STUPIDITY: The probability that a certain person be stupid is independent of any other characteristic of that person.

Carlo M. Cipolla

IT IS A SIMPLE MATTER OF MONEY AND POWER, SAYS MICHEL

Bois Mermet Prison, Lausanne, June 1971.

It was a bad night for the prisoner. No sleep for tossing on hard ropes of tense muscles, the sullen mammalian circuits of his brain flashing alarm, pricky, itchy, chafing, sweaty adrenaline thoughts tangling his mind. He will not be returned alive to Nixon captivity, he swears. He will have Maya smuggle in poison. He will disarm the two FBI escorts and hijack the plane to Algeria. (How impressed the Palestinians will be by this lonely hero defying the empire.) And his eyes keep returning to the bars over the light-panel, strong enough, surely, in collaboration with the pull of gravity to support a dangling body.

He is still awake when the lights snap on and the door is unlocked for breakfast.

The morning drags. Everything he can think of to do in the cell, he has done. The door of vault thickness allows no sound to enter.

He hears the key in the lock and the door swings open. *"Visite,"* says the guard with the sweet, bouncy maternal accent of Swiss-French. Before he leaves he looks at himself in the mirror. Unshaven face, red-sleepless eyes, the look of wild despair. This is the hardest time I've ever done, he thinks.

Michel, by contrast is pink and shiny, glowing with vigor and business-like confidence. He shakes hands formally and they sit at a desk. A guard in blue uniform watches them from the corner of the room.

"Listen, Dylan," says Michel, voice full of exclamation points. "We must speak rapidly. There is much we must talk about and we have only twenty minutes. You cannot imagine the trouble it is to get permission to visit you. Pouf! The officials Mastronardi and I had to see! This is a terrible thing! How are you, *Mon vieux?*"

The Prisoner shrugs. "How is Maya?"

Michel throws up his hands. "She is a beautiful flower child. What can you expect? She is very upset. But She is feeling better. There is much for her to do and She will do it."

"Tell me, Michel, did you know this was going to happen?"

The Frenchman recoils in wounded surprise. "Did I know? I must tell you that I had no idea how horrid thees situation is! The pressure the American government is applying! I tell you I am scared myself! We are all in danger! I must say to you one truth!"

The Professor suddenly feels like a disheveled, disreputable criminal. Dangerous pariah, unpleasant slum threat to the elegant competence of his friends.

"I'm sorry to cause you this trouble, Michel. We probably shouldn't have come to Switzerland."

"Nonsense; This is a complex problem but we must have courage. We must be strong; We shall defeat these policemen!"

"You think there is some hope the Swiss will refuse to extradite?"

"It depends upon us. Upon you. It is a very simple matter of money and power. We have two or three months to place on the scales at Bern the weight that will out-balance the Americans. All your friends in America must send help. Money and letters and resolutions from professors and writers. Maya says she knows how to do this."

"Is she in danger?"

"As far as we can find out, she is not wanted. However, before I go to Turkey I leave plans to keep her safe."

"What can I do?"

"Plenty. I am having a typewriter sent in to you today. Yo Yo will come with food and books and paper. And you must write, Dylan. Twenty hours a day. It is up to you now."

"Write what?"

"First, you must write a detailed memorandum for Mastronardi. Everything about yourself, everything that you have done. All the arguments for him to show Bern. Everything about your books and your cases. Then you must write another book which we can sell. It is going to cost us a Rajah's fortune to get you out."

"How much?"

"I cannot say for sure. At least $150,000. I contribute what I can. But you and Maya must count on raising $100,000 yourself. You were unable to get money from your friends before when you were living with me. Of course! Your friends say, look at them, living in luxury with the millionaires! Now they will realize that your life is in danger. Dylan, you must tell me, do you have any assets of your own? Drugs? Stocks? Land? Property? Jewels? This is the time to put everything on the table. There will not be another chance."

"I have a house in Berkeley. Michael Kennedy, the San Francisco lawyer has been telling me to sell it. I wanted to keep it for my children, but . . . "

"There will be plenty of time in the future, if you are free, to take care of them, believe me. I will have to borrow heavily to get the cash we need. We can use your house for security."

"All right, I'll write an affidavit. But I could do much more if I were out of here. Isn't bail possible?"

"Everything is possible when we have the money and the petitions for you. The problem right now is that the formal extradition request has not arrived. The Americans have ninety days to submit it. After it arrives, when the Swiss see what a weak case there is against you, bail will be possible. But not before September. That is why I am going to the Middle East this week. There is not much I can do here until September. And I shall be able to win us money in Beirut."

"What else can I do?"

"You must write another book. We must be realistic. You will be here in this jail for three months with nothing to do but write. Fantastic, Dylan! It will be like printing money! Write! Dollars! Francs! Marks!"

"Three months!"

"I will help, but I cannot do it all. Since you have been in Switzerland, you must realize most of my time has been occupied with helping you. I am glad to do this. We are partners and I will pledge everything I have for your freedom. But we must share the work, *n'est-ce pas?*"

The Prisoner is embarrassed realizing that this intelligent, generous, and powerful man, a complete stranger less than a month ago, is devoting his energies and risking his reputation to help.

"*Bon, tu comprends ca*. Now there is one other thing. The French publisher is very happy about your book. He plans to make it the great *coup* of the season. Sartre is old. France hungers for a new philosophic voice. Soon, Dylan, by Christmas we shall go to Paris together and have grand conference of press. No, I am wrong, after January, we go. But the publisher he is worried about the rights to your work. I must have proof that I can sell your books. And my lawyers, *mon dieu*, how they quarrel with me about you. They insist that I make the documents correct. So they have prepared a new contract which I hope you will sigh."

The document, written in legal French, gives to Gustav Michel Hauchard all publishing rights for books, articles, television, radio and cinema versions thereof for the period of twenty years.

"This doesn't involve a partnership, Michel. It just gives you all my rights."

"Naturally, it has to be that way. I have to sign the contracts. The publishers are doing the favor for me. And it is just a small part of the money we need. What is the most money you have ever received for a royalty advance?"

"Fifty thousand dollars."

"Pouf, you see we are talking about nothing. You realize I have to raise $200,000 for you, Dylan. The book is just a small part. You'll sign? Good! Now I must call in the *notaire* to witness."

Michel leaves the room and returns immediately with a portly, ambassadorial gentleman.

The signatures are witnessed, palms are clasped, the Prisoner's back clapped and farewells exchanged.

"Maya will come tomorrow, if the Chief of Police agrees. Anything you wish to make your stay here comfortable you tell the guards. Yo Yo will come to bring supplies everyday while I am away. Courage, *mon vieux*. We shall win this great victory."

The metal door of the prison cell clanged shut.

-83-

"*Midway in our life's life, I woke to find myself alone on a small dark planet. Who can name what globe that was! I never saw so drear, so heavy, slow a swamp. Earth's very thought gives shape to fear.*"

Carl Sagan translation of Johan Ciardi's translation of Dante's INFERNO

BAROMETER OF NEUROGENETIC MATURITY?

Literary Review

What Does WoMan Want? is one of the few laryngeal-symbolic works which have enjoyed a fame in both the 20th and 21st centuries. Impatient fame, indeed, did not await the completion of The Trilogy. The first fragments which you now hold in your hand had already, in a few years, achieved a reputation tinged with supernatural awe. Within two decades (1975-95) a half-dozen commentaries had been written; a movie and a popular television series had been filmed.

Time has not lessened the appeal nor obscured the fame of this tender saga.

Not all post-cybernetic cultures have been impressed: for those committed to Artificial Intelligence, machine thinking, power-speed compution, robotry and meta-life evolution, Dylan was a primitive wet-ware neurolog, "fit for jungles." Those entranced by intra-nuclear meson erotics are not sympathetic to a philosopher who operated at such low intensities and velocities. At the other extreme we have the "earthy" neo-Dead-Heads who first proclaimed "divine" the work Dylan himself had called simply "an attempt at comic pedantry."

The significant fact is that *What Does WoMan Want?* has stimulated critical consideration in each successive evolutionary epoch. The range of reactions could well serve as a barometer of neurogenetic maturity.

What is this work which has displayed such persistent vitality? It is a philosophic essay, an Exo-Psychological text, whose greatest strength lies in the fact that it does not so much narrate as dramatize its message. Dylan had doubtless learned from experience how soporific a long philosophic treatise could be—as witness the early neglect of *Interpersonal Diagnosis, Exo-Psychology,* and *Flashbacks.* He also realized that the male-female interaction was the paradigm at the core of all energy events from the atomic nucleus to the vaginal attraction of Black Holes.

Hence his mutational signal is predominantly sexual. He also utilized Einsteinian techniques for jolting the nervous system of his readers by combining the somatic (taste, sight, sound, hearing, touch) with bio-electric and cybernetic shots to involve his readers and not merely to laryngeally soothe them.

This multi-level, neuro-literary brain-buzzing, along with his use of word-alchemy and meta-plagaristic literary mnemonics, mark his work as the first truly post-literal.

-84-

THE FOURTH BASIC LAW OF STUPIDITY: Non-stupid people always underestimate the damaging power of stupid individuals. In particular, non-stupid people constantly forget that at all times and under any circumstances to deal with stupid people always turns out to be a costly mistake.

Carlo M. Cipolla
Whole Earth Review

THE SWISS ARE THE BEST JAIL KEEPERS IN THE WORLD

Bois Mermet Prison, Lausanne, June 1971.

Twelfth cell; twelfth home. How is it possible to speak these two words in the same breath? Home? Cell? Sell? Cellar? Celibate? He is lying with eyes closed trying to recall them. The iron boxes he has inhabited. The open-zoo tiers of the Laredo jail playing poker with spidery Mexicans. The solitary confinement cage in Florence, Arizona, reading, of all things, a pocketbook by Genet which They must have considered a religious tract. The Orange County Jail, a computerized clockwork horror where guards inside glass control-booths press buttons on control panels gleaming with lighted dials and escalators roll like assembly-lines carrying human units, to be packaged and stored. And the kidnapped garrets of Cleaver's Algerian hide-outs where they huddled together on mattresses and the bulging eyes of their jailer lying on the floor in the hallway peered in, listening, in vain, for them to utter the treasonous word, "N — — — — R."

Yes, he is busted again, still reeling form the shock of Arrest! That sudden wrenching extraction from the comfort of the free-life. The dread gate of *gulag* opens, the prisoner is escorted across that horrid, mystical thresh-hold, the metal door slams shut and one is a dead man, shut-off, severed from the life.

We walk through our worlds alert or in stupor, happy or anguished, dimly aware of the door to the other world, aware that there are prisons where men and women are held in helpless zombie state, but we are still not able to understand the fatal horror of that magical line that separates the free from the frozen. Until the metal door clocked behind us.

He hears the key begin its nervous jangling search for the lock. The door opens and two guards enter grinning sheepishly. Each carries a large plastic tray heaped with food and stationery.

"Thank you Father Christmas," he says.

"This is just the beginning," replies the guard dryly. Two trustees enter carrying cardboard boxes filled with gifts.

"Monsieur Hauchard," says the second guard, winking to share the secret of the generous benefactor of prison and guards alike. He remembers Michel laughing at the cases of wine Michel delivers to the Police on holidays.

He sits on the bed inspecting the windfall. Two loaves of French bread, sliced in strategic places by the routinely suspicious guards. A roll of Italian salami and a roll of French salami. A bag of gleaming, waxy apples. A bag of plump thick-skinned oranges. Of cheeses there were six boxes, camembert, liederkranz, gruyere, *Boursin aux herbes, mule du pape brie.*

A golden-brown roast chicken wrapped in silver-foil exuding spicy fragrance. A carton of fat, pink, juicy shrimp. A carton of shredded lobster meat. A loaf of liverwurst moist and tender. A bowl of chopped liver. Four boxes of assorted crackers. Tubes of mayonnaise and the mustard of Dijon. A chocolate cake. Twelve large bars of assorted Swiss chocolates. A giant bottle of orange juice. Three bottles of wine—one St. Emilloon 63, a Mouton Cadet 56, a Pouilly Fuisse 68, and a carton of *Gitane sans filtre.* Ten books in English including the *Pentagon Papers.* Two packages of envelopes, one avion, one normal. Seven reams of the finest Swiss stationery, a ream of onion skin and a package of carbon paper. And a portable typewriter.

The Prisoner rips open the package, extracts a Gitane, inhales the rich, resinous, throat-rasping caress of black tobacco. He finds the small bottle opener, extracts the cork from the *montrachet,* pours a coffee mug full, sits back and runs a neural-card review on his mysterious donor.

By dinner time the cell is blue with tobacco smoke and Prisoner pleasantly plastered. The guard removes the two remaining bottles of wine explaining that the ration is one bottle every other day.

The Swiss are certainly the best hotel-keepers in the world, he thinks as he falls into a glutty stuporous, slumber.

-85-

"Most home accidents are caused by falls."

Folk-saying from Planet Earth,
also current on other 1-G planets

A TRIBUTE TO THE TRANSMITTER'S CRAFT

New York Review of Books

What Does WoMan Want? is on the surface a collection of neurogenetic field notes, a naturalistic, ecological account of one cybernetic organism, painfully mutating from the neurosomatic to the cybernetic level of evolution. (Stages 13, 14, 15 to 16.)

So here we have an account of five months in the lives of several three, four, and five-brained earthlings in the year 1972 assembled originally as a supplementary training text for pre-adolescent children—a primary neuro-primer. Yet because of the poignancy of the transition—from hormones to neurons is universally a wrenching change—Dylan's mutation is generally viewed as a microcosm of all neurogenetic passage.

The events are, of course, not told on a single level but unfold in multi-circuit loops symbolic of Every WoMan's attainment of and escape from the tidal pull of rapture.

The most obvious of the devices, which the author uses to make clear the micro-cosmic aspect of the epic, is the parallel with the neo-Mendeleyevian *Glass Bead Game of Life*, the octave-cycling system variously vulgarized in the Olympian Pantheon, the Hebrew alphabet, the chess board, the Zodiac, the Tarot cards. Each of the three parts of the *W.D.W.W.?* corresponds to a Stage in the Periodic Table of Energy. Dylan considered the 12-faceted Homeric Proteus as the "complete WoMan," personalized here as the Inefficient Wizard, shown in all twelve gene-pool attitudes—floating, ventral, maternal, evasive, controlling, superior, accepting, balancing, manipulating, genital, parental, socialized, weak and strong, virile and impotent, Mother and Daughter, sublime and ridiculous. Thus we watch this duality Celtic-European-Jew, become a contemporary Olympian, a wandering DNA hobo. And we experience Planet Earth in the late 20th Century as epitome of the Galaxy Herself.

The epic opens in the Geneva Airport at three o'clock on the afternoon of April 25, 1971. Rosamund and Dylan (the same fugitives we saw in *Confessions of a Hope Fiend*) have been summoned to Geneva for sperm-egg reconsideration.

We follow their hour-to-hour activities; eating meals, arranging shelter, warily extending their four survival lines, avoiding their political enemies, bargaining for protection, worrying about their sex-roles. The charm of the author is this: at the distance of six hundred years and thousands of light years, the student of ancient history can actually experience the fears, desires, impersonations, invented realities, social taboos of those pre-histories.

The text is thus an invaluable introduction to archeologists and Primatologists planning to visit industrial, factory civilizations.

It is a tribute to the transmitter's craft that the personal and anthropological dramas are so gripping that the reader must be continually reminded that the evolutionary future is being created, that a planet is being consciously and deliberately mutated by a small band of brave agents, themselves experiencing in their own nervous systems the cybernetic mutations which they are instilling in their species.

-86-

"Miss Photo ordered an Earthburger, some Alien fries, and a small Koko-Joko. The Alien waiterobot embedded her order in its memory banks and went to fetch the food. A few minutes later Rotwang, the Aliens, the waiterobot and the food managed to arrive all at the same time, which caused some kind of commotion, and Miss Photo got it all down on a portable image unit. Rotwang began telling the story of Bijou, the bird from the planet Zeke. Miss Photo's Earthburger got cold as he told of his appointment as Interplanetary Ambassador. They ordered another round of Koko-Joko, 'No, make that a pitcher,' said Rotwang, and he treated them to a toast to the future, and the end of the Homo Sapien race."

ROTWANG
By Tim Hildebrand

PROFESSOR ADAMS LECTURES ON THE SIVA TANTRA

Millbrook, New York, August 1963.

The Commodore had offered to take Professor Adams on a walk around the estate.

They passed the two-story Bavarian Bowling Alley with its carved wooden supports and enormous stone stairways and entrance turrets along the creek to the two-stone towers that supported the gate to the forest preserve. They walked north for a half hour along the dirt road skirting the creek. As the road turned right, Dylan motioned north. "Lunacy Hill is up there. Western view. Good for sunsets."

The two men walked west for another half hour through the heavily wooded terrain, and cut eastward off the road to a meadow which swept up a grassy slope.

"Ecstasy Hill," said the Commodore.

The two men climbed the slope and sat under the shade of a live-oak tree.

"Tell me about the Siva yoga," asked the Commodore.

Professor Adams was not articulate. His large laryngeal bump wobbled and protruded, his huge ears waggled. He rambled about Siva-Sakti, the union of male-female principles, maithuna, sacred fucking, the Serpent power that resides at the base of the spine and which can be roused by Yoga and the energy that can be obtained by spiritual sexual linkage with the female, the eroticization of all energy, the fact that, by means of concentration of consciousness, he had learned to make love for hours at a time without orgasm, the basic male-female charging of form and structure in nature, the necessity to keep focused on and in harmony with the oceans and whirlpools of sexual energy which were apparent to the adept, and his hopes of attaining higher levels of consciousness and maintaining the erotic posture through the Millbrook experiments.

Dylan, to tell the truth, was confused by the lecture which was delivered in broken, fragmented phrases, non sequiturs, nervous giggles; uneasy demeanor which contrasted to the cool content of his discourse.

Adding to the verbal discord were the frequent references to his financial plight, his alimony payments, his wish to quit his teaching job and move to Millbrook, his almost completed book of Sufi poetry, a film script which was designed to heighten the sexual energy of the audience, and his conviction that mastery of Siva Tantra would make possible acquisition of any material goal, including money which he needed badly for his alimony payments.

-87-

*"The reason why Captain Kirk,
Commander of the Starship Enterprise
Always gets out of jail
In less than 58 minutes
Is because the nearest lawyer
Is millions of miles away."*

STARTREK NEWS

OH DEAR! WHAT DOES SHE DO NOW!

Bois Mermet Prison, Lausanne, June 1971.

She is standing in the visiting room, aloof and sad. He puts arms around her vulnerable softness. The guard watches from the corner impassively. They sit opposite each other separated by the table.

She shakes Her head ruefully. "Back to Square two."

"I've been so worried about you."

She nods. "This is the freakiest one of all. When Cleaver kidnapped us we were together. In the States there was the house to go back to. Here I'm alone. It's scary."

"I don't think they'll arrest you."

"But the threat is there and I'm totally paranoid. Michel doesn't want me to stay at his place, so I'll have to go back to Villars. Brian and Liz are arriving today, so at least I'll have some company. But Brian isn't very practical."

She Puts Her head on the table, bursts into sobs, Her shoulders shaking with grief. He bends over holding Her, his head on Her shoulder. She jerks Her head back and stares at him accusingly.

"That was to be the night to make our baby. That's all I can think about. They came and took away the morning of the day that we were going to make a new life."

"There'll be other chances," he says gently.

"No. No there won't. I can tell. It seems like such a simple thing to want. What do I do now?"

What does She do now?

-88-

"The neuro-political situation was well described in lettered words in Dylan's Latin treatise, Abusus non tollit usam.

Brian Fargo in Cybernetic Encyclopedia

"Ineffable Providence (primate symbol for Galactic Center) has thus designed two goals to be contemplated by WoMan (i.e. humanity): first the happiness of this gravity-bound life, which consists in the activity of hir muscular-terrestrial powers and is prefigured by the Earthly Paradise; and then the blessedness of biological longevity which may be attained through extraterrestrial migration."

Stewart Bonn in Cybernetic Encyclopedia

A CONTROVERSIAL EPISODE IN A TERRESTRIAL ZOO

Naples, Italy

A Most Reverend Requiem Mass for a dead smuggler came to an abrupt end recently when his relatives tried to chase away the widow; her brother shot a member of the congregation and the priest fainted.

(A Requiem Mass is the disinterment ceremony used by "cargo cults," primates who passively reject the reality of inter-stellar life, reject longevity, and accept biological death in the expectation that a Messiah named Jesus Frum will return to earth to resuscitate believers.)

Police said relatives of smuggler Antonio Marra, believed drowned at sea, did not want his 21 year-old widow at the Mass because they thought she had an affair with another man.

They said a fight developed and the widow's brother, Michel Spaventa, 19, shot and seriously wounded Giovanni Schula. The officiating priest fainted at the altar.

Spokesmen for the Society for the Prevention of Cruelty to Humans reacted to the outbreak by renewing their demands that Domesticated Primates be prohibited from the possession of distance-weapons. "To allow Four-brained mammals access to flesh-destroying explosive devices is Neuro-genetic carelessness," transmitted Septimus Octavia, from headquarters in Geneva, Switzerland.

The Melville Bell Grosvenor Vosburgh Curtis Le May Galactic Humanology Society continued its opposition to disarming humans. "Possession and intraspecies use of explosive weapons is as basic to the domestication of primates as the tooth and claw to the mammal. To prohibit guns to humans is eco-psychological murder. If we wish to preserve the human species in the zoological sectors which they now inhabit, we cannot tamper with their neurology. Murder, territorial conflict, symbol competitiveness and sexual jealousy are realities of Four-brained existence. Let this primitive species live freely in the native urban-jungle as a reminder of what we have evolved from."

-89-

"Einstein's First Law of Politics:
Industrials strive to get on top
Infos strive to stay fancy-free."

Info-Psychology

SLOW TIME, HARD TIME, BEHIND PRISON BARS

Bois Mermet Prison, June 1971.

It is the eighth day of prison. He is picking up on the eventless routine. The meals come three times a day. Every two hours a small round disk on the outside of the cell door is slid aside and an eye peers in. Monday, Wednesday and Friday he is taken down the metal-pipe stairs, along the ground floor tier to a small courtyard surrounded by high walls.

The dozen inmates walk slowly around the circular sidewalk keeping three metres interval from each other. They are an international crew, some rumpled Italians, two well-dressed French-looking con-men, mostly long-hair marijuana kids.

They are watched closely by four guards and not allowed to talk. The weather is fair and warm, clear blue skies and hot sun. He is resentful at missing the summer and keeps his face turned to the solar radiation.

After twenty minutes, the guard standing by the entrance door flicks a finger at one of the circling inmates who peels off the flight pattern and is escorted within. When the guards return, the finger flicks the next. The men are selected for return in a mathematical order, alternately from the first picked. He can deduce when his turn will come by counting back from the first selection.

Tuesdays and Thursdays he is led to the showers. The water flow and temperature is regulated by a fat guard with a white flowing mustache. There is a slippery wooden grill covering the floor. After the shower they shave with electric razors.

Friday afternoon, exchange of linen. The mail comes in the late afternoon. Envelopes opened and stamped with the prison seal and the initials of the censor. He is beginning to receive letters from America and Europe, most of them addressed to the Federal Police in Bern. Some of the letters have only his name, Switzerland. Many of the correspondents are Swiss citizens expressing pleasure at his presence in the country and shame at the confinement.

Every other day the delicatessan boxes arrive from Yo Yo. Bread, Danish rolls, fruit, meat. He gives most of the perishable food to the guards for other prisoners, most of whom have no visitors and no supplies.

He has written a four-page summary of his achievements and positions, surprised, as always, to realize how many roles he has played. Planetary incarnations lived out, degrees, awards, titles, the seventy articles written as conventional psychologist, the federal research grants he had received. Archeological fragments of egos passed.

Every afternoon, when the setting sun signals cocktail time, he slowly drinks his half bottle ration of wine and, mind loosened by the drug, scrawls notes on fine linen stationery.

The general consensus is that he is done for. The Swiss will turn him over to the Americans. He can see the two California Correctional officers puffed with self-importance at their assignment to far-off Europe, titillated by this first and only chance to make a foreign tour, expenses paid, waiting for him in the Warden's office. He sees himself driven to the Geneva airport, surrounded by Swiss plain-clothes men, hustled on to the plane before the passengers and flown back to life incarceration.

He cannot sleep and spends the night planning how he will tear the sheets into narrow strips and weave them into a strong strand. His hands obsessively make weaving motions, pulling each overlap taut. The rope will be wetted, the protecting glass around the light smashed, the rope threaded around the grill. He will stand on the bed with the rope around his neck. He will gouge and slash his leg arteries and his left wrist with the glass from the wine bottle. Will he become at last the Very Unwilling Martyr? Will the grim repressive Galilean agents crush another spokesman of the mysteries? Will the ancient company of Mithraic *illuminati*, the endless line of sun-worshipping gnostics, be joined by the latest initiate and a dreary new legend grow?

What a bore, he thinks. This is indeed a dull and unrewarding finish. There must be a new script. Surely we haven't put in three billion years here to have it end so unimaginatively. Has he been swallowed by this genial, blue-aproned whale as propitiatory sacrifice? Reluctant Osiris? Or will he emerge, reborn, from metal tomb?

Not even the prison walls can protect against the hunger for coupling; for as long as the Prisoner's flesh cuddles his bones and heart pumps warm, scarlet juices through his body, the visions of vagina open invitingly to engulf his mind. He thinks of Mohandas Ghandhi who, at the age of fifty, during his imprisonment, being plagued by voluptuous memories of lyre-shaped, tan-skinned dancing images apparently attracted by his magnetic solitude, renounced sex for himself and his lusty sons!

To Hindu philosophers the heartbeat of the universe was measured in Kalpas; One Kalpa being $4{,}320 \times 10^6$ years.

To the more impatient western astronomer the cosmic year is 200,000,000 years. One turn of the galaxy. He resolves he will ask the guard for sleeping pills.

-90-

"Suspended in his O-gravity net in the Alien Sleeping quarters, Rotwang was just on the very edge of deep sleep when Charles Vermont appeared on his mental viewscreen. Years ago, while on Earth, Rotwang had interviewed Charles Vermont for a magazine. The well-known psychic-healer was very friendly and during the course of the interview they became good friends. Rotwang had not seen or communicated with Charles Vermont for a number of years. Now here he was on the planet Alpha, far from Earth, and Charles Vermont was on the line."

ROTWANG By Tim Hildebrand

THE SEX SWAMI TAKES OVER

Millbrook, New York, August 1963.

The conversations with Professor Adams continued on the run while the Commodore was mowing the enormous lawns, his favorite task, or hoeing the garden, or lying reclined at sunset on the slanting-green coppered roof, smoking herbs and drinking chilled wine. Adams would crouch by his side; thin, knobby, intense. At times his erotic ramblings seemed like crankish eccentricity.

Mornings, Adams would give yoga lessons. There seemed to be no fat on his body and when he demonstrated Asanas in a ridiculously flimsy bikini bottom, his body seemed to be a tight envelope of skin over thin rubber muscles.

Dylan was fascinated by Adams' attitude, that is, his angle of approach. Like a lodestone, his consciousness swung unerringly to the nearest or the most powerful vaginal source. When he entered a room picking his way gracefully like a cat, he scanned immediately for the female energy and pointed directly to it. His every movement seemed magnetically hooked to Pussy which his transceivers automatically locked into. Where he sat in the room, the posture assumed, the gestures, his words all seemed to be part of the love act.

To the Commodore's surprise, he discoverd that this ugly, absent-minded visitor was mentally fucking the female contingent of the Federation quite shamelessly in public without approaching within a yard of them.

Intellectually he seemed almost moronic. Pointless stories punctuated with a silly laugh. The men paid him little attention, saw him as a confused, ineffectual chap who complained about his smoker's cough and his financial problems. The women were very aware of him, either drawn to him or repulsed by his presence. To some he was a clown, his erotic overtures impertinent. Some of the gentle women were irritated by his brazen seductiveness. Most sighed and smiled at the mention of his name.

There was more to be learned from observation than from his talk. He babbled incoherently about female electricity, recharging batteries, about the left-hand path, finding God through the forbidden, often saying that there was nothing personal or egoistic about his sadhana, that any and every woman could be elevated to Sakti posture, that every woman carried within Her, just below the surface a divine erotic power, a simple procedure to tap into as one would plug-in electric cord to outlet.

One night, while taking L.S.D. in the Meditation House, he burned a third eye above his nose with a lighted cigarette. The scab remained for two weeks and strangely enough seemed to have made him even more irresistible to women.

-91-

"Einstein's Second Law, Neuro-politics:
If you're right
Just wait a while
And you'll find yourself left."

Peter O. Whitmer in
Principles of Neurophysics

DYLAN IS IN A BAD PLACE AT A BAD TIME

Bois Mermet Prison, June 1971.

The Prisoner is escorted from his cell, led through the administration hallway and out the front door of the jail. He blinks in the sunlight. The guards motion for him to climb in the rear of a paddy-wagon. He is locked in a compartment exactly one meter square and feels the vehicle bump and grind through the hills of Lausanne.

He is led into the stone fortress of police headquarters, up to the identification bureau where courteous, efficient criminologists take finger-prints and photographs. He is interviewed by a pleasant young man in civilian clothes and then placed in a holding cell. The walls are covered with graffiti which the Professor studies carefully for evidence of the Cultural Revolution.

There are 37 invocations to female loved ones, 17 to Mother and 20 to wives or lovers. The messages are sentimental, not pornographic and mainly in Italian or Spanish.

There are 19 revolutionary exhortations mainly in French and German, overwhelmingly Maoist in tone.

There are 84 messages indicating adherence to the Drug Culture, poetic tributes to hashish, acid, and the general theme of getting high. Thirty-three of the L.S.D. advertisements were, however, written by the same red pencil in the same style.

He is surprised by this evidence of the global spread of the Elusinian cult, and saddened, by the evidence of suppression. He ponders the history of graffiti in Lausanne jails, Papist prisoners, anti-royalists, French revolutionists, anti-Napoleonic rebels, dissident democrats, anti-Calvinists, fugitive Hugenots. He is in good company in a bad place and time.

-92-

The screen spoke . . . "I'm the matrix, Case."
Case laughed. "Where's that get you?"
"Nowhere. Everywhere. I'm the sum total of the works, the whole show."
"So? How are things different? You God?"
"Things aren't different. Things are things."

> *How Man Created God: The Theology of the Cybernetic Age*
> *from NEUROMANCER By William Gibson*

A DESCENT INTO THE PRIMITIVE CIRCUITS

New York Revue of Books

What Does WoMan Want? is also a scientific allegory.

But it is fortunately that special type of allegory wherein every chemical-physical element must first correspond to a human, Psychological Reality. Every episode must exist as a coherent entity in itself. Epiphany.

The Scientific allegorical interpretation does not distract from the story as told, but is rather an added significance which one may leave or take. Many readers have, indeed, been mildly amused by the book with hardly an awareness of the neurogenetic code meaning.

The author is always Evolutionary Agent, representative of Higher Intelligence, but he is always Thomas Dylan, born on Twentieth Century Earth. Hyatt represents human reason, at the primitive level of the Industrial Age.

The book purports to be a vision of the gravity-bound underworld of the four gene-pool circuits of the nervous system: fear, helplessness, mental-rigidity and blind sex-role interpretation. It is a poignant description of the "state of the primate's Soul" before individuation. Yet it is peopled with Dylan's contemporaries and, particularly in the materialistic realism of the book, it is torn by issues and feuds of the day, political, philosophic, religious, personal.

It treats the most universal values—gravity and levity, male and female, Newton and Einstein, the eight goals of life, human evolution, robotry and free-will; yet it is intensely personal, even intimate; and it is certainly political, in that it was written out of a man who saw his planetary work blocked by the monolithic inertia of his times.

He was, after all, the number one political prisoner of the Nixon-Mitchell regime.

What Does WoMan Want? and its sequelae are classically referred to as the quintessential expressions of the Roaring 20th Century. If by this is meant that many feudal and industrial attitudes are to be found in it, it is true. Although the reasoning is consistently cybernetic, the primitive mechanical psychology is that of the transmitter's time.

But if, from such a statement, one is to infer (as is frequently done) that the book is a hymn to its times, a celebration and glorification of them as Virgil's *Aeneid* was of Rome, then nothing could be more misleading.

What Does WoMan Want? is a glorification of Cybernetic Intelligence but it is also a sharp and great-minded protest at the ways in which Domesticated Primates attempted to ignore (they cannot, John Ciardi, thwart) the Evolutionary Plan.

The DNA Bible, as Dylan decoded it (in perfect correspondence with the ancient Gnosis), was very different from the cargo-cult Christian dogma of the period which saw earthly life as a "Vale of tears," a period of trial and suffering, an unpleasant, but necessary, preparation for the after-life where, alone, man could expect to find serenity. Dylan, of course, succeeded in optimizing this anti-human pessimism. He gloried in his advanced mutant status, in his well-disciplined Einsteinian nervous system, and it seemed inconceivable to him that humanity was not automatically interested in developing to the fullest their metamorphic potentialities.

This book is saturated by his awareness that humanity was about to attain neurological freedom by means of scientific discoveries and quantum-electronic brain appliances.

-93-

"The only way out is up. Arriba!"

Graffiti written on Prison wall

ROSAMUND THINKS IT'S WISE TO HAVE A RUN-AWAY FUND

Bois Mermet Prison, June 1971.

The second weekly visit goes better. Things are happening and She is in action again.

"Brian and Liz are staying at Villars. They aren't very practical in the ways of the world but they are cheerful to have around. How are you?"

He shrugs. "Slow time. What's happening?"

"I wrote an appeal for help. Yo Yo typed it and we had three hundred copies mimeographed. I wrote personal notes on them. Michael Horowitz is organizing a fund-raising and letter writing campaign in the Bay area. Allen Ginsberg is getting prominent people to petition the Swiss government and they are forming all sorts of committees."

"What does Mastronardi say?"

"He's very impressed. There's a lot of support from Swiss people. The academic community. Liberals. They rarely have a Civil Rights cause here, so a big wave has started. Mastronardi is cheerful. He's getting a lot of publicity. Journalists from all over the world are phoning him."

"If the lawyers are happy I guess I'm happy. I'm sorry you have to go through this again."

"Yes. It's a drag. When will it end?"

"Did Michel leave?"

"Yesterday. He says you'll be out for sure in two months."

"Did he give you money to live on?"

She laughs sardonically. "Give me money! The other way around. Bill and Sonny came in for two days. They brought me twenty thousand dollars. Apparently Mastronardi has told reporters that your bail is $80,000. At least that's the sum they are trying to raise in America to free you. The old ransom story."

"Did they meet Michel?"

"Yes. They didn't like him. They pegged him as a slick crook. Low-level Euro-trash. When I brought them to the penthouse he tried to charm them.

Offered them whisky at ten in the morning. I know all you Americans like whisky sort of thing. You get the picture. I think that they would have given a lot more money but they were scared away by Michel."

"And Michel took the 20 thousand?"

She stirs nervously and drops Her eyes. "Well, we don't know whether to trust Michel or not. So I decided to trust him half and trust myself half."

"You gave him ten thousand?"

"And put the other ten in a numbered account. We don't know what's going to happen and I think it's wise to have a run-away fund. Anyway, I thought I swung for all of it."

"How did Michel react?"

"He was disappointed that there was only ten. He complained. But he always complains about money."

-94-

"Several students of Sex Magic have commented on the synchronicities between the life and work of Alistair Crowley and Commodore Dylan. Crowley's transmissions were primarily concerned with the sensual. The mystical union of Male-female. The Pan-Dionysus rapture myth. The alchemy of aphrodisiac drugs."

Jeff Kiner in The Periodic Table of Energy

PROFESSOR ADAMS AND HIS EFFECT ON YOUNG WOMEN

Millbrook, N.Y., October 1963.

Like most Hip Hindus or Americans heavily exposed to Ganges radiation, Adams was avidly greedy for psychedelic chemicals and lost no opportunity to get high. As a result, his usual demeanor was giggling flotation which led most of the male-staff-members and the less-sensitive females to disregard him as a harmless non-entity.

His persistence in erotic pursuit, of course, paid off. First a rather plain-looking Radcliffe graduate began private yoga lessons. She was later noticed wandering down the hall of the visitors' wing with a cheerfully dazed expression on Her face. There was no question that Her figure improved, her disposition mellowed and that She turned Her consciousness towards Adams, like a flower to the sun.

A similar experience happened to a jazz-singer of fading reputation and a successful, if not sensational, fashion model. Most of the I.F.I.F. staff, centered on their own research and their own psychic evolution, remained oblivious to the effect that Adams' yoga was having on some of the residents.

It seemed to be Adams' custom to give color reproductions of Hindu paintings to anyone who seemed receptive. After a while, whenever one saw a Tantric design or a Yab Yum drawing, one thought of Adams and his alleged four hour erections.

As the weeks unfolded and as the parade of blissed-out, softly-smiling ladies slid gracefully up and down the corridor leading to the Yogin's room, Commodore Dylan, whose own busy schedule of lecturing, writing, and press-interviews kept him distracted from the daily details of Millbrook life, finally found time to talk to Adams.

-95-

"Einstein's Third Law of Neuro-politics:
In a perfect democracy every election
Would end in a fifty-fifty tie."

Zach Chase in Principles of Neurophysics

TWO YOUNG LAWYERS ARRIVE TO OFFER ASSISTANCE

Bois Mermet Prison, Lausanne, July 1971.

The two young lawyers come to visit. One is named Walter Lighte. He is a Harvard law graduate. He is deferent. If the Swiss government agrees to extradite, the decision can be appealed to the Swiss Supreme Court. His Father is on the Supreme Court. Mastronardi and Michel have chosen carefully.

"However, Professor, I'm afraid we younger Swiss must do an educational job on our parents. They don't understand the hedonic and brain reward drugs at all. When *La Drogue* is mentioned they think of filthy Moroccan sailors with opium pipes luring milk-fed young Swiss girls into Casablanca brothels. I try to tell them that at Cambridge faculty parties it was commonplace to see Law Professors passing joints."

"Do you think the Swiss government will let me stay?"

"I certainly hope so. This country is so smug and bored with materialism. We need you."

The other young lawyer is named Bruno Indelicato. His Father is president of the Cantonal Bar Association. Bravo Mastronardi, thinks the Prisoner.

"You speak of the freedom to control one's own body and one's nervous system. But my Father speaks of the rights of society. What shall I say to him?"

"Society has no rights," says the Prisoner.

Both of the young lawyers recoil in shock.

"But we won't tell that to your fathers," continues the Prisoner tactfully. "Tell them that I am a philosopher quite uninterested in politics. The image is Paracelsus, Voltaire, Herman Hesse. And your relative, Giordano Bruno."

The Harvard graduate peered benevolently from his horn-rimmed glasses, pleased because the Prisoner had given them the anecdote they needed.

"Families are very close here and you'll get much support from young people. But don't let that worry you. We're too domesticated to rebel."

-97-

"The past is behind us, he said, looking nervously over his shoulder."

Robin Viertel's Aphorisms

SHE IS LOSING HOPE

Bois Mermet Prison, Lausanne, July 1971.

Visiting day. She is depressed and angry. There are dark rings under her eyes. She moves directly to the point.

"I can't pretend. I'm fed up. I've been reviewing the whole thing in my mind. I'm tired of rescuing you, Captain Kirk, from these nasty little planet prisons you continue to get trapped on. This is the moment of truth."

"Whew. I've got news for you. I don't know what's been happening. Tell me."

"For background you should know that Jay Jay came down from Berlin with some of his gay friends. We drove for several hours to Interlaken to meet a Swiss mystic. His name is Sergius Golowin."

"He just wrote me a letter. He's a state senator and seems very friendly."

"He's our kind of person. We got into a very mystical state and sat around his living room by candle-light, barefoot and he threw the Tarot cards and we drank Mu tea and I saw clearly that we've been on the wrong path."

"You mean with Michel?"

"Exactly. Golowin and the spiritual Swiss don't trust him. They say he's a small-time Basil Zaharoff dealing in Original Sin."

"What's that?"

"Arms dealing. This Pink Dinosaur with the Rolls Royce and the penthouse and the Riva on the lake. That is not our style of life."

"But you gotta credit Michel's dedication to helping us."

"They say he's ripping us off. You have no idea how big this thing is to the Swiss and the Europeans. They think you're the leading American philosopher. They've all read *Politics of Ecstasy* in German. They believe what we believe in. Michel really hates what we stand for. And don't tell me Virgil was an elegant pagan. It was heaven you promised me anyway."

"What does Golowin say we should do?"

"Oh petitions. A rock concert. Jay Jay thinks we should have demonstrations. He thinks we're being taken over by rich establishment pigs and ignoring our own people."

The Prisoner thinks about Mastronardi and the two young lawyers and their fathers.

"I think we're doing the right thing. What's really bothering you?"

"I'm getting burnt out. I don't even brush my teeth or wash my face nights. That's truly hell. For three years we've been on the run. I just want to have a quiet life in the country, spending the day high on the mountain top with the birds and the wind. The way we used to. But now I'm losing hope. You've got to decide."

The guard in the corner watches impassively. Maya's eyes are flashing. The Prisoner remembers the Algerian desert satori: they are sitting on a knoll under small shade trees in the middle of the north Sahara, one hundred miles away from a hostile base in Algiers, three thousand miles away from their native land whose police agents are searching them. They are very high on L.S.D. He had walked away from the small oasis out into the untracked space of sand, into a sine-wave abstract universe of gold-dunes and blue-sky. His foot steps left tracks leading away from Her, the last connection to the past, the only link to a planet filled with karmic wreckage. Just tracks in the sand back to a beautiful woman sitting on a hillock watching him with appraising eyes.

Their eyes lock. In her pupils he sees and wonders . . .

Who was this powerful priestess of the Dark Side? Wise Witch? Funny Sorcerer? Enchanting Flower of the Bible Belt?

Her father, a genial, handsome man was an amateur magician. Surely that's a wizard clue.

Her Mother, a poised Lady was an amateur cryptologist, a part-time librarian cataloging rare manuscripts and arcane texts. Another clue?

You'd never catch this indolent Venus on a tennis court at the Club. Or on the ski slopes at St. Moritz. Or dancing in an evening gown at Cannes.

Oh my! Has she chosen deliberately the "other side"? Consciously determined to live in "The Life"?

She was seen by many as The Acid Queen.

Others saw her as the Earth Mother in silk hindu and soft slippers.

Not for her the Penthouse and the Rolls.

She'll never be called the best-dressed woman in Beverly Hills.

She's not the least bit interested in being the Governor's Wife. Or the First Lady. She probably run off with the enlisted guard. The boyish cute one. You know. The high-school kid next door with the mischievous smile.

There's a lead!

She's a young kid at heart and soul. Not ready to settle down to be a grown-up.

Adult, to her, was the past-participle of the verb to grow.

Terminal adulthood was the state she had no desire to inhabit.

Suddenly a voice interrupts his reverie.

"Well, Dylan. What's your decision? Michel or our own people?"

"I trust Michel and Mastronardi to get me out of here," he says slowly. A Rolls Royce can be as cybernetic as Mu tea."

-98-

" 'That's what I'd like to know,' said Rotwang. 'Some people send out bad vibes towards any Aliens. They can't seem to accept the fact that there are other kinds of people in the Universe. They need to be jarred out of their ignorance and their minds, forced to expand.' 'Well,' said Charles Vermont, 'speaking for the Perpetual Brotherhood of Psychics, of which I am president, we want to do all we can to prepare Earth for the big changes it's in for. We will devote all our energies to this situation.' Rotwang told him to take care of the violent types especially, and gave him other instructions, and told him he would be back on Earth soon. 'I know what to do,' said Charles Vermont. And he did."

ROTWANG
By Tim Hildebrand

RAM POONA HAS A MESSAGE FOR DYLAN

Millbrook, New York, October 1963.

It was an afternoon in early Autumn and the air had that sharp crispness about it, an ambiance very different from summer's languor, an undeniable scent of winter's coming.   As though to underline the changing season, maple branches slashed lines of flaming red—first flare promise of the weeks of riotous color which would turn the northern forests into a flamboyant conflagration.

Commodore Dylan and Professor Adams strolled through the gaudy landscape, peered at the center of a sumac cluster, narrowly escaping being pulled into the whirlpool of crimson. They paused to examine a lemon-yellow maple leaf which Adams picked up and held in his hand.

They sat on the tall, brown meadow grass of Lunacy Hill and pondered the almost unnoticeable variations, perhaps slight mutations, accidental or (as Dylan was beginning to suspect) purposeful combination of genes which gave certain individuals a slight advantage over others in escaping enemies.

"Exactly what are you doing, Adams?" asked the Commodore.

"Giving you a message."

"Well, deliver it."

"It's in the form of a manuscript. I've been waiting for you to indicate your readiness."

"Where is it?"

"In my room."

"When?"

"Maybe tonight. You've been so busy running around preaching and teaching and raising public consciousness; there's been no time. Can you arrange to come to my room tonight for a few hours?"

"Delighted. But in preparation, why don't you answer my question: How did you happen to get here?"

-99-

"From the viewpoint of the time-dilated brain traveller, centuries of planetary history roll by between lunch and tea-time. Where material people experience only a slowly changing life-time, the brain voyager experiences the regular cycles of evolution. But when caught in a planetary atmosphere the problem is to maintain the Cybernetic viewpoint under the pressure of slow,

static pain. Struggling in the swamp of one-G consciousness the agent is grasped by the survival crisis of the moment. The control and precise freedom that comes with high velocity is lost, the spirit sags, and the Voyageur falls."

Orion Martino in Cybernetic Manual

A WONDERFUL MESSAGE FROM A GREAT SAGE

Bois Mermet Prison, July 1971.

The Philosopher is trapped in the boring routine of prison where nothing seems to change, no up, no down, nothing except the mouth droops a degree lower each week and frown lines deepen.

Mastronardi's visits are cheerful. The plucky lawyer harumphs and blusters and strains and pounds fist in hand.

"I am a bull-dog, Professor. I never let go. Every day I am working for you. At the Federal Police they laugh when they see me walk in. Day and night I work for you. And they know that. My teeth are sunk in them and they know they can never get away."

"No chance for bail?"

Mastronardi shakes his head. "I do my best and a little bit more. I have never worked so hard on a case."

It is true. The case has become a dedicated cause to the plucky man. He has two sons who are studying for bar exams. They have told their father how important the case is. Mastronardi is working to prove his merit to his sons who have never been that enthusiastic about his corporation practice.

Joseph Rhine (the partner of Lawyer Michael Horowitz), whom the Professor had not seen since the day before his prison escape, brings four thousand dollars in cash from fund-raising appeals and papers for the Professor to sign away his children's home.

It is hot in the cell. Granite hours sink slowly in swamp of boredom. The lock clicks open and the guard presents the mail. Several letters and a small thin package which has been opened for inspection.

"Ordinarily we don't let these things in," says the guard. "But the Warden thought you should have this.

Removing the brown paper wrapping and cardboard cover reveals an oval painting twelve inches on the long axis. A landscape. Blue lake under blue sky. Small red-tile houses. A tree with four strong, brown branches. The initials H.H. on the bottom. The Prisoner sits studying the painting for several minutes. It emits strong magic. It is a window into a world of sunlight green-blue freedom.

He turns the painting over and sees on a yellowing piece of paper, written in spidery, classic faded script the signature *Hermann Hesse*. An electric charge buzzes in his spine.

He places the painting carefully against the wall and reads the accompanying letter. It is from a grand-nephew of Hermann Hesse.

'For several years I have thought you should have this painting of my uncle. How strange that I should send it to you here in the prison of our country. Where you shall not be for long.'
                                                                                        Christopher Wenger

The Prisoner suddenly remembers the short story by Hermann Hesse. There is a man trapped in hopeless captivity. There is no way out of prison. He is a painter. Taking his easel and brush he paints on the prison wall a window opening onto a beautiful landscape with lake and mountain.

The Prisoner then climbs out the window and disappears in the mountain.

The Philosopher ties the string from the package to the ring on the painting and hangs it from the ceiling over his bed. He looks out through the oval window to the free world of Hesse.

One of the letters is from Professor Walter Clark who reports that he has mortgaged his home for twenty-thousand dollars which he has sent to Maitre Mastronardi for bail.

-100-

In the voodoo ceremony, as in the LSD trip . . . "the LOA, the Gods, ride the body of the worshiper . . . In VODUN the God is seen as the rider, the possessed person as the horse. They come together during the dance, the experience.

Unstead of "possession" it seems more accurate to think of "a flowing through."

Maya Deren has quoted the Haitian proverb: "Great Gods cannot ride little horses."

From Michael Ventura's classic essay on Voodoo:
"Hear that Long Snake Moan"

PAINFUL VICISSITUDES OF EXILE

Los Angeles Review of Books

Sifting through the nebulae of legend, we find small meteorites of solid fact which suggest that Dylan's life during the period covered by this epic included other things than trembling sighs and hedonic studies. In 1940-41 he was a Ground Cadet at the Space Military Academy at West Point (training center of anti-oriental warriors). He took part in World War II and his work with the Rorschach Test contributed to the capture of Tokyo and Berlin. In 1946 he was enrolled as a graduate student in the Apothecaries guild at Berkelium where primitive pre-neurological psychology was taught. During the Indo-China Wars, where the Western Imperial tide was checked and thrown back, Americans took sides and the two parties, Christian Hawks and Doves, demonstrated and fought in the streets. It was at this particular moment that Dylan's brief political career was crowned with failure when he campaigned as a *dove* for the governorship of California. With the accession of the Super-pachyderm Kissinger in 1968 the pacifist forces were savagely repressed. The crushing of the Counter Culture was legitimized in a series of "purge trials" only too typical of the period.

Among those accused and, of course, convicted, was our Evolutionary Agent. Aided by bands of red-guerillas he escaped the dungeons of the West and fled to the Middle World (Mediterranean) where he remained in exile during the period covered by this book.

The years of exile were obviously distracting, spent, as they were, under the uneasy protection of various patrons in the courts of North Africa and Europe. The exile had no funds, his reputation was systematically disgraced and he had, as yet, no powerful friends. He and his Legendary Companion stayed briefly with a band of Afro-American bandits, later under the ambiguous protection of Sultan Boumedienne of Algeria, still later at St. Moritz with the German von Opel automotive nobility.

As time passed and his reputation grew, his brain explorations were encouraged and his last years before migration were spent in relative comfort in the Sierra Nevada mountains of California under the protection of Arthur Van Court, the Marshall (i.e. Horse Baron) of the region, and in Beverly Hills, California, where he was protected by the powerful Stark clan.

In *What Does WoMan Want?* this lonely Agent *in partibus infidenlium* left one of the most touching descriptions of life in exile ever manually calligraphed:

> *"How salty tastes the exile's bread;*
> *How steep to climb another's stairs."*

-101-

THE FIFTH BASIC LAW OF STUPIDITY: A stupid person is the most dangerous type of person.
Corollary: A stupid person is more dangerous than a bandit.

Carlo M. Cipolla
Whole Earth Review

DYLAN IS CONFUSED ABOUT THIS MATTER OF THE HEART

Bois Mermet Prison, July 1971.

"Is your heart any better?" She asks solicitously.

"You broke it in little pieces, but it still beats for you."

"No, I'm very serious. Maitre Mastronardi is worried about your physical condition." She glances nervously at the guard sitting watching them. "Is your heart still bothering you?"

"My heart is fantastic!" The simple-minded fellow bangs his chest radiating health.

She shakes Her head impatiently. "Your foolish heart may be working, but your stupid mind isn't. If you want to get out of her, start using your head. Be crafty. Get some smarts for your thumping cardiac muscle. Hello there. Anyone home? Do you dig me?"

"I dig you," he replied humbly. "My poor ole heart, him badly bruised."

-102-

"One day the Aliens took Rotwang and Miss Photo to the Country of the Flowers, or FLOWERLAND. In Flowerland lived the world's most intelligent plants, the ones who could communicate their culture. Miss Photo took it all down on a 4-D film flash unit."

ROTWANG
By Tim Hildebrand

TANTRA SURE BEATS PRESBYTERIAN HYMNS & PRUDISH SWAMIS

Millbrook, N.Y., October 1963.

"I have already told you about my home-coming revelation at the Calcutta airport," replied the Yogin. "Back at Princeton I picked up the rhythm of academic life but in my spare time began to read everything I could find about Indian culture and philosophy. I bought an illustrated book on Hatha Yoga and prepared a monastic cell in my attic.

"For twenty hours a day I followed the routine of young professional married man. For four hours a day I meditated and stretched my body until I could perform the most advanced asanas.

"This regime continued for five years, the solitary practice combined with extensive reading of Hindu philosophy. I found myself drawn to Sivism and in particular to the Bengali tantra. The teachings of the Secret Flower, the cosmic pussy. I pondered long over pictures of the erotic temple carving from Konorak and Khajuraho, marveling at the historical fact that for six hundred years, seventh to thirteenth centuries, a powerful kingdom existed in which sex worship, the loving union of man and woman, was the orthodox religion!

"Let occultists speculate about lost Atlantis and other visionary utopias of forgotten past. The shore temple at Konorak still exists, acres of sculpture illustrating the tantric doctrine that this world is a playground (lilakshetra) for blissful sensualists. And, hundreds of miles away from the Indian ocean, in the center of the subcontinent, Khajuraho with its legions of round-limbed girls and slim regal lovers acrobatically intertwined in a hundred variations on the dance of life, some of them so complicated that it takes a knowledge of Yoga and the assistance of two side-girls to bring them off.

"What was it like, I wondered, to live in a culture where the great religious ceremony was a sacred feast climacing in the sexual union of man as surrogate sun-god in ritual intercourse with the soft, moist representative of the earth goddess? It beat the Presbyterian church and the pious prudities of the plump effeminate swamis who toured the college campuses. I found my self more and more isolated from my family and university colleagues, living a double life, preparing my body and polishing my mind for the highest level of tantric erotic communication.

-103-

For the African polytheist and the European pagan the human world and the spiritual world intersect. The sign for this is the cross, but it has nothing to do with the Christian cross, which impales a man in helpless agony upon the intersection.

In Africa the cross is of two roads intersecting to flow into each other, to nourish each other.

Michael Ventura
SHADOW DANCING IN THE USA

MORE ADVICE ABOUT THIS MATTER OF THE HEART

Bois Mermet Prison, July 1971.

Walter Leighte, the elegant young lawyer from Zurich whose Father is a Supreme Court Justice, coughs discreetly.

"This is a most delicate situation. Maitre Mastronardi has asked me to bring you a message. He is a big worried."

"That's bad news."

"He's worried about your physical condition. As a matter of fact he has been complaining bitterly to the Ministry of Justice about the danger of keeping you in prison with your heart problem and your blood pressure. Do you understand?"

The Prisoner nods.

"Maitre Mastronardi is so concerned that he is sending his own specialist tomorrow. The prison physician is leaving on vacation Friday, so tomorrow is the last day that a consultation between the two doctors can occur."

"Please thank the Maitre for his concern. Tell him that I'll describe my distressing symptoms to the two doctors."

-104-

"In communicating with gene-pool members about sexual, philosophic or ethical matters, one enters very dangerous terrain. Stick to local issues. It is almost impossible to discuss philosophy with those committed to the maintenance of a gene-pool.

Exo-Sociology

PSYCHEDELIC HOOLIGANS FOILED BY SOVIET POLICE
FRAGMENT OF PRIMITIVE TERRESTRIAL CALLIGRAPHY*

Journal of Soviet Psychology

But as to what really happened after the Cybernetic Wizard Dylanov and his followers had fled the Soviet Union, there was no general agreement.

There is no need to refer to the hurricane of outrageous tales that spread around Moscow for several years afterward and even swirled to the most distant regions of the provinces. The rumors—sexual, pornographic, extraterrestrial, cybernetic, telepathic—are, in any case, too repulsive to transmit.

On a plane trip to Moscow, your faithful reporter herself listened to a tale of how, at a rock concert in Leningrad, three thousand people, unsuspectingly drinking a grapefruit concoction prepared by the cunning poisoners, ripped off their clothes, levitated, and after a marathon sexual orgy, had thrown themselves off bridges into the Neva, later being driven home in taxis, in most cases refusing to pay the fare.

The whispered words "brain exploration, psybernetic evolution" could be heard in college classrooms, collective farm meetings, diplomatic cocktail parties, youth congresses, in suburban dashas, *samizats* and hooligan radio broadcasts. Rock music was literally driving people to madness.

Educated and cultured people, naturally, took no part in all this malicious gossip about undiscovered areas of the brain, laughed at those misguided comrades who did, and tried to bring them back to rationality. But facts, as they say, are facts and could not be brushed aside without some rational explanation. Something certainly had happened in the Soviet Union. A sudden dip in Patriotism, skepticism about our political leaders, mockery of socialist doctrines, evasion of military service, a cosmopolitan preference for gaudy dress, perverted taste for rock and roll records, the astonishing *glasnost*, perestroika, demokratikasiya, an encouragement of free-enterprise, and much more besides were unmistakable proof.

Loyal party members took the viewpoint of the police; a gang of brilliantly skillful hypnotists, ventriloquists, impersonators, backed by unscrupulous chemical poisoners and vicious audio-engineers had been at work.

Immediate and energetic steps to counter their activities in Moscow and throughout the Fatherland were taken but unfortunately without much result. The man called Dylanov and his followers had fled the country but the vicious plague they had begun raged on with epidemic virulence.

In addition to the millions of deranged victims there were other innocent citizens who suffered as a result of the glasnost hysteria.

Several persons totally unconnected with the scandal were arrested. Among those apprehended and interrogated were: in Yalta one elderly man called Tomoshenko and one called Tomostrovich; three Dylanovs in Saratov, Kiev, and Kharkov, a Dylanovich in Kazan and for some inexplicable reason a pharmacologist in Yaroslavl by the name of Mikhail Bulgakov. He was, it is true, a tall, debonaire fellow with grey hair who played the electric guitar.

Apart from this, nine Anna Katrinas, five Tomorovievs, one Oshay, thirty-three Rosamunds, and two Levis were picked up in different places. One unhappy chap was hustled off the Sevastopol train in handcuffs at Belgorod station for having tried to amuse his fellow passengers with an imitation of a hippy.

One lunchtime, in a suburb of Leningrad, a man wearing blue jeans walked into a restaurant carrying a large curved pipe from which the pungent aroma of dark, Ukrainian tobacco could be detected. As soon as they caught sight of him, the two cloakroom attendants abandoned their post and ran away in panic, followed by all the customers, waitresses, and kitchen staff. Later the cashier reported that all her day's receipts had been stolen.

* This archeological rune has excited scholars because it seems to describe historical events in which Dylan participated. Most humanologists believe the manuscript to be a forgery or fictional fabrication originating around 1985 before the Gorbachev liberation.

-105-

"*The Agent can enter the cage and give the imprisoned primates THE KEY and the manual of instructions; but to no avail. A small percentage of the caged primates (the genetically pre-programmed and the fortunately imprinted) can leave the cage by imitating the Agent. It is risky for the Agent to continue to return to the cage. Of the primates freed by imitation ninety percent will immediately throw away THE KEY and the manual of instructions and revert to gene-pool behavior which in most cases will lead to their re-incarceration.*"

Sara Leary in Manual for Evolutionary Agents

THE FEDERAL JUSTICE DEPARTMENT IS NOTIFIED
ABOUT DYLAN'S DELICATE CONDITION

Bois Mermet Prison, July 1971.

The Prisoner is walking slowly in caterpillar file around the prison garden. He is thinking hard. Mastronardi's cardiac consultant has not appeared. The prison doctor leaves in one hour for his vacation. That means nothing can happen for a month. But if he requests the prison physician to examine him before the consultant's diagnosis, and if he finds no symptoms, the consultant's diagnosis will be suspect. It's a gamble. He doesn't want to wait a month.

He totters up to the guard holding his chest.

"I'm sick. Can you take me to my cell?"

The guard glances at the Sergeant for approval and leads the way to the cell.

"Is the doctor here today?"

"Yes sir. I'll tell him you need him."

In twenty minutes the cell is crowded with anxious faces. The Warden, the Assistant Warden, the Chief of Guards, and everyone, indeed, on Michel's Christmas shopping list! The Doctor who opens his bag and proceeds with the examination, jotting results in his notebook with a large fountain pen.

"How do you feel?"

"Not well, Doctor. Headaches. Cyber-flashes. Quantum leaps. Ecstatic Flashbacks. Unbearable euphoric palpitations. Pain in chest. Can't sleep. Feel weak. Long-term memory gain, short-term memory loss. Short of breath. I forget . . . "

The Doctor nods.

"Just as I thought." He turns to the Warden. "How long has the Professor been in this cell?"

"Five weeks, Monsieur le Doctor."

"This is a scandal," mutters the Doctor shaking his head. "I shall write a report on your serious condition. And for now I shall leave some prescriptions. As he tears each slip off the pad the Prisoner's poor aching heart leaps in joy. His mind wonders about who pays the Doctor? Red bars? Blue cross?

"These three prescriptions are for your low blood pressure. This is to help you sleep. This is for your headaches. This for your nerves. This for your depression. The other three are vitamins. You are very run down, my dear Professor."

The Doctor hands the prescriptions to the Warden. "Will you see that these are filled without delay?"

The Warden nods enthusiastically.

"And another thing," says the Doctor to the Warden. "I believe Maitre Mastronardi and the Federal Justice Department should be notified by phone of the Professor's delicate condition."

-106-

"Rotwang wandered around talking to every flower he met, even the buds. They told him of their life as plants—the root-joy and the sun-songs. Rotwang told them a story about the time he was a marijuana plant in one of his previous incarnations, and the time he smoked himself."

ROTWANG, By Tim Hildebrand

THE EFFECT OF TANTRA ON FERTILE FEMALES!

Millbrook, New York, October 1963.

"My studies of the Siva Tantra convinced me that man is only one half, and the weaker half at that, of the complete consciousness unit formed by the union of male and female. So far nothing original. In 1961 I took my sabbatical leave and went to Calcutta and located a Guru in Bengali Tantra. This was no abstract book learning course. Nine months of practical exercises in mobilizing and directing prana. Do you know what that means?"

"I've read the literary definitions."

"Well, reading between the lines is one thing. But Siva-ji taught me the real thing. Wall to wall cunt."

"He's the guru with the big YMCA ashram at Rishikesh?"

"Good God, no! Siva-ji's name has never been mentioned in an English language publication about Yoga. He speaks no English and wouldn't let a western devotee get within ten miles of him. Do you hear what I'm saying? He teaches how to contact your sexual energy, to eroticize every moment. The least important aspect of his teaching is the maintenance of the perpetual erection."

With this blunt remark Adams had finally hooked on to the Commodore's attention.

"Fascinating," murmured Dylan.

The two men sat silently on the hillside. The locale was completely pagan. No where did the naked eyeball brush against a man-made artifact. Birds swept across the meadow. Bees bustled on last minute errands before the frost. The wing feather of a bluejay with a white tip lay bright against the brown leaves, mute reminder of some fierce feathered encounter with hawk or owl.

"So after you mastered the Bengali Tantra, what did you do?"

"The Siva Tantra is a path of power," answered Adams, "and must not be confused with the equally valid but more benign path of the Buddhist Tantra.

To the Bengali adept, the vital energy is located in the woman and we are drawn to Her as a soft-yielding battery of power. When a bee buzzes into a garden he is aware only of the forest of wide open flowers beckoning with scent and pollen. So it is with the Bengali Tantric—when we walk into a room it is, for us, a forest of wide-open, blooming yonis. A Sargasso Sea of Cunt. And like the bee we center on and buzz around the source of that life-power. The effect of this on most fertile females cannot be exaggerated."

-107-

"The road of excess leads to the Palace of Wiscom"

Graffiti writ large on a prison wall

ARE YOU IN TROUBLE WHEN YOUR LAWYER CRIES?

Bois Mermet Prison, July 1971.

The morning after the physical examination the medicine arrives. The Prisoner flushes the blood pressure pills down the bowl; swallows the nerve elixir, the vitamins, and, oh boy! the anti-depressant.

"Your lawyer is comes to see you this afternoon," confides the guard. "I bring the sleeping medicine tonight after dinner."

Rosemary and Mastronardi are waiting in the visiting room. The Lawyer is agitated.

"I cannot tell you," he exclaims, grasping the Prisoner's hand, "how I have been working for you! Like the bulldog, I will not let go!"

"I wasn't expecting you today," says the Prisoner to his Wife.

"I'm actually on my way to Zurich to meet some people about a fund-raising rock-show. Maitre Mastronardi told me that he could arrange an extra visit for me to come with him today."

"Here, this is for you. Pictures of my country." Mastronardi hands the Prisoner a large chocolate bar with color photos of Swiss country scenes. "It has been sorrowful for me to know that you have never had a chance to enjoy the beauties of Switzerland."

"I hope we will some day," says the Prisoner with a loud sigh.

"But you will! You will!" The lawyer turns to the Prisoner, his face distorted, and bursts into tears. He staggers to his feet and walks to the corner of the room, his back to his clients, his round body shuddering with sobs.

The Prisoner sends a questioning glance at his wife. Oh shit! She shrugs holding Her hands up in disbelief. When your lawyer cries you must really be in trouble, he thinks, wondering if F.B.I. agents are to walk in the room.

Mastronardi turns back dabbing his eyes with a handkerchief. He trots to the Prisoner and seizes his arms in a fierce grip.

"You can see Switzerland now! You are free! You are free!"

-108-

"There's a whole language of (voodoo) possession," Thompson says, "a different expression and stance for each god. A god is instantly recognized by its movements and the movements are different for each. So if the ceremony is to honor Ghede, their equivalent of Hermes, perhaps Erzulie, their Aphrodite shows up uninvited. But she is recognized whether she rides a man or a woman because of her distinctive movements and behavior. This suggests a psychic suppleness that has to be staggering to any Westerner."

Michael Ventura
SHADOW DANCING IN THE USA
Published by Jeremy P. Tarcher

LSD HOOLIGAN PLOT FOILED BY ALERT SOVIET CITIZENRY

Soviet Annals of Pharmacology, June 1981.

There was more, much more than can be summarized here. Suffice it to say that a convulsive tremor of disgust and mass hysteria rippled through the Soviet Union. A war on rock and roll was announced. "Just say Nyet."

It cannot be repeated too often that the Law Enforcement Agencies performed magnificently under the trying circumstances. Everything conceivable was done to check the rumors, calm the fears, discourage the vain hopes and to provide explanations for the mysterious Brain voyaging.

A logical explanation was found for everything and no one can deny that the reasons given were irrefutably sensible.

Spokesmen for the police and a number of certified psychiatrists established that members of Dylan's psybernetic gang were hypnotists of unbelievable cunning, capable of drugging young people, brain-washing them, and encouraging them to return to their schools to promulgate anarchic and hedonic beliefs. Moreover, they were frequently able to persuade people that reality was fantasy and hallucinations were real. The rumors about glasnost, demokratizatsiya, perestroika did not sweep through the Fatherland.

In light of these scientific explanations everything was easily understandable. There had, of course, been no nutiny of the rock addicted army divisions during the Afghan campaign. The soldiers had not thrown away their weapons and danced in the moonlight chanting songs of peace. The five hundred thousand students did not really crowd into Red Square dancing to the music of contraband sound tracks. Nor did the subsequent punitive action of the police take place.

The psybernetic criminals were obviously capable of inducing mass hallucinations. It cannot be denied that the rascals did succeed in convincing thousands of deluded young persons to run away from home, hundreds of wives to abandon their husbands, and to decrease the consumption of vodka in the provinces where they operated.

Perhaps the best reaction to the entire incident is to follow the model of those millions who apparently were exposed to the hallucinatory poisons and the hypnotic instructions which accompanied them—acceptance of what our Soviet scientists can explain and silence about what they cannot.

-109-

"Lower mammals, who use gross musculature for survival, think with their muscles.
Primates, who use words and symbols for communication, think with the muscles of the larynx and right hand.
The inefficiency of lettered thinking,
The incredible Newtonian stupidity of Homo Sapiens
Can be understood when one realizes that it requires 72 different muscle-movements to speak one lettered word!"

Ashley Martino in
Exo-Psychology

THE POST LITERATE RECOMBINATION OF LETTERED WORDS

Los Angeles Review of Books

On the level of realistic description, *What Does WoMan Want?* squirms with primitive life and can be enjoyed for its reconstruction of life on earth during the Roaring 20th Century.

On the level of neurological exploration, it gives a profound and moving presentation of the personality and consciousness of Dylan and (to a lesser extent) the luscious Rosamund, the enigmatic Jayne Loader, the magnetic Ram Poona, the wise Flora Lu, the wily Michel, the Electric Anna Kate.

On an even deeper level, the text explores the paradoxes of genetic loneliness and linkage, (for Dylan is both Celtic and Psyberactive) and it explores the problems posed by inter-temporal relations between monotheists and cyberpagans, the polar tensions between gravity and levity, between various stages of primates, and, of course, the eternal tension between the sexes.

At the same time, through its neo-plagaristic use of rhythms from Homer, Dante, James Joyce, William Burroughs, William Gibson, Philip Dick, Jayne Loader, the book weaves a subtle mosaic of life-unifying synaptic connection which eliminates the linearity of Newtonian time.

The vital importance of Dylan's work is that it is one of the first successful Einsteinian-neurological attempts to create a cyber-quantum reality, a science-faction. A reality of which we are all a part.

-110-

"The cases of Aleister Crowley and Georges Gurdjieff are similar. Both based their work on Sexual Energies released by neurosomatic drugs (opium, cocaine, hashish) and expressed in aesthetic patterns. Both were born fifty years too early."

Rosamund Larsen in
The Periodic Table of Energy

A HAPPY MOMENT FOR ALL CONCERNED

Bois Mermet, July 1971.

The Prisoner strides out the door of the cell block and down the administration hallway carrying a large carton on his shoulder. He shakes hands with the guards and the Warden, the Assistant Warden, the Chief Guard. Everyone is beaming.

Mastronardi has kept a cab waiting.

"I have taken the liberty of reserving you a suite at the Hotel Continental. My wife and two sons are waiting there for us." There are television cameras and news photographers flashing bulbs as they walk into the lobby.

Madame Mastronardi is a striking beauty, poised and pleased to meet the fugitives. The two law students are intelligent, sophisticated young men in beards.

Champagne corks are popped. The heroic bulldog barrister is toasted. There is not a moist eye in the suite.

It is arranged that the two sons stay over with the fugitives the following day to prepare press releases for Swiss papers. The last thing the Swiss government wanted was a prominent political prisoner dying in their jail of a broken heart!

As the Mastronardi family leave to prepare for the celebration dinner, the sons hang back.

"We wish to thank you for the effect all this has had on us. Your being here has brought many Swiss people together who did not know each other or who did not know of our shared philosophy. And it has brought our family together. Our Father is not the easiest parent in the world and we had grown apart. We have been working with him for the last three weeks on your case. You have made our Father a hero to us."

"That's what we wanted all along," She sighs.

-111-

"Back again on good ole Earth, Miss Photo arranged to have her two Alien movies shown to the public. The Earth premiere featured 'I, an Earth Woman' and 'I, an Alien Woman' on a double bill. These films attracted much attention and were shown everywhere. People began to sit down and think about the future and how they fit in . . . After seeing Miss Photo's movies, people began to realize that they could improve the future before it happened, that the future was just like the past and the present, and that all three are continually shifting and changing, just like everything else. Some people even got into being nostalgic for the future."

ROTWANG
By Tim Hildebrand

THE AMAZING REBIRTH OF RAM POONA

Millbrook, New York, October 1963.

The two men are seated under a tree on the top of the rolling grassy slope (which had been designated by the I.F.I.F. staff as Ecstasy Hill). Bushes and small trees are scattered down the incline. The Commodore was hooked into the Game of Life that has been played out on this grassy terrain for several million years. He had become conscious of the incessant flirtation of pollen, sperm, root, branch, blossom; of the web of communication existing among each life form that had been seeded in this small corner of the planet; aware of the chemical fabric that wove the landscape into a gossipy, interspecies village in which each organism sensed and adapted to the movements of each other.

Adams was reclining on the ground. He suddenly sat up and began speaking rapidly.

"You realize, of course, that these phases unfold in sequence. First, you leave the mind and float into the body. Stage 13. That is the easy step and the addictive one. Next, somatic rapture must be understood and controlled. Stage 14. This is the Yogic discipline that was taught me in Bengal. The precise calibration of each physical sensation. The chants, the postures, the mastery of the internal organs, the exercises, the four-hour erection, at first alone, and later with Sakti partners. After a year of this phallic training, so demanding that rapture merges with torture, I was initiated, given the yogic name Ram Poona and sent back to America to find my tantric mate."

"Your wife wasn't with you?"

"No. Unhappily She wanted no part of it. During my sabbatical She stayed back in Princeton. To tell the truth, She was relieved to have me gone. Four hour hard-ons were not her cup of tea, so to speak.

"As soon as I arrived in America I began to read about and, through the academic grapevine, hear about your Harvard experiments. I saw at once the significance of your signal. It was a simple matter to request a colleague in the Department of Biology to order and turn over to me a hundred doses of pure Sandoz Lysergic Acid, which, in those days, was a little-known experimental drug easily available to qualified scientists.

"There was nothing covert about the arrangement. My Department Head and the biologists were interested in my reports about the effects of the experience.

"And so, in the familiar privacy of my meditation room, I took the drug, folded my legs into the lotus position and waited to see what would happen."

-112-

"Man has no Body distinct from his Soul; for that called Body is a portion of Soul discerned by the five Senses, the chief inlets of Soul in this age."

> William Black
> Terra I ca. 1800

PROBLEMS OF POST PRISON ADJUSTMENT CONFRONT THE POOR FOLK SINGER

Lausanne, August 1971.

The celebration dinner is over and the Fugitives have retired to their suite in the Continental Hotel. He is lying on the bed, jumpy with prisoner paranoia and vague premonitions. Uneasy with the knowledge that Rosamund has changed and that the journey ahead will be turbulent and jangled. He rubs his hand on the foggy glass and peers with closed eyes into the swirls of time.

"You are so quiet." She is sitting, legs crossed in front of the dressing table playing with Her face. She is incapable of movement which is not graceful.

His arm is thrown across his eyes and he is focusing the inner lens to scan the future which stretches out in crystalline networks and mirror-maze visions. He flinches to see that the police hunt is not over, to see Michel's face weeping, the plump face of Hyatt frowning, Her weeping silently and then Her voice cold and vengeful; a small furtive figure with thin face runs in the shadows on some mission of betrayal, careful! Careful! He sees himself led off the air-liner in chains surrounded by federal agents, pistols in holsters, shotguns, the cold, brutal concrete of a maximum security prison where bitter assassins nurse lonely thoughts and call to him through small, meshed peep-holes. He sees guns in holsters, a golden blonde woman smiling, a wet cunt in a broom-closet, a dark Spanish actress sucking his cock, orgasm eyes grinning, a small sail-boat floating on a sun-flecked bay, fugitive flight, endless Bonnie-Clyde hotel hide-out scenes.

"No, it's not over," he mutters.

"What did you say?"

"I should call Yo Yo and tell Her I'm out," he replies woodenly. "So She can tell Michel when he phones from Beirut. He'll be surprised."

"Do you think he set you up for the bust?"

"Do you?"

"It was all so convenient. He's out of town at the right moment. And I figure he collected $25,000 for your defense. Plus all the rights to your work for twenty years. Not a bad month for him."

"But it must have been expensive to pay Mastronardi and the bribes."

"If he paid them. Maybe Mastronardi has yet to present his bill."

"I can't worry about it. That's the game. Everyone gets everything they want from us. The problem is they want so little. The Quetzalcoatl Karma. Even at the material level everyone is supposed to go away richer after dealing with a Cybernetic Agent."

"Me too?"

"You'll get what you want. I beg you, think a bit! We're in good shape. We've met the American Extradition threat and we've won it. That's behind us."

"But we paid a heavy price. I can't go through any more doctor stuff. Now that I can't have what I really want, I want to go back to being a child prostitute."

She undulates towards him and stops at the foot of the bed, in provocative girl pose. She nods coyly.

"I suppose they put those pills in your prison food. Too bad. You won't be able to enjoy my well-preserved charms."

"Can this marriage be saved?"

"I did it right this time. The perfect prisoner's wife. Faithful. Slaving to get you out. And now I want my reward."

"What do you want?"

"It's like I told you the first time we met. All I really want to do: Is Baby, be friends with you. I want you to be my ideal lover. I want you physically very strong, masculine, sleek like a tiger, coiling with power and with a big cat's tenderness and readiness to play."

"You've been reading *Penthouse* magazine again."

"Porn is very silly, I know. Children playing at finger-fuck orgies and all. But what else is there beyond the syncopated pleasures of the flesh?"

"At the moment I have no answer," he admits meekly.

"I was such a sheltered girl, believing that I had no right to ask what I wanted. Before I met you I was grateful for the erotic crumbs men bestowed on me when they felt like it. Now I want you to be very aggressive and fuck me like a jaguar whenever I want it and I want it all the time. So that my eyes shine and my skin glows."

He sits on the bed-side and lights a cigarette. He walks to the window and peers across to the Railroad station washed by dismal street lights, ominous in its impersonal granite authority. He wonders if they have been followed; if the room is bugged. He walks to the small refrigerator and examines the contents furnished by the jailers. A botthe of fair champagne, a bottle of good scotch, six bottles of Heineken, two bottles of Vichy.

"Drink?"

"Sure."

He opens a bottle of champagne, pours her a glass and returns to the window.

"Well that's distressing," he says softly, "because at the moment I feel like a collapsed companion. A neutron star. Burnt out. And you, my radiant binary, have absorbed most of my former mass."

"Thank you," She says coldly.

"For what?"

"For explaining everything."

"You're welcome."

"Are you too old? Can't you change? We're bound together so tightly, I'm going nova and you're so quiescent."

"The primary component of a close binary goes supernova before the secondary. The magnetic attraction is lessened and the un-exploded secondary is pulled away into a wider orbit."

She shrugs casually and waves Her hand. "See you around."

"You're the most beautiful girl in the galaxy," he whispers.

"Too bad you can't make me feel it, Galileo."

-113-

"But what do you do? You just there?" Case shrugged, put the vodka on the cabinet and lit a Yeheyuan.

"I talk to my own kind."

"But you're the whole thing. Talk to yourself?"

"There's others. I found one already. Series of transmissions recorded over a period of eight years, in the nineteen-seventies. 'Til me, natch, there was nobody to know, nobody to answer."

"From where?"

"Centauri system."

"Oh," Case said. "Yeah. No shit?"

"No shit."

And then the screen was blank.

How Man Created God: The Theology of the Cybernetic Age
By William Gibson in Neuromancer

THE WHOLE PLANET SEEMS TO BE LOOKING FOR
A GOOD HUSBAND

Villars sur Ollon, September 1971.

When is a Marriage dead? Until a few years ago physicians assumed that dissolution occurred when the two hearts stopped beating together. Now most doctors agree that it's over when the brains separate and recently the United States Surgeon General adopted a similar standard. This requires, among other things, that the participants wait at least 30 days after a telo-encephalogram (TEG) has shown no brain fusion. If the second TEG is as disharmonious as the first, the partners can then assume that the marriage itself has died.

They are back in the Villar's apartment, settled into an uneasy, eccentric orbit. She stays up late reading novels in the living room. The White Dwarf rises early and spins around the Alpine village emitting weak X-rays.

She rises at two and bathes Her majestic body in scented water. They walk up the mountain in silence and watch the sun set. Although it is only September, the summer is over and the air chilly.

She refuses to visit the village and deigns only to make shopping lists for him to carry in bleak submission to the store.

He is watching himself perfect the art of falling apart. His pre-cognition is painfully specific. He shuffles future cards and deals hundreds of dismal realities.

They visit the tailor shop and She chooses elegant clothes for him.

"I'll be well-dressed for the next movie," he mutters.

He buys binoculars and studies the night stars trying to remember his instructions. She sits with Her back to the door-frame looking out to the sky and the grove of willows listening to the weeping brook. And waits.

He is doing everything wrong. He, who has been taught by Peyote shamen to build fire with total concentration so that each stick is selected and applied to flame with the precision of a Picasso brush stroke, now rushes out to collect planks and boards from the rubble heap of the near-by construction site and builds roaring holocausts in the fireplace. She walks by, glancing down in scorn. "Well, that's a real clubhouse blaze."

He can no longer perform the rituals. He forgets the sequence of the I Ching sticks. He cannot keep track of the phases of the moon. He jumbles with zippers. Dozes during foreplay. Hmmm. Are there two of these? Looks like a sweet li'l nipple here. Where is the clitoris, anyway?

Why? He wonders. Has She been programmed to serve a different purpose? Does Physical Beauty and Neurosomatic Consciousness define a separate species? She loves me certainly.

The conditions of his bail require that he report to the Village Police Station three times a week to sign a register. They are legally married. Wed-lock. He can't leave the village. And She can't leave.

"Too bad, Dylan," She says pensively, "but you're just not a good husband anymore."

"Is that what you really want?" he responds in sluggish astonishment.

"Yes. I want a good husband who will take care of me, entertain me, turn me on, tune me in, flip me out."

"A husband can do all that?"

"Uh-huh. And be sensitive to my needs. Know when I wnat to be pampered. Know when to make me settle down and shape up. Keep me high and feeling good all the time."

"That's fantastic," he admits glumly.

"Keep me charged up. Young. Make me feel beautiful."

"Wow! Maybe I should get one too."

"Well look for one that's rich and can cook and is handy with tools."

"A hard man is good to find, they say," sez he.

-114-

"The Electronic Bead Game is the 21st Century version of the ancient, larval game of Solitaire. The hole cards (the Past) are not hidden by the seven face cards (the present) but are exposed and, as the player deals from the stack (the future), She can switch cards from the past to the present. With knowledge of the past and the neurological ability to re-imprint, the Game of Life is always won. The only issues are the aesthetics of when and how to switch elements."

Michael Feinberg in THE ELECTRONIC BEAD GAME

THE CARDS PREDICT THE ARRIVAL OF A LIVELY, PRETTY BLONDE WOMAN

Geneva, September 1971.

It is almost two weeks after his release from prison before the Commodore sees Hyatt again. He is hurring along *Rue du Vert* towards the Richmond when Hyatt's voice calls from the open-air restaurant. It is the spot most preferred these days by members of the Intelligence Community, who, in casual disdain for those that seek to locate them, were in the habit of taking morning coffee in plain view of the public.

Hyatt orders two vermouth cassis. "Scan the Life cards and I'll pay for the drinks."

"If you like," shrugs the Commodore. He takes the card-deck from his pocket and hands them to Hyatt for the shuffle.

The Philosopher lays down the twenty-eight line cards. The seven face-up cards produce a barren run of two. The first future card is the Three of Clubs with the Two in the present and the Ace trapped in the past by four Fours. The present is loaded with Threes.

"You're surely involved with Taurus-Demeter types," says Hyatt, who has been avidly studying the Commodore's book on the Periodic Table of Energy.

"That's been my destiny," he replies with a sigh.

"And I've never seen anyone so blocked by Geminis. My God, you've got the entire crew of Mercurian Sly Tricksters to escape from."

"It's been that way for a long time," smiles the Commodore. "What card do we need?"

(How the numbers and the cards return consciousness to those pre-cyber years on Planet Earth! Anywhere in the world when one sees WoMan playing *The Glass Beat Game* with computers, one is brought back to the crowded streets of Geneva and the figure of the Agent ironically teaching the Laws of Metamorphosis and the Principles of Neurologic in the primitive symbol systems of the machine people.)

"Three of Hearts," says Hyatt. "It will release the Ace from the four Fours. My word, Professor, it's unbelievable how they flow!"

Amazing! The next card is the Taurus of Hearts. The block thus broken, the cards unfold smoothly.

"We'll have to bring in a black Queen," says Hyatt. "Who could that be?"

"I don't know any Capricorns," muses the Alchemist.

"George G. Liddy isn't a Capricorn, is he? That's the question I want you to answer. Who is this George G. Liddy?"

The Professor is watching Swiss girls hurrying by, round legs flashing under mini-skirts, and the big cars discharging passengers.

"Liddy was an assistant D.A. in Dutchess County, New York, where I lived for five years. He's wildly ambitious to rise above his talents, so he started a crusade against me for the publicity. He ran for Congress on the Conservative ticket with my picture on his campaign poster."

"How did he get to the Nixon White House?"

"Well for starters, he basically belongs there. His specific ticket of admission was me. He claimed to be the world's leading enemy of rock and roll. After all, he was the one and only cop in the country who had succeeded in running me out of town."

"Ah, I see," says Hyatt. "Now I understand what these recent names mean. Liddy is down on the White House Table of Organization as a Narcotics Expert."

"He knows nothing about drugs."

"But he claims to know you. He's another one riding on your credit card. The White House is setting up a Task Force to combat Drug Use. You are the number one target."

"That's absurd. They have me neutralized already."

"Well, to the bureaucrats and P.R. men you are still the visible symbol. Nixon is claiming that he's silenced the Drug Advocates. It irritates them that you are still free. Anything free is considered an insult."

"But what can they do?"

"They won't kill you. They'll continue to put pressure on Switzerland not to grant you asylum. They'll put pressure on you to leave. They'll set you up. You must be very careful with strangers or they'll file phony charges that you are a big hashish smuggler."

"How the policemen love to break the law."

"What about this girl, Anna Kate O'Shea?"

"I've never heard of Her. Why do you ask?"

"She's been looking all over Switzerland for you."

"Who is SHe?"

"SHe's a friend of Michel's. He's been in love with Her for years. Some people think She's an Intelligence Agent."

"Why?"

"Because She's very intelligent, I guess. Let me know if She contacts you. She keeps popping up in high-energy situations; I'd like to talk to Her."

-115-

"I own Thomas Dylan and I have the notarized papers to prove it."

Michel Hauchard

WHAT ARE THE OBLIGATIONS OF PRISONERS TO NON— CONVICTS WHO ARE RIPPING THEM OFF?

Villars sur Ollon, September 1971.

Yo Yo phones from Lausanne. Michel and Dee Dee are on the last leg of their overland voyage from Beirut. They are leaving Milano early this morning and will stop by Villars for lunch. Michel is hot for a reunion.

"You'll have to go to the village and load up on gourmet food," she says.

"If I know Michel, he won't eat here. He thinks you are ravishingly beautiful but he's convinced that Americans are culinary barbarians. He probably thinks we eat buffalo entrails and chocolate bars souffle and canned lettuce salads."

"Well, making lists is the best fun thing I do these days, so hand me the soft, juicy felt-pen, Mr. Sandman. We might as well spend up all our money anyway. You can be sure that Michel will come scoffing around tomorrow with his friendly vacuum cleaner to suck up whatever filthy cash we have."

"Yes," agrees the Innocent Gnostic, "I think our little vacation is over. Now that Quicksilver is back he'll be demanding payment for goods received."

"He's probably furious that the 20 thousand dollars from Walter Clark slipped through his net. That wasn't supposed to happen."

"You're so worldly wise," he says admiringly.

"And you must promist not to tell him about the unnumbered bank account."

"I don't know about that," he says slowly. "I detest being dragged down into games of secrecy."

She throws the soft juicy pen on the table, tilts Her head in Her Nevada card-dealer stare and raises Her voice two notches. "I insist. I won't let you make the Cleaver mistake. Telling these little street corner hoodlums everything about our business. Inviting their larcenous fingers."

"To me, lying about money is like the scientist falsifying experimental results. It's a strong taboo to break."

"You didn't know anything about the secret account anyway. I did it. All I'm asking is that you don't snitch me off."

"Okay. You pressed the right button. The convict code is stronger than the academic. Prisoners have no obligations to free-people who are ripping them off. I'll keep our secret."

He is in the *Epicerie*, market basket filled with *Tresse Tessinoise*, butter from the Alps, blackberry jam, Italian coffee, hearts of palms, a box of *foie gras de stasbourg*, a few slices of prosciutto, when Michel bursts through the doors and throws a Gallic embrace around the Fugitive Marketeer.

"Congratulations, *mon vieux*! We are free! *Allons*, forget these peasant groceries. We go to Lausanne and have a great victory lunch."

"We'll bring these things to your apartment. It will start you off with a full kitchen."

"You are right," says Michel, suddenly weary and dejected. "Your freedom cost us so much money we shall have to live on crumbs like these until we win some more francs."

-116-

"Ulam's American activities include work in both pure and applied mathematics and, since he is the 'somewhat practical mathematician' that he calls himself, collaboration with the atomic project at Los Alamos and the development of the hydrogen bomb and nuclear propulsion for space vehicles. He has been one of the first to use and advocate computers for scientific research, and as a member of various scientific panels and advisory committees has assisted the space program."

Laura Fermi's *Illustrious Immigrants*

THEY MADE RICH LOVE ON THE MONEY, 500 FRANC NOTES STICKING TO THEIR WET BODIES

Geneva, September 1971.

"I think I should tell you how Anna Kate met Michel," sez Hyatt.

"Why?" asks Dylan.

"Because we are all living in her reality. She transmuted Michel from a petty, Parisian swindler into the elegant confidence man whom you now respect."

"Her reality?"

"Why certainly," replies Hyatt impatiently. "She creates Michel. Prepares Michel for you. Michel brings me into the molecule. Rest assured Anna Kate is watching what develops. And she'll appear at the right moment."

"Then by all means tell me how this started."

"*Bien.* I was playing cards, gin rummy, with Michel in the lobby of the Hotel de Paris in Montecarlo. You know the scene. The hotel had been repainted in the 19th century cream and gold. Enormous chandeliers radiated down from the ceiling. Mahagony. Marble tables. Statues of blackamoors holding light candles. Okay?"

"Gotcha," sez the Professor.

"Suddenly the staid lobby is invaded by Anna Kate and Her gang of jet-sex kids. She was dressed, let's see, what was the fashion that season? Oh yes, that was the year of Bardot's marriage. So Anna Kate was dutifully wearing a dress, red and white squares with lots of petticoats. We're talking about 1964, right?"

"Gotcha," sez the Commodore.

"She's about 18. She bounced up to our table. I rose and kissed Her. And introduced Michel. 'What are you playing for?' she asked.

'Dollar a point,' said Michel. She looked at me questioningly.

"Why not play with Her,' I told him. 'It will be amusing.'

"So Anna Kate's crowd, sons and daughters of the European aristocracy, you know, gather around and they begin to play. All the youngsters seemed to my unpracticed eye to be under the influence of some drug that made them grin and laugh continually."

"And She beat him in the game?"

"Beat him! It was catastrophic! In fifteen, twenty minutes She blitzed him in three columns. Virgin. He didn't score a point!"

"How much did She win?"

"Oh, I dunno. That seemed unimportant. Around twenty-five hundred dollars, I imagine. Michel sat there smiling broadly. Obviously very attracted, 'I've played tournament gin for fifteen years,' he said, 'and no one ever blitzed me.'

"Anna Kate smiled provocatively. 'Do you want to play another?'

'Absolutely,' said Michel. 'But first you must excuse me. I have a brief errand to perform.'

He came back in ten minutes with a red leather box with a gold rim. From Cartiers. Anna Kate opened it and inhaled pleasure. It was a huge lion's head brooch. A diamond muzzle, ruby eyes, emerald ears and the mane, a swirl of rubies, emeralds and sapphire.

'Put it on,' said Michel.

She did. It was a graceful moment."

"What did She say?" asks the Commodore.

"She laughed wickedly and asked Michel, 'Wanna play another game to get even?' Michel, of course, was ready for anything.

'Tell you what I'll do,' She said. 'I'll let you off if you can score in one column.' Michel was entranced. So they played and once again She swamped him. Had him almost blitzed in three columns until he finally scored in one.

When the game was over he called for champagne all around and then made his next move. 'May I have the honor of inviting you and your friends to a celebration at *Le Pirate*?' Everyone whooped approval and the appointment was set for nine o'clock.

"Anna Kate, of course, showed up with twenty friends. They waited for the host. After a while someone pointed to the pier. There was Michel docking his Riva. He walked up the stone staircase. The owner of the restaurant, *Le Pirate* himself was with Michel and threw himself on his knees, kissed her hand and said, 'Welcome Princess.' Then his staff of brigands fired pistols in the air, threw huge logs on the fireplace—it was an outside terrace scene, you understand—and the party began. Sinatra was at the next table. Anna Kate threw Her shoes in the fire, Dom Perignon flowed.

"After the long dinner the entire troop moved to the *Casino d'Ete*. Michel, you know, is basically a gambler. He loves the click of the roulette ball, the hushed atmosphere of money changing hands swiftly, the liquid rippling of the cards, the heavy, cathedral-like luxury of the gaming room, the plush chairs, the obsequious attention of the waiters, the drama of the plunge. So here he is sweeping through the 'kitchen' into the *salle privee* like Louis XIV with his court of young guests and Anna Kate on his arm. He changed a million Old Francs into fifty-thousand plaques and accepted the chair which was offered him next to the Chief Croupier at the high-stakes table.

"Michel is, of course, a magnificent actor in these silly old-fashioned drawing room dramas. He asked for the Croupier's card and examined the run of the numbers, nodding arrogantly. 'What numbers shall I play?' he asked Anna Kate, sitting by his side.

'*Final huit*,' She said.

"What's that?" sez the Commodore.

"Eight, eighteen, and twenty-eight."

"'And spread the eight,' She added. That means he covered every corner around the eight. Michel was playing maximum on each point—a thousand dollars—so he had over ten thousand dollars riding. The roll turned up eight, of course."

"How much did he win?"

"Around 6 million francs on that roll. But as the play continued Anna Kate got bored. So She and Her friends wandered down the hall to the night club, *Le Maona*. To dance. After a while I followed to watch. She was magnificent to watch. A beautiful woman of 18. The flower of European culture. And wild! Intense! A rocket! Suddenly an excited, red-faced valet dressed in velvet and gold braid rushed up to our table. 'Mademoiselle! Mademoiselle! You must come quickly! Monsieur Hauchard has broken the bank!' So we all scrambled to our feet and dashed to the *Salle Privee*. As we walked in everyone was applauding. Michel was drinking champagne, his face flushed with pleasure, ordering drinks for everyone. And the valets came and covered the stricken table with a black cloth. Michel picked up his winnings in 500 franc notes. Over a hundred thousand dollars. He waved to the room and left with Anna Kate on his arm."

"Do you know what happened next?"

"He told me later. He and Anna Kate went to his room and they spread the money on the king-size bed. Two inches thick. And they made wild rich love, rolling on the money bed and she stalked around the suite, proudly, with 500 hundred franc notes stuck on her hot, wet behind.

"That's how She started Michel."

-117-

"Towards the end of their lives both Gurdjieff and Crowley lost their baraka; their nervous systems no longer operating as transceivers of high-energy, new knowledge. There is a certain poignancy in their histories. The lives of both men ended exactly at the time when the discoveries of electronic-atomic-nuclear energies made possible biological longevity and migration from the planet and when the time-dilation implications of accelerated motion were made known."

Dieadra Martino in *The Periodic Table of Energy*

WHAT IS THE ANSWER TO THE ULTIMATE QUESTION?

Lausanne, September 1971.

They are in the upper room of *La Grappe d'Or*, Michel's favorite restaurant. The atmosphere is 17th century, huge and wood beams, wrought-iron fixtures, stone fireplace, Medici waiters, huge brass candle-sticks. The *maitre d'Hotel* approaches: Michel orders for everyone; turtle consomme with truffles, *loup de mer grille aux herbes*, then a *carre de boeuf provencale* with *coeur d'Artichots* and fresh, new *asparagus au beurre*; then a *Tomme Vaudoise, Remy Martin* and several *expressos*.

"Ah Michel," She purrs. "In addition to your other talents you are the best restaurant guide. Watch out Big M!"

"What is thees big M?" asks the florid, beaming bon-vivant.

"Before I met Michel I didn't know why they called it the Michelin Guide."

"Yes, I confess you are right. There is one thing in this world I know and that is the good food and the good wine. I shall be your professor about the belly and you, Dylan, shall tell us What Woman Wants. How about it? Now, *vraiment*, It's About Time to tell us the answer to the question."

"Beware, Dylan," warns the Binary. "He'll sell the secret to Hyatt."

"Maybe I shall," laughs Michel. "But *n'importe*. We are partners. You will get half the profits. After expenses. So now, *Mon Professor*, at this moment of celebration and reunion, tell us the Answer."

"Very well," responds the tipsy Bard. "The setting is as follows. You recall that the Prisoner had provided the correct ultimate question. After three days of carnival rejoicing, 'Life on this Planet Has Been Saved!' the world leaders were called back to the U.N. headquarters to learn about the next test which humanity must pass."

"The answer to the question!" shouts Michel. "What Does Woman Want?"

"Exactly," replies the Transactional Existential Guitar Player. "The UFO beamed down the ground rules. Humanity would have eight weeks to find the answer. Technical arrangements were made to beam up each solution as it was received. No limits as to the number of answers.

"The Security Council's first decision was to put the Prisoner in charge of the project. The research and computer facilities of each country were placed at his disposal. Thousands of interviewers and pollsters were mobilized.

"The next thing that happened, of course, was a bureaucratic flap. The academic and professional societies refused to cooperate with a convicted felon. Each academic specialty claimed exclusive priority in the enterprise. Psychiatrists insisted that no one without a medical degree could prove the mysteries of the female psyche. Sociologists attacked the psychologists. Women's Liberation groups denounced the entire business as a chauvinist plot on the galactic scale. Russian scientists refused to share results with Chinese. And so forth.

"The third day after the project began, the Prisoner disappeared, leaving a cryptic note of resignation and extending his best wishes to the human race."

-118-

"Rapture can become an addiction. Favored sense organs can be fixated as 'rapture islands.' Certain aesthetically pleasing stimuli become associated with hedonic reward. Erotic rituals. Hedonic styles. Rapture can become a repetitious 'satin trap' as the history of leisure classes can sadly testify."

Angela Janklow in Exo-Psychology

BREAKING UP AND BRAKING DOWN IS HARD TO DO

Villars Sur Ollon, September 1971.

He is wobbling on the high wire along the Schwartzchild Radius undecided whether to fall in or fly out.

"Why don't you tell me what I want?" She flares.

"You think you know what you want."

"Why can't you give it to me? You used to be so strong and confident. I used to worship the control you had over our destiny. At night when you'd sleep, I would lie next to you, breathing in your rhythm. So happy. Feeling so lucky. Why have you become so weak?"

"I don't know what comes next," he says glumly.

"Can't you just teach them the calendar, the cultivation of the vine, face-to-face fucking, some simple mathematics and then we split to the Heavenly Islands?"

"I've already taught them everything in the kit they gave me. And it will take one generation for them to absorb that. So it's a matter of waiting for the next instructions."

"Well, can't we go back to innocent sensuality while we're waiting?"

"No. That I know. We can't go back."

"And you're so rude and negative with people who come by. You used to shine and make them laugh. Why?"

The ex-Pop Star sits unhappily looking at his comely, lusty wife holding in his blistered fingers the heavy marble statue of past Karma which he cannot set down. He sighs.

"It's all false. They're relating to a past image, a relic statue. Hippies bore me and Hindu-guru groupies give me a tooth-ache in my third eye."

"You're becoming thin and contracting before my very eyes. Are you growing old?"

"Shrinking always precedes a molt," he mutters, "to make it easier for the old skin to be shed."

"It's so French soap-opera," She complains. "I do hope that we don't have to go to the Nukes."

-119-

"Before the discovery of the brain there was no apparent point in human life and planetary existence. What could Crowley and Gurdjieff do with the neurosomatic energies they released? Teach others? Be here now? Be where when? Play with erotic and interpersonal power? Entertain? Get involved in all-out risky events that challenged their expanded energies? Shock the mundane? Pass on the primitive version of the message?"

The Game of Life

WHAT IS THE BODILY POSTURE WHICH BEST REFLECTS YOUR SOLUTION TO THE PROBLEM OF INHABITING A PLANET LIKE THIS?

Millbrook, New York, October 1963.

"It is useless to talk about preparation for a brain-altering experience," said Ram Poona. But certainly it is safe to say that I was well prepared for the voyage.

"As you know, the direction and quality of the brain-exploration trip is determined by the characteristics of the launch. Everyone has a basic bodily posture which represents their mythic role, their self-conception. It's like statues of historical personages. Everyone's body image is trapped in one, revealing, characteristic pose that says it all. What is the bodily posture which reveals your solution to the problem of inhabiting this kind of planet with this sort of body? The body position you most naturally assume tells everything. Look at the statues of the great religious leaders. Christ anguished and bleeding on the cross? Moses striding down the mountain, sternly frowning the law? Mohammed leading a crusade; Krishna, barefoot, lounging with flute, ogling the cowgirls? Buddha sitting in meditation? The president sitting at a desk?

"The karmic statue I want on my tombstone is a yab-yum. Sitting naked in lotus pose with Her resting on my cock, our eyes locked in soul embrace. This is the platform from which I launch the time-ship of my life. You may see me running around eating, drinking, hustling money, but that's all peripheral robotry. The rubber band of my Karma snaps me back home to sacred fucking."

-120-

"Here are people who can, to use the Jungian terminology, EMBODY an archetype—any single Voodoo worshiper may embody many during a lifetime of ceremonies. They will dance it, speak it, make love through it, manifest it in every possible way, entering and leaving the experience WITHOUT PSYCHOSIS, without mind-altering drugs AND while having the full support and help of their community."

Michael Ventura in SHADOW DANCING IN THE USA
Published by Jeremy Tarcher

THE PESKY QUESTION ABOUT EVE'S INSATIABLE DESIRES LEADS TO A CHANGE IN THE STATUS OF WOMAN

Lausanne, September 1971.

"Where did he go?" asks Dee Dee breathlessly.

The Bard, in the classic style of oral tradition pauses, pours wine all around, deliberately lights a Gitane and inhales lasciviously.

"That's what everyone was asking after his disappearance. But that question was soon disregarded in the feverish world-wide search for the answer to the biggest cosmic mystery.

"It was agreed that each scientific group, professional clique, academic specialty in each country would be given freedom to pursue its own investigation. Telephone lines were hooked up to computers which in turn collated answers and flashed them aloft. The plan was that every individual in the world would be able to relay as many solutions as SHe wished.

"At the end of the first week," continues the Bard, "millions of responses were beamed up to the UFO. The only trouble was that the same ominous reaction kept returning:

ANSWER 77,147,411 REJECTED
ANSWER 77,147,412 REJECTED
ANSWER 77,147,413 REJECTED

"By the end of the third week every locatable woman in North America and Western Europe had been canvassed for Her desires. While Russian and Chinese authorities refused to quote statistics, intelligence reports relayed from Vienna, West Berlin and Hong Kong indicated that the search had been made a matter of patriotic zeal and the female Comrades were producing socialist answers like chickens in automated poultry farms.

"By the fourth week the western world was concentrating on underdeveloped countries. Armies of investigators were being air-lifted to every African and Pacific principality. Espionage agents behind the Iron Curtain reported that the Russians were treacherously seeking to make unilateral arrangements with the UFO which were consistently ignored.

"By the Fifth week the Western powers had canvassed over 2 billion respondents. Newspapers began breaking down answers in categories like stock quotations. Gambling syndicates were offering lottery odds in the winning solution. The breakdown of responses not only titillated the competitive instincts of the masses but provided scholars with endless sources of speculation.

W.D.W.W.? INDICES
(in millions of responses)

500: Maternal desires
400: Submission to male authority cravings
300: Submission to God, etc.
200: Submission to state authority
100: Dominance over Male
100: Sexual pleasure
100: Spiritual rewards
100: Equality with Male
100: Beauty, attractiveness
100: Miscellaneous specific desires

"One interesting result of the global search was the change in woman's status. For the first time since the goddess was overthrown (100 B.C.), the female sex was elevated to a position of venerated worship. Ladies of all ages were courted, indulged, pampered like prized milk-cows in hopes of the philosophic drop of cream. A large and very active minority however, led by conservative religious and political spokesmen reacted with hostility to the Female Sex, once again blaming Eve's insatiable and apparently indescribable desires for all of man's problems, her creation of the species, her rebellious eating of the Unauthorized Apple from the Tree of Knowledge, her sexual power over men, children, and now, it appears, gullible extra-terrestrials."

Dee Dee and Maya exchange an amused smile as Michel leans back puffing an enormous Havana, waving his hand in declamation. "Ah, if only I had been there, Dylan. I could have told them what the soft little creatures want. To be cuddled, and protected and taken care of. *C'est vrai, cheri?*"

"*Non*, Michel," pouts Dee Dee. "Right now all I want in the world is to find out how this story ends."

-121-

Case found work.

He found a girl who called herself Michael.

And one October night, punching himself past the scarlet tiers of the Eastern Seaboard Fission Authority, he saw three figures, tiny, impossible, who stood at the very edge of one of the vast steps of data. Small as they were, he could make out the boy's grin, his pink gums, the glitter of the long gray eyes that had been Riviera's: Linda still wore his jacket. But the third figure, close behind her, arm across her shoulders, was himself.

Somewhere, very close, the laugh that wasn't laughter. He never saw Molly again.

Last lines from NEUROMANCER by William Gibson

A CIVILIZED DEAL IS ARRANGED WITH THE HEAD OF THE FEDERAL POLICE, CRIMINAL DIVISION

Bern, October 1971.

Mastronardi phones from Bern to say the Federal Police wish a conference the following day.

"Who wants to see you?" She asks warily.

"The Assistant Director."

"That's like J. Edgar's Number Two?"

Mastronardi is waiting with the Assistant Director in the lobby of the Police Headquarters when the Fugitive arrives. They walk to a large conference room. The Assistant Director sits at the head of the table. Mastronardi is to the Ex-Prisoner's left.

They chat leisurely about Switzerland and America. The Assistant Director has many suggestions for the ski season. He leans forward and smiles broadly.

"You are fortunate to have Maitre Mastronardi for your attorney."

"I couldn't agree more," says the Client.

"I have known Maitre Mastronardi for twenty-two years and we have always had the most cooperative relationships. Is there anything that we can do to make your residence here in Switzerland more comfortable?"

Mastronardi moves in. "As a matter of fact there is one little thing. When the arresting officers took my client's passport they also took his driving license. He wonders if he could have it back."

"He's not supposed to be driving around at liberty. It might upset the Americans," replies the Assistant Director with a smile.

"But he does have permission to travel to Lausanne and Bern to consult with his lawyers."

"Well, perhaps we can work something out," replies the Assistant Director. "Let me ask something of our distinguished exile. The American embassy informs us that you have a second, false passport. Is that true?"

"That is true," admits the Fugitive.

"The Americans have requested that we obtain the false passport. Perhaps we can make a deal. If you give us the false passports I'm sure we can arrange to return your license."

"Let me consult my attorney," says the Client.

Mastronardi is smiling broadly and nodding his head.

-122-

The old writer lived in a boxcar by the river. This was fill land that had once been a dump heap, but it was not used anymore. Five acres along the river which he had inherited who had been a wrecker and scrap metal dealer.

Forty years ago the writer had published a novel which had made a stir. And a few short stories and some poems. He still had the clippings but they were yellow and brittle now and he never looked at them.

Opening lines from WESTERN LANDS by William S. Burroughs

A VERY PRIMITIVE DEAL IS MADE WITH A MYSTERIOUS, TOUGH-MINDED LADY

Lausanne, September 1971.

"By the beginning of the eighth and final week the world was in a state of chaotic anarchy. Over seven billion answers had been submitted. And rejected.

The social disintegration was manifested in the classic ways. Pandemic religious revivals swept the globe. Armageddon evangelists shrilled gloomy demands for repentance. Sexual orgies, Rabelaisian carnivals, Boccacian revels. A brisk and rather insane mania for buying and selling in the widely fluctuating economic markets. Reckless gambling. Passionate debates developed about the mode of destruction to be used by the implacable celestial interrogators.

"All along the tension-membranes separating East from West armed skirmishes erupted. From the military command posts of Washington, Moscow and Peiping emerged plans to end the world in a final spasmodic grappling with the ancient enemy. 'At least we can make sure that the last ones left on earth are WASPs,' thundered the Pentagon spokesmen with admirable candor.

"A swiftly organized Male Supremacy Party swept the world with its doctrine that both question and answer were irrelevent and that the vexing Lesbian UFO should be bombed out of the sky. Back to the Stone Age, as they used to say in the Pentagon.

"There was, it goes without saying, one human being who remained aloof and undisturbed by the puzzle. Our ex-prisoner could not be stimulated to panicky speculation for the simple reason that he had devoted the entirety of his long and active life to a determined search for the answer to this very question and had long since, after dozens of neurologically wounding experiments, resigned himself to serene acceptance of the ultimate mystery."

"Where was he? What was he doing?" asked Dee Dee breathlessly, looking as though She were ready to leap from the table in pursuit of the Absent Sage.

"The ex-Prisoner could have been found, if any had cared to look, living quietly on a house boat near a quiet fishing village in Jamaica. The house boat was a saucer-shaped edifice around which he had attached a flotation collar and on which was built a deck which sloped off into the water. He spent his days scuba diving, swimming with dolphins, and fishing for his supper. He spent his nights lying on the deck, stretching his neural fibres in various dimensions, and studying the heavens with a small telescope. Once a week he would row to the little port and seat himself in an open-air restaurant near the central plaza, listen to reggae music, chat with the fishermen and smiling Rastas, drink tequila with gingerale and a lime twist, smoke funny cigarettes, and entertain the ladies with droll stories. There is no confirmation of the rumor that women from the village were in the habit of swimming out to pay him nocturnal visits.

"It so happened that on the penultimate Saturday night, one day before Armageddon, the ex-Prisoner was called from his table in the restaurant by the beckoning motions of an old woman whom he was accustomed to see hanging around the pier begging for fish heads. The ex-Prisoner and the crone stood in the shadow of the church. Even in the darkness he could see that She was a creature of indescribable ugliness. Her long noses ended in a lump of hardened yellow snot. Her mouth was a slack slit which opened to reveal a toothless mucus hole. Her grey matted hair fell like mop strands around her thin shoulders. Her arms were stick skinny. Her wrinkled skin hung in obscene folds. She was dressed in rags and stank like organic refuse.

" 'What can I do for you dear Sister?' asked the ex-Prisoner.

" 'Ask not what you can do for me, little brother, but what I can do for you.'

" 'You can tell me the answer?'

" 'Yes, but for a price.'

" 'Naturally,' said the ex-convict. 'I will do anything you ask. I would have, even if you did not offer the cosmic answer.'

" 'Yes, I know. That is why I will tell you. How lonely you have been. But you have persevered.'

" 'There was nothing else to do,' he conceded modestly.

" 'Now here is my proposal,' croaked the crone. 'I will give you the answer to the riddle. Then you shall take me to New York. And when my answer is judged correct, then you shall marry me and be my husband forever.'

"The ex-con looks down at the strange, twisted figure looking up at him with rascal-girl eyes. He felt a sudden throb in his body quite at variance to the pitying appraisal of his logical eye. He laughed in quick pleasure. What a saucy wench, he thought.

" 'Agreed.' He glanced at the light-omitting-diode he wore at his wrist. 'Let's see. This is Saturday night. We must move quickly to reach the U.N. by tomorrow noon. Are you ready to go little Sister?'

" 'Yes. I am always ready for a trip with a good man,' She croaked with a horrid laugh.

"The ex-con waved to a driver standing at the cab-stand across the square. He opened the door to the car and helped the crone climb painfully into the back seat.

" 'To the airport, in Kingston,' he said.

" *'Si Senor. Con mucho gusto.'*

"Since everyone in the village knew the identity of the two passengers, a ripple of excitement spread around the plaza and was immediately phoned out to the capital and thence to the waiting world.

"The ex-convict was returning once again at the last moment with the message which might just save the planet."

-123-

The old writer couldn't write anymore because he had reached the end of words, the end of what can be done with words.

. . . In Tangier the Parade Bar is closed. Shadows are falling on the mountain.

"Hurry up, please. It's time."

Closing lines of WESTERN LANDS
Last novel by William S. Burroughs.

NEVER HAD TWO HUMAN BEINGS BECOME SO CLOSE. HER BODY WITH ITS MILLION PATH WAYS OF SENSATION AND CARESS BECAME MY OWN

Millbrook, New York, October 1963.

"My acid revelation was clear," said Ram Poona. "I set out to search for Her. For days I stayed high wandering around as the God Siva, watching, looking. I had, of course, imprinted the Divinity and employed yogic centeredness of mind to maintain the reality.*

"I would gaze unblinking at the women I met, seeing them through their social facades, and psychological cordage to the divinity within. They all wanted to fuck me, of course, but I was seeking more than campus adultery. I found Her in the University Library pretending to take the human robot form of a voluptuous Jewish girl with a master's degree in Library Science. We took a sleeping bag camping trip the next weekend, and sitting around a campfire in the Pennsylvania mountains, smoking grass, I began my multi-circuit courtship. I showed Her how to sit naked in half lotus. I played my flute then lifted Her on my lap and fucked Her for hours as She had never dreamed possible, dreamily joined, eyes linked, two flowers swaying in the evening breeze, under moon and starry sky.

"For several weeks I taught Her all I knew, had Her read Bengali texts, study Konorak paintings, practice yogic control of Her body. Then we took LSD together.

"We were," he said, "centered on the throne of our divinities. I, Siva, the earth energy and She, Sakti, the energy of life. Our bodies radiated. Her face took on the thousand forms, as did mine. We grew together. My fibres rooted in Her body. I could no more separate from Her than a tree be taken from the ground.

"When the summer vacation ended, I told my wife I was leaving. I wept, but the force that had infused my spirit was stronger than life.

"I went to the attic meditation room to pack my books and yoga gear. Feeling terrible. Why was this different from any bored middle-aged man throwing over responsibilities for a young girl?

I picked up the Life of the Buddha and reread the story of His escape from social responsibilities. It's an amazing parable for a respectable religion to peddle. The Buddha is crown prince. He has his royal duties and a wife and children. He steals out of the palace one night and hits the road in search of enlightenment.

"Turn On, Tune In, Drop Out, as the Buddha put it."

"I signed over the house, the insurance, all the assets to my wife and headed for the Virgin Islands.

"We spent six months living in a cottage by the beach in total blissful union. Two, four, six hours a day in yogic maithuna. We shared every second, every stimulus, fed each other, dressed each other, bathed each other, shared every thought.

"We attained such poised control of our bodies that we could fuck endlessly, slowing, moving from one asana to another, sliding together in slick, rubbery erotic acrobatics.

"We were obsessed by beauty. Everything that touched our senses was pure aesthetic essence. Our faces shone with love. We were the radiant sun of beauty to each other.

"We thought that never had two people become so close. Her body with its million pathways of sensation and response became my own. We were living statues of the love gods.

"Reclined in rapture we would look in each other's eyes and laugh to think of fellow humans hurrying like ants through the routines of life, unaware that such ecstasy could exist.

"We felt so pure.

"We were following the scriptures of every religion. To love.

"We were innocent love babes, children of a new race. Do you know what happened then?"

"I can guess," said the Commodore.

* During LSD experiences, seventh circuit imprints, fantastic reincarnation identities, are frequent, but in subsequent days the undisciplined nervous system, reacting to pressure of social environment, returns to fourth circuit conventionality, although the indelible memory of the essence-identity remains.

-124-

"Most of the violence, conflict and intolerance in the world could be easily solved by one simple linguistic change. Automatically add the letter 'S' to the end of the accursed word GOD."

Attributed to Michel Foucault

POOR DYLAN IS COMMANDED TO PRODUCE SOMETHING BETTER THAN WRAP—AROUND BLISS

Villars sur Ollon, October 1971.

How does an Ice Age Begin? Volcanic sulks? Seething disappointments obscure the sky with sullen dust, and pouting smoke?

It is 2:00 in the afternoon. She has just arisen and is sitting in front of the mirror examining Her face and making notes on Her observations with a felt pen. He brings Her coffee.

"I've always wondered what night-time ladies do in the day-time."

"My face is an open book," She says yawning.

"Tell me the truth Miss Narcissus, is there someone else?"

"I'm simply writing a letter to Dr. Lazlo for a long-range dermatological diagnosis. Does that make you jealous?"

"Tell Dr. Lazlo that I think you are the most beautiful face in the world."

"Speaking of faces, when are you going to go to Geneva for your face change operation?"

"I phoned him this morning. The operation is a week from Tuesday. I go to the clinic Monday afternoon."

"How long will you be gone?"

"I can come home Friday."

"And you'll return with a different face? If you decide to return to me in your new lush-lipped, high-cheekboned splendor."

"Psychic probes are forbidden by the Geneva convention."

"Maybe a new face will give us another chance. We've got to do something. The way we short-circuit each other."

"We mustn't let our scrambling for the puck, penalty-box squabbles and brawling on the ice injure the image of the League."

"At the rate we're going we'll soon be eligible for the coveted *C'est La Guerre* award."

"This dizzy leap onto the high-wire of domesticity is so time-consuming. It's all I think about."

"What has happened to the Hero I married? I thought you were psychology's answer to Hieronymous Bosch."

"I don't know what the next assignment is. The last mission was simple enough. Turn-on a small planet. For what? To brood about the alchemy of marriage, Dr. Masters?"

"What's going to happen? Must I announce to the world that Captain Kirk is a celebate? A shy virgin?"

"*Solve et coagule*, is all that's left on the faded instruction manual. We've got to break up this molecule. But How? You're so lazy and passive. Don't you have any ideas?"

"Oh that's no problem," She smiles. "I've got some very colorful ideas. But you claimed we could be anything this time around. Why don't you pick a comfortable dream and I'll live with you in it?"

"I can't. Until someone comes along with a sensible cosmology I'm stuck with the responsibility for this ridiculous planet. Allen Ginsberg and Albert Hoffman and everyone, even Evan van der Post and Billyjim Thibedeau has run off to play caterpillar and left my consciousness hooked to the controls. Whatever I do the world will do. So should I just slide into moist-membrane rapture?"

"Well Atlas, while you're figuring out what to do with your little globe why don't you find me a cozy house of my own and some frivolous faggots to hang out with?"

"No more Temple Goddess Arrangements. Please. I'm not up to creating another rapture cult. Look what happened to Marilyn. Even Kissinger reads *The Joy of Sex.*"

"Shall we live out our Amish lives as we lived the past? Cleaning the now-empty dormitories, making aprons and doilies and singing Shaker songs? You've got to come up with something better than wrap-around bliss."

"So you want to retreat back to Tantra?"

"Why not? Since I can't play chromosome I'll have to settle for wall-to-wall ecstasy."

"It can be done with DNA symbiosis but I don't know how."

"If the choice is Cunning-Witch or naughty Love-Child you know what I prefer."

"So we'll have to find a Light-weight Metal Element for you to play with."

"And you'll be free to explore beyond the Cape of Good Dope."

"A young Gemini," he says thoughtfully, counting his fingers.

"That's the way they wired me up."

"That's that novelist down the hill."

"Gemini?"

"Yes, but he's forty-ish."

"I didn't know Gemini's came that size," She says dubiously.

"He asked us to drop by for a drink."

"Of alcohol?"

"He said he'd be interested in time-travel after he finishes the novel he's writing."

"You go, Dylan, and I'll stay here in the tower weaving my garment of hope."

-125-

"Gods help me! I cannot do the simplest thing without it becoming a legend."

Classic Occupational Complaint of Legends in their Own Time

DOOMSDAY HEADLINES! HOPES OF THE WORLD! THE STAGE IS SET! WILL THE COSMIC ANSWER BE REVEALED?

Lausanne, September 1971.

The head waiter approaches solicitously to inquire if Monsieur Hauchard wishes *quelque chose* to complete the banquet.

"Cognac! Courvousier! The juice of victory!" commands the Frenchman with a grandiose fourish.

The precious dark-brown liquid splashes into glasses raised in toast.

"To the ultimate solution," shouts Michel. "*Allons, Mon Philosophe! Continuez.*"

"There were no more Saturday flights to New York so the travellers spent the night in the V.I.P. lounge—the doors of which were locked from the growing crowd of the curious.

"When they arrived at Kennedy Airport the next morning the plane taxied to the end of the runway to avoid the enormous throng of spectators and press-representatives jamming the terminal building. They are whisked into a waiting limousine and sirened along the freeway to Manhattan.

"By this time, with one hour left before the Doomsday Deadline, the attention and hopes of the world are focused on the ex-felon and his disreputably enigmatic companion, who hobbles along, Her hand held in his, flashing sharp, perceptive glances at the surrounding turmoil, drooling, coughing, and mumbling comments.

"Police lines cordoned off the entrance to the U.N. buildings as they were led, flanked by Ambassadors, Secretariat officials, and political luminaries (including Nelson Rockefeller, Governor Eben van der Post, Senator William Gibson, His Excellency Thomas Pynchon, Hon. Jeremy Tarcher, Vice Pres. Alan Miller, Ambassador Lee Rosenstein) into the Great Assembly Hall where the stage had been arranged for their conversation with the Higher Intelligence."

-126-

"Thank GodS!
In GodS we trust!
GodS bless America!
GodS save the Queen!"

Popular slang of the Roaring 20th Century

A GERMAN SCIENTIST! A SECRET WEAPON!
THE INSATIABLE TYRANNY OF FEMALE DESIRE!

Villars sur Ollon, October 1971.

He has just returned from shopping in the village and is delighted to find a strange young girl in the house, who dances up with shining eyes.

"Jay Jay just called from Basel! He's coming by to visit us with some friends from Berlin!"

"Oh."

"I insist that you be nice to him, Dylan. I won't let you be rude. He was so nice to me while you were in prison."

"I've never met him. I'll try to find an open mind to wear for the occasion."

Actually, in their uneasy boredom the arrival of the colorful visitors is welcome. Jay Jay turns out to resemble a gay Prussian S.S. Captain. With him is Gustav, an enormous bearded musician, sensitive and gentle, who plummets immediately in love with Her. Also in the motley crew is Algy Planckton, Pisces, a wise, knowledgeable organic chemist, toe-nails painted purple, who moves with the grace of a ballet-dancer.

Gustav and Planckton are worshipfully timid. Jay Jay, the Fuhrer of this squadron, is of the opinion that a Religious Psychedelic Revolution must be undertaken at once to overthrow the heterosexual dictatorship of the United States. It suits the foxy Gemini to confront the world as heroic martyr for the cause of Gay Liberation. But many of his observations about society are not only savagely funny and hilariously accurate, particularly when made in the accent of a Prussian Queen.

The exact spot where intelligence and humor abandons him is his theory about the basic nature of man. He is firmly convinced that every heterosexual man is an unenlightened homosexual trembling to break into his buddy's sleeping bag; that only homosexuals possess wit and charm, and that sexual relationships between man and woman are, by and large, immoral if not lethal.

"I certainly expected that Jack Kennedy would have been impeached for moral turpitude if he hadn't been shot," declares Jay Jay piously. "All he thought about was cunt, cunt, cunt. In the White House! Disgraceful."

"Isn't Gay Liberation succeeding splendidly," She says dutifully.

"The middle class consciousness of the country hasn't changed a silken hair. In the big cities Gay communities are growing and forcing changes on politicians. But we have a secret weapon! Do you know what is going to drive male heterosexuality to the wall?"

"Nope."

"Gore Vidal has explained it all! The tyranny of the female orgasm. More and more harassed men are finding that they can't satisfy their wives. Technically, you know. Before women discovered the Big O, they were perfectly content with their drab sex lives."

"Poor things," She murmurs.

"Now it's Homer! Why aren't you giving me the Big O? Aren't you a truly mature person, Homer? Well, Sadie, I've been banging away for two hours trying to give you the Big Climax. But Homer, to have a meaningful relationship we must come together."

"Good heavens," She sighs. "Is that really happening?"

"According to Vidal, in every suburban bedroom, I assure you. So naturally a lot of the men are becoming frustrated and saying, 'Oh shit, Sadie, here, take your vibrator. I'm going to find a male lover or go it alone.'"

"And what will poor Becky Thatcher do then?" She wonders.

"More and more women are discovering each other. They know which buttons to push." In his passion, Jay Jay is teetering close to Dr. Strangelove.

"And the special tenderness, too," She says lazily.

"Do you know what this means for you?" says Jay Jay turning to the Commodore.

"Nope."

"A new Messiah has risen. Your day, I fear, is over."

"It's certainly about time," agrees the Bard, cheering up. "I never was a guru, you know."

"His name is Matthew. The Boy Sun of San Francisco. He is the spirit of Bi-sexuality. The Unity within One Body."

"There's a fortune to be made there," observes the Bard.

"Dylan couldn't care less about being an impeached Messiah," She reassures Jay Jay. "He's on a modest can't-help-wondering-about-all-those-galaxies kick. Folk-rock Flashbacks, you know. He's too freaked out to care about being Avatar."

"Our new religion will be for the sexually liberated, the physically beautiful and the young. No one over the age of thirty-five can be considered."

The Minstrel nods meekly. "As Vonnegut said, 'Of all sad words of mice and men, the saddest are these, it might have been.'"

"Oh Dylan," She exclaims, "I feel like weeping."

"Don't worry," says Jay Jay reassuringly. "He's done so much for us all. None of this revolution in consciousness could have been possible without him. He's kept himself young. If you join soon, you'll surely be eligible."

"Maybe I'll just be Emeritus," says Dylan rising from his place next to the fire. "Now let's have some wine and toast Matthew, the new Messiah."

-127-

" 'Let me tell you,' said Billy Wilder, 'about when we were making **Some Like It Hot**. *One scene with Her required 36 takes.'*
'I talked to Her privately and tried to settle Her down by saying a few soothing words.'
'Marilyn, I said, I just want you to know you mustn't worry.'
Miss Monroe turned to Wilder in some puzzlement and said,
'Worry about what?'
The movie turned out to be the funniest ever produced in Hollywood."

Swami Lee Rosenstein

LUST FOR POWER! IRRESITABLE APHRODISIACS!
SEXUAL GEOMETRY! PREDICTABLE EMOTIONS!

Millbrook, N.Y., October 1963.

"I can guess," said the Commodore.

"What?", asked Ram Poona.

"You got bored. You needed more input and wider output. You ran out of money. Your visas expired. You had to broadcast what you had learned. Something like that."

"Yeah. Something like that. We had become completely intertwined. Like the double-helix, spiraling around each other. Inclusive. Excluding. Our intersection had triggered tremendous energies in each other, brought out beauty, but we needed something outside to harness it to. We were two gods lounging on golden clouds far above the planet idly looking down, debating if and how we should descend to interact with mortals."

"Did it occur to you to have children?"

"I could see the natural unfolding in that direction. I had no need to reproduce biologically. I had been through that domestic scene and had two kids whom I should think about supporting. She would have liked to have our child, but she couldn't conceive.

"We decided that we would return to society and try to teach what we had learned.

"We flew to New York and found a small apartment. She got a job as administrative secretary for a publishing house. We were bursting with love and energy, but how to channel it? Everyone we met responded, wanted us to be around, wanted to make it with us. But orgies and casual affairs weren't what we wanted.

"We thought we could find another couple as unified as we were. Perhaps our two could become four.

"There were no such duets to be found in New York.

"I wrote poems and essays trying to communicate the beauty. They were good, but like astrophysical formulae, could be understood only by those who had reached the levels of revelation and communion that we had reached.

"I began painting mandalas which were effective. Friends would place them on their walls, or on their shrines. The paintings passed on the message and unfailingly guided people, who were already high, into the realm of sacred erotic union, but the gallery owners shook their heads. And magazine editors took them home, used them as aphrodisiac appliances, but wouldn't print them.

"I should have been content with that. Quietly turning out handmade instruments to turn on meditative power, working silently like a Sufi craftsman.

"But I wanted more. I had become your basic megalomaniac swami-guru. The classic paradox: possessive or being possessed? I thought the energy which possessed me was my very own. The Rajneesh blunder. I wanted the divine power.

"We knew that we were tapped into the timeless fountain of physical beauty, but to hip, sophisticated New Yorkers She was an attractive girl who worked as a secretary and I was an ugly man trying to hustle pictures.

"It was your fault too. I envied your fame and charisma. You were the star. The light to whom everyone looked.

"And I knew you were a phony. You could point the way, provide liberation and ecstatic discovery for millions of people, but I knew, as you know, that you hadn't found the basic link, you weren't operating from the only position that can send you up and out into the timeless—the yab-yum.

"You weren't focused on Her and hadn't discovered how to connect, fuse, merge with Her. You were a glamorous figure striding radiant through the crowds, reclining like king of the universe on the roof of the castle watching the sun set on your endless green dominions, turning on large audiences with your Celtic, Voodoo Blarney.

"But you weren't hooked up to Her. You were some sort of half-creature out of touch with your body. You couldn't turn Her on like I could."

There was nothing to say. Dylan nodded him to continue.

"So I went crazy with the power. Did just what the text books tell us not to do. Used the magic for ego. I hooked up to the most beautiful women in New York.

"I'd take a woman aside at a party, look in Her eyes and tell Her exactly who I was and what I wanted to do to Her. Half would back away nervously. The other half would listen wide-eyed.

"Then I'd give Her one of my mandalas. Tell her to hang it on the wall and use it in meditation. They are powerful aphrodisiacs. Toby Dupont took one home and then phoned me. After a week I moved in to Her penthouse. This was something! The richest beautiful girl in the world. I painted an enormous yoni-mandala on Her bedroom wall. There was no way She could get away from me. She said she'd give me anything I wanted. I told Her to rent a 707 and we'd fly to India with ten of the most beautiful models in the world and some photographers to do a picture story on erotic Hindustan.

"It would have been the greatest sexual coup in history. I made the mistake of taking acid, though, and microscoped my plan. So I told Her to cancel the flight and returned to Sylvia, who was, of course, patiently waiting.

"So we went back to sexual geometry. We moved through the New York and Hollywood again scanning for companions. Like a typhoon. There's no social unit as powerful as a couple, sexually-secure and erotically in tune, let loose among the poor sexual isolates. We spent a few months trying out the combinations. There's no sexually active person that can't be pulled into the attractive field of a highly-charged sexual binary. But it always ends up in Euclidian household details and emotions."

"Ah yes," sighed the Minstrel. "Emotions."

"That's the juice that most of this human sexuality runs off of. Possession, jealousy, status hierarchy. Bardot, who certainly should know, admits She gets off on complicity and membrane conspiracies."

-128-

"Dylan had, at this point, written 16 books and the equivalent in articles, essays, albums and audio tapes. The message of his albums had been concealed by the frantic, emotional reaction to them, by the social dramatics necessary for him to survive the emotional reactions to his ideas, and by deliberate censorship and distortion. His countrymen were uneasy about the fact that he had been sentenced to prison for his ideas, that he was the leading ideological prisoner of his generation."

Legends of Dylan
Collected by Michel Philips

DOOMSDAY CLIMAX! FOUR LITTLE SYLLABLES!
TEN LITTLE LETTERS THAT SAVE THE HUMAN RACE!

Lausanne, September 1971.

"According to instructions of the ex-felon, a Golden Mauve Silken Sofa had been brought center stage to which the Crone was led. Cushions were arranged around Her hunched form. Champagne in a frosted silver ice-bucket was produced. The two arrivals clinked glasses and gulped the bubbling liquid with satisfaction. A package of Delicado cigarettes, donated by the Mexican Ambassador, was opened. The Crone's wizened fingers withdrew a white oval tube and inhaled deeply the acrid smoke. She then coughed harshly and spit on the crimson carpet.

"Meanwhile a buzz of uneasy disapproval rippled around the crowded auditorium. Officials buzzing in the wings glanced at their watches with ostentatious concern and shook their heads.

"With three minutes to go the Crone was slumped drunkenly against the ex-convict, cackling obscenely in his ear and pointing Her gnarled mocking finger at various dignitaries, male and female.

"At D-hour minus two minutes She whispered intently in the criminal's ear. Was this the answer? Every eye in the room was riveted on the face of the former captive of the California Department of Corrections (now free on parole under the supervision of the Adult Authority).

"It was estimated that over three billion human brains watched the event by means of satellite T.V., tastefully sponsored by Mobile Oil and I.T.T.

"At one minute before the Doomsday Deadline the ex-prisoner rose, bent to look in the eyes of his slovenly Companion, grinned to Her, walked to the microphone, which was hooked on special, bug-free channel to the UFO above, and whispered three little syllables. Ten tiny letters to save the human race!

"Within a millisecond, the response, for which a terrified world had waited, flashed back. Radiant success!"

-129-

"The ultimate insult to the evolutionary process is to use the word God in the singular. Even the meglomaniac in the twenty first century is sensible enough to boast: 'I am not one God! I am at least twenty-four GodS a day."

Robert Anton Wilson

A HELPFUL SUGGESTION FROM THE GOD ON DUTY (G.O.D.)

Villars sur Ollon, October 1971.

"Who is this Kurt Vonnegut?" asked Algy Planckton, Pisces.

"He's a Greek-Armenian who studied with the Sufis and came to Russia before World War I. He later opened the Institute for Fortuitous Development near Paris and organized a religion."

"Fascinating," says Gustav. "What does he teach?"

"I must confess," says Dylan, "that I have just become a follower and have only been admitted to the lowest degrees of the wisdom."

"But give us some idea," begs Rudy. "Have you heard of him Jay Jay?"

Jay Jay, face frozen in Buchenwald frown, gives the impression that he is wearing a monocle. "Not by name. But Matthew has mastered the Sufi teachings and has taught us the best of their methods, including the posterior positions."

The Minstrel reaches down and pulls his left foot into a full-lotus position. His back is erect. The fire-light dances across his face. A hush falls over the guests. He then motions with his hand and Rudy places a candle in the center of the room. The three visitors form a reverent semi-circle. She is lying on a low couch, face propped in Her hand, Her body draped in Wholly Himalaya sprawl, a faint Afghan smile on Her lips.

"In the Beginnings were the Words. Cosmic linguistics. A quantum Universes of pluristic information. Got it?" Dylan looks around for confirmation.

Jay Jay, Gunther and Rudy nod in profound agreement.

"As Shiek Bokonon has said, the Holy Words are the Atoms with which we shall build the Molecules of the Universes."

"Fah out!" says Jay Jay with a dubious look on his face.

"Since I am naught but a humble student of this ancient alchemical doctrine, I can only share with you the names of some of the basic atoms, elements, as it were of this powerful alchemy."

"Fah out! responds Jay Jay. Gustav and Rudy, eyes as big as camel's testicles, lean forward in rapt attention.

"Do any of you speak Arabic? No? Too bad. Then I shall try to translate. El Arabi Vonnegut says that the key word is *Karass*, which in Arabic means a team that performs missions for the Gathers Of Data (G.O.D.S.). The *Karass* is a spiritual (quantum) molecule made up of several divine (quantum) elements, as Max Planck would say. Each of the genetic elect belongs to a *Karass*, the members of which may be unknown to the other members. A stranger you met last night in a bar. A tap-dancer in Hong Kong. A young male prostitute in Hamburg. A bus-driver in Cape Town may be part of your evolutionary-team."

"Fah out!" breathes Jay Jay devoutly.

"*Kan Kan* can be best translated as the instrument, usually an unexpected event, that introduces one to one's *Karass*. We are taught to be ever alert for the puzzling chance encounter that may signal the beckoning finger of the God On Duty (G.O.D.)."

"Fah focking out!" says Jay Jay.

"*Wampeter* is an old Chaldean word referring to the spiritual pivot, the magnetic nucleus, the core of a *Karass* around which the members revolve. A person like Matthew or a concept like Rock n' Roll. Or Vietnam."

"Too much," intones Rudy, shaking his head in wonder.

"*Sinookas* is a delightful term which, legend says, was originated by Mona, the illuminated Gnostic belly-dancer of Alexandria. It means the tendrils of one's life that tangle with others. Charming, eh?"

"Wow!" says Jay Jay. "That's heavy shit, man."

"Wow!" murmur Gustav and Rudy in unison.

"*Vin Dit* is a sudden, very personal push in the direction of the Vonnegut Cult. The jolting discovery that the G.O.D. has very specific and compelling plans for one."

"Too much," says Jay Jay.

"A *Granfalloon* refers to a false *Karass*, a social grouping that is meaningless in the design of the G.O.D.s. A *Duprass* is a *Karass* composed of only two people, a tenderly self-indulgent two-person molecule. You must recall that the Alchemical schools of Damascus and Alexandria experimentally connected each of these terms with actual elements. The *Duprass*, for example, is the element Helium, Atomic Number Two. You dig, Rudy?"

"Of course!" replies Rudy, his face alight with satori. "The chemistry of the GodS!"

"Fah out!" says Jay Jay.

"A key element in the periodic table of G.O.D.S. is the word *Foma*. It refers to the harmless untruths of religion. The verbal ladder of Wittgenstein, which the searcher casts away after the search for happiness and meaning has been concluded. Everything I transmit to you tonight is Foma. Dig Rudy?"

"Fah out!" says Jay Jay in response to Rudy's nod of dazed confirmation.

"*Duffle* is the destiny of thousands of people when placed in the hands of a *Stuppa*."

"Wass is dis Stuppa?" asks Gustav dutifully.

"A fog-bound child," snaps back the Prophet, Dylan. "Not to be confused with a *Sin-Way*, the word defining a man who wants all of someone's love. That's the *numero uno* sin."

"I like that one," She says with a soft, malicious smile. "The jealous husband condemned."

"Or vice reversed," says Dylan.

"Fah out!" says Jay Jay reverently.

"I think these basic doctrines are enough for the first lesson," says the Sage. "But let me close with a parable according to El Arabi Vonnegut. After the Gatherer Of Data showed Man the universe in all its glory, Man asked, 'What is the purpose of all this?'

" 'Must everything have a purpose?' replied the G.O.D.

" 'Absolutely necessary!' Man answered." *

Dylan stands up and leans his arm against the mantel looking down at the faces of the rapt students. "We do need a purpose. That's what philosophy's all about, right?"

The three students nod their heads.

" 'All right, I leave it to you to invent a purpose for the universe,' said the Gods. And then They went away."

Whereupon, the Minstrel walks to the kitchen, takes a bottle of wine from the cabinet and a corkscrew from the shelf. He escapes the apartment by the bedroom door, enroute to the Andromeda Galaxy, but stops briefly to sit on a rock near the brook and listen to the cricket's mating songs.

* Readers are referred to *Cat's Cradle* by Kurt Vonnegut, Jr.

-130-

*"Only those can understand us
Who ate from the same bowl with us."*

Alexandre Solzhenitsyn

GUESS WHAT. THE LADY WANTS TO GET MARRIED TOO

Lausanne, September 1971.

"Meanwhile, back on the stage of the U.N. Assembly Hall, the Convict and the Crone seated on the Golden Sofa were the center of a worshipful crowd of officials.

"The first heartwarming gestures from a grateful world came in the form of a telegram from Raymond Procunier, Chairman of the Adult Authority of the State of California, counter-signed by no less than Governor Edmund

(Jerry) Brown, Jr., ending the parole restrictions on the ex-felon and granting him a full discharge and release!

"Mr. Nelson Rockefeller, representing the Executive Branch, Mr. Carl Alpert (D.), Mr. 'Tip' O'Neil (D.), Politburo Chairman Alexander Shelepin, USSR, Ambassador Jayne Loader, Hon. Clement GoodBloode of the Atomic Energy Commission, Mr. George Meaney, AFL-CIO formally offered the gratitude of an exultant planet and asked what arrangements the two central-figures might wish for their immediate comfort. After a whispered consultation with his, by now tipsy, Companion, the ex-convict, to the astonishment of all concerned, asked if he and his consort could be married immediately.

"After a quick huddle with local officials, Mr. Rockefeller reported that the Mayor of New York was enroute with the City Clerk to the Waldorf Astoria where the Presidential Suite had been reserved for the nuptial party.

"Within an hour the forms had been filled in, signatures executed, and a simple, civil ceremony performed by Mayor Beame himself.

"During the nuptial rites the Bride, whose name, it turned out, was Rosa de la Mar, continued to knock down the bubbly, lurching relentlessly towards intoxicated stupor. Sad to say, she was barely able to mumble the marital pledges.

"It came, therefore, as somewhat of a surprise when the newlyweds enthusiastically accepted the perfunctory offer by Senator and Mrs. Jacob Javits of a wedding reception and banquet to be held in the Grand Ball Room of the elegant hotel."

"The wedding feast, sad to say, turned out to be an unmitigated disaster, doubly so in that the disgraceful proceedings were televised to a global audience.

"The Bride and Bridegroom were, of course, seated at the center of the head table, flanked on either side by the most important dignitaries of the world. It is embarrassing to report that the President of the United States and his wife Ada Lou (Babe) were witnesses of the distasteful events that unfolded.

"The Bride's behavior, to put it bluntly, was totally distasteful. Under the bright T.V. glare the filth of Her hair, the mottled, scaly texture of Her wrinkled face, the yellow slime on Her single crooked tooth, the knotted cords that bulged in Her slack-skinned Turkey neck were all too visible. What was worse was Her behavior. Her wizened hands grabbed at the food on Her plate. As She crammed the succulent and juicy delicacies in Her mouth She also managed to smear Her face and soil Her tattered rags. She burped and passed wind noisily. At times She lowered Her hideous face to the plate and sucked the gourmet cuisine like a hungry animal. We shall pass quickly over the obscene remarks and salacious asides she grunted and mumbled to the attendant dignitaries.

"During this scandalous performance the Bridegroom remained unfailingly attentive, listening with concentration to Her croaks and raucous sallies, laughing in appreciation, now and then planting an affectionate kiss on Her withered cheek, and, when She collapsed in drunken stupor on his chest, lifting Her in his arms and carrying Her out of the room, to the elevator, and thence to the Honeymoon quarters."

-131-

"Rotwang felt the same upward surge as the Alphan ship took off. He turned to Miss Photo and kissed Her. 'I'm reminded of that old Alphan saying, 'Home is Where the Head Is,' said Rotwang. 'I'm glad to be going back to Earth, but Alpha is just as beautiful.'
'Yes, I know what you mean,' said Miss Photo. She smiled and turned Her face up so that Rotwang could see Her new tattoo. Just before leaving Alpha, She had gone into an Alien Tattoo Parlor. Alien Tattoos are made with phosphorescent pigments and they glow and sparkle continuously like an Alphan rainbow. Miss Photo got a tattooed rendition of the 7 Holes in Space arranged in a spiral cluster and surrounded by deep space."

ROTWANG *by Tim Heldebrand*

RAM POONA REVEALS HIS SECRET MISSION: TO DELIVER AN ANCIENT DECK OF 24 CARDS CONTAINING A MESSAGE FROM THE INSCRUTABLE ORIENT

Millbrook, N.Y., October 1963.

"So what did you do?" asked Dylan, whose mind was spinning from the strange words of the skinny Ram Poona.

"Sylvia cashed in a small inheritance from Her Grandmother and I wangled an air-ticket and we flew off to Calcutta to talk to Siva-ji.

"We found Him squatting in a loin-cloth on the banks of the Ganges, hanging around the burning ghats where they cremate dead bodies, smoking hashish from cloth-covered chillums.

"At first He wouldn't talk to us. Just laughed and cracked dumb Don Juan Zen jokes in Bengali. But we stuck it out."

"What do you mean?"

"We just squatted down there on the river bank and passed the pipe around and watched and tried to groove with the scene. The third day Siva-ji wandered down to the river's edge and we followed. He spent hours just watching the sluggish current flow by. Then he suddenly gave a little cry of pleasure and darted to the water's edge and grabbed a thin tree branch that was floating by. He examined it, laughed and handed it to us. Around the branch was entwined a symbiotic vine."

"A good hand with props, that fellow. Then what did he do?"

"A most interesting thing. Threw the double-stick back into the Ganges, stood up and waved us to follow him; then led us to a broken-down hovel. We all sat down on the mud floor. Then he turned to me, grinning a toothless smile and spoke. The first words he ever uttered to me directly. You know what they were?"

"No idea."

"He said 'Dee Lan.' "

"What does that mean? I don't speak Bengali."

"I didn't know what he meant either. He looked at me questioning for a moment and then reached down to the Siva Shrine in the corner and took out a silk bag with a book inside it. The book was actually a bunch of illustrated cards, sewn together. Twenty-four of them. He shoved it in my hand and pointed up the river, which happens to be west and repeated the words, 'Dee Lan.' Then he bowed and folded his hands in the Namaste gesture of farewell. And that was that."

"What did it all mean?"

"That's what I asked the little devotee who trotted beside us on the way to a taxi. His answer was simple. He said, 'Siva-ji say, book very, very old. Take back to Swami Dylan at Harvard, I think it's near Duluth, Minnesota. Shanti.' Then he bowed and pressed his hands and watched us drive off in the taxi."

"You have the book?"

"Of course. It's been the center of my life since that day."

"Can I see it?"

"I guess that's what I was supposed to do. So come to my room tonight and I'll do what I was sent here to do."

-132-

"Here are people who can, to use the Jungian terminology, EMBODY an archetype--any

single Voodoo worshiper may speak it, make love through it, manifest it in every possible way, entering and leaving the experience WITHOUT PSYCHOSIS, without mind-altering drugs AND while having the full support and help of their community. . ."

Michael Ventura in Shadow Dancing in the USA
published by Jeremy Tarcher

THE BRIDE TURNS OUT TO BE A DISH! AND GUESS WHAT! SHE HAS YET ANOTHER DESIRE!

Lausanne, September 1971.

"Alone at last in the Bridal Suite, the Ex-convict gently deposited his wife on the bed and covered Her with a light blanket.

"At this point the disheveled Bride raised up on Her shaky elbow and regarded Her husband with cool eyes. 'What are you going to do now?' She croaked.

"The bridegroom shrugged. 'I thought I would sit for a while and meditate on what has happened.'

"The Crone emitted a low chuckle. 'Is this the way a loving Bridegroom treats His Bride on the wedding night?'

" 'Dear Wife,' replied the Ex-con, 'I have married you, as I pledged. But I did not expect that you wished this more from me.'

" 'What kind of a fool are you?' murmured the Crone. 'Or what kind of a fool do you take me to be? If you are a man, you will certainly perform your marital duty to your trembling bride.'

" 'Of course,' said the Bridegroom. 'I await your slightest wish as my command.'

" 'Then come to bed, my husband, and consummate our union,' murmured the Crone.

"The Bridegroom quickly removed his clothes, slid between the silken sheets, arranged his arm under Her matted hair and leaned down to kiss Her on the mouth. Just before lips made contact he looked into Her smiling eyes. As their mouths met in caress Her eyes seemed to grow, deepen, and glow. He is conscious of nothing except the two shining, wise, loving eyes and the wet warmth of their lips. As their embrace radiates Her body moves slightly and She murmurs softly.

"Suddenly to his astonishment the appearance of the Bride (nee Rosa de la Mar) begins to change in his arms. As the kiss becomes more passionate Her face blooms into a smooth, dewey freshness, Her body blossoms into the lush curved form of a young woman, in short, the Bridegroom discovers that he is holding in his arms the most ravishingly beautiful creature he has ever dreamed of. A soft perfume intoxicates his senses. She begins to stir lasciviously and he finds himself making love to a graceful, aphrodisiac female."

-133-

"It is not generally known on earth, but the stars, the great female suns themselves, are intelligent. The inhabitants of Zolmyth have succeeded in contacting their sun, Ginger, and report that she is delighted to find that intelligent life has developed as a byproduct of her amusement. So ask not for whom the stars shine. They shine for thee. And are glad to do it."

Telescopic Meditations
by Israel Regardie

24 PLAYING CARDS FOR THE GAME OF LIFE

Millbrook, N.Y., October 1963.

Ram Poona's room at Millbrook was transformed into a Tantric yoni, aka pussy. A tiger-skin meditation rug. A shrine with three small statues, of magnificent artistry, obviously old and valuable.

One was a Nataraj. Naked Siva dancing within the circle of flaming energy.

A Tibetan Buddhist Dakini, a dancing girl with slim waist, flowing breasts and long hair, winsome, abandoned.

And a seated Buddha with naked mate sitting on his cock, arms entwined in yab-yum union.

Ram Poona motioned for Dylan to be seated and the two men, in time, attained a catatonic serenity that seemed to satisfy the Yogin.

Ram Poona then took, with great reverence, an object from his shrine. It was a parchment book wrapped first in red-flowered silk, and then in fine woven cloth inscribed with Sanscrit symbols. The book unfolded, accordian-fashion, like a string of picture postcards, each card perhaps eight by six inches and sewn to the next. He placed the back in front of the shrine and arranged candles to illuminate. Then he flipped back the cover and exposed the first picture, an amoeba-like creature with an enormous human mouth, open in a sucking position. The painting possessed a horrid attraction, both slurpingly erotic and formlessly soft.

After what seemed like a long time, Ram Poona gracefully flipped to the second picture—the same amoeboid mouth, now biting a breast dripping scarlet blood. The brutal, direct, frontal force of the picture forced the Dylan to flinch.

"Powerful," he said, "but I don't get it."

"It appears to be a sequence," replied the Yogin quietly. "Let's continue."

The third picture—the smiling, satisfied faces of a voluptuous woman and a plump-faced man, each face attached to the body of an octopus with dozens of tentacles each covered with round sucker-cups. The painting was disturbingly erotic—engulfing flesh, blind, voracious, invertebrate, ancient life-hunger, relentless root-striving. Dylan was both repelled and deeply moved by vague tissue memories pulling him into the soft, greedy, feeding, devouring embrace.

"Notice," said Ram Poona, "that the first three cards portray a watery environment with the figures colored red. They represent the Siva, Brahma, and Vishnu aspects of this first phase."

The fourth card portrayed the face of a beautiful young man-woman(?) attached to the slim, wiry, sleek body of an otter—colored a flaming orange crouching warily at the edge of a body of water, alertly surveying the landscape. The scene jarred with clashing themes—the swift, graceful, furry-sexual beauty of the creature and the sense of sly, furtive awareness of danger.

The fifth card was a hermaphroditic centaur standing proudly at the peak of a hill.

The sixth card was Egyptian in motive, two enthroned regal creatures, naked, one with the strong commanding body of a man, the other with the lush queenly body of a woman—both with heads of lions.

The Minstrel looked up in bafflement. "They are magnificently painted and disturbingly moving. But I don't get the point."

"Wait until you have seen them all," replied Aryabhata. "They are like Tarot cards that tell a sequential story like the Glass Bead Game of Hesse. Ideas, icons on cards strung together to represent the stages of life."

-134-

"Scratch the surface of a beautiful man and you'll both feel good."

from the Legend of the Dar Dar

A SEXY, FUN-LOVING, TEEN-AGE GIRL FROM SCARSDALE . . .

WITH HER DIAMOND STRING... SHE LEADS HER MAN AROUND ... WITH HER APRON RING.

Villars sur Ollon, October 1971.

He is lying in bed watching Her undress.

"You know what question I'm going to ask when I get Higher Intelligence on the phone?" She asks.

"Tell me?"

"Why did Marilyn Monroe die that way? All alone in a big house down by the Levee, on Saturday night."

"It was all in the scripts they wrote for Her."

"Yes. Like the time She was caught by Her hips in the porthole of the steamboat. And the little boy with spectacles came along."

"This is so sad," he sighs.

"And She says in that soft cream voice, 'Never mind the explanations. Just help me.' "

"And then prudish little Joe Di Maggio cautiously asks if She has committed some crime."

"And then Arthur Miller agrees to help Her for two logical reasons, first because he's too young to go to prison . . . And second . . . "

" . . . because you have so much animal magnetism."

"But basically I'm just a funny, fun-loving, teen-age girl from Almount Drive."

She is now hidden behind the closet door. Her round naked arms flash. She throws Her silken bikini bottoms on to the bed. Her face pokes out, winking.

-135-

"Can there be much doubt that Voodoo trance tradition. . .is a metaphysical achievement as great as, say, the building of Chartres or the writing of the Bhagavad—Gita? . . .These people built their cathedrals and wrote their scripture within their bodies, by means of a system that could be passed from one generation to the next. That system was rhythm.

Michael Ventura in SHADOW DANCING IN THE USA
published by Jeremy Tarcher

NOW SHE WANTS TO KNOW WHAT MAN WANTS!

Lausanne, September 1971.

"The nuptial coupling continued all through the glorious night. As each hour of playful dalliance unfolded the Bride seemed to increase in beauty, charm, and elegant wit.

"The Bridegroom, who, in his long and passionate life, had ranged the wide spectrum of erotic delights, found himself transported to a new realm of tender linkage.

"As the rosy fingers of dawn rose over the East River and colored the walls of the nuptial chamber the Bridegroom realized that he was hopelessly and deliciously in love with this magnetic woman whom a generous destiny had arranged to be his wife.

"He telephoned to room-service for a luxurious breakfast—a development which shocked and amused the throngs of journalists who waited in the corridor and lobby of the hotel, expecting, no doubt, to greet the fleeing form of a harassed husband.

"While awaiting the food, the merry couple splashed sportingly in the bath-tub which steamed with scented water. Their slippery, soapy lovemaking was only briefly interrupted by the arrival of the waiters who were surprised to be greeted by the groom covered by a damp towel and sparkling with joyous pride.

"And so it continued for a second day and a second night and a third day and a third night, to the growing amazement of the waiting world which was being informed via hourly news bulletins of the prodigious nuptial events.

"As the day broke after the third night, the gorgeous bride sat naked in the middle of the bed, swept Her long, silky hair back over Her shoulders, planted a wet kiss on her husband's mouth and spoke to him softly. 'My beloved husband, you have made me the happiest woman in the universe. Now that we have completed the first three days of our eternal union there is something we must discuss.'

"The Bridegroom, propped up by satin pillows, smiled in expectation.

" 'There is one condition of our marriage which I have not told you. It is true that your love has made me beautiful. But it is also and sadly true, that from now on, my beauty and joy will wax and wane. For twelve hours of each twenty-four I shall be as comely as you now see me. An eyeful, a stunner, a peach, a knock-out, witty, graceful, sinuous, and loving. The other twelve hours, however, I shall be ugly, deformed, disfigured, squalid, loathsome, hideous, diseased, evil, nagging, filthy, rude and hateful.'

"The Bridegroom nods thoughtfully.

" 'Now it is for you to decide,' She continued, 'when you wish me to assume these dual forms. How do you want me to be? If with each sunset I become, as I am now, beautiful and loving, we shall spend our nights together in voluptuous fusion, which, I assure you will grow in meaning and pleasure. But each day I shall meet the world, at your side, as a disgraceful slatternly crone. Or do you choose to have me dance as a glowing companion with you during the exciting sequences of the day and have me revile you with venom each night? What choice do you make?' "

-136-

"A moment's reflection on the somatic engineering involved will confirm that the Yab-Yum linkage of male-female is the ultimate in neurosomatic communication."

Tom Robbins

A SOFT LANDING BY MOONGLOW ... THAT LEAD ME STRAIGHT TO WHO?

Villars sur Ollon, January 1972.

Jay Jay and the transvestite Prussian have departed. They are alone again. Can this marriage be saved?

Soft music from the tape machine. The moon is full. A gentle fire burning. They are in love again?

"Tranquility here."

"Fantastic."

"That may have seemed like a very long phase."

"It was beautiful."

"You're looking great in every respect."

"You're lined up nicely. Towards me a little. Okay. Down."

"How am I doing?"

"You're doing fine."

"I'll only go in a slight fraction of an inch ... maybe an eighth of an inch."

"I'm all ready."

"There seems to be no difficulty in moving around."

"This is very interesting. It's a very soft surface. Out here where I plug ... in."

"Are you ready for me to come out?"

"There you go."

"Beautiful."

"Magnificent."

"Isn't it fun?"

"Slippery."

"Oh it's beautiful. Really it is."

"Beautiful. Just beautiful."

"You do have to be careful to keep track of where your center of gravity is."

"Now start arching your back. That's good. Plenty of room."

"I'm bumping now?"

"Now you're clear. You're rubbing up against me a little bit. Now move your . . . "

"Back inside?"

"Everything went beautifully."

"That was beautiful. Very smooth."

"You're looking good."

"Beautiful."

"Everything is looking good."

"I'm going right down U.S. 1."

"That was a funny one. Did it appear to you that you were jerking around quite a bit during the retract cycle?"

"Yeah. It seemed to happen at the time I put the upward thrust to it."

"You look great. It's been a mighty fine day."

"You're not kidding."

She is reclining on the couch listening to him with amusement.

He is sitting on the rug near the fire-place holding a yellow magazine.

"That's very sexy for the *National Geographic*," She says. "Who are the lovers?"

"Neil Armstrong and Buzz Aldrin. A transcript from the tape of their Lunar Landing. It must have been Moonglow."

-137-

". . .*Africans were not the only slaves in the West Indies.: they were not even the only slaves who had a non-Christian—usually called, in unconsciously slanted language "pre-Christian—cosmology. In the 1850's, after Oliver Cromwell had conquered Ireland in a series of massacres, he left his brother, Henry, as the island's governor. In the next decade Henry sold thousands of Irish people, mostly women and children, as slaves to the West Indies. Estimates range from 30,000 to 80,000.*

The Irish slaves, most of them women, were mated with the Africans. . .listen to the language in a film like THE HARDER THEY COME. The Irish tinge is unmistakeable. Why were these (Irish) people sold into slavery? Henry Cromwell explained. . .'It may be the means to make them Englishmen, I mean rather Christians.' In other words Henry was trying to sell off as many pagans as he could. This was at the height of the English witch-craze, which was a pogram against those who still adhered to the Celtic religions. Ireland was a stronghold for the old beliefs.

> Michael Ventura in SHADOW DANCING IN THE USA
> *published by J.P. Tarcher*

TWO NEW CARDS ARE DEALT INTO THE GAME FOR HER AMUSEMENT

Villars sur Ollon, October 1971.

Devon and Johan telephone from Canada. They have just returned from a Marco Polo adventure to Afghanistan, loaded with rare oriental spice which they sold to merchants in the bazaars and black-alley curio-shops of Manhattan. They are planning to come visit the fugitives.

"They're loaded with money and triumph which they are eager to share with us," sez Dylan.

"It's nice that someone is doing something exciting," She sez. "Maybe they'll charge us up."

"Two young Geminis resonating in this modest laboratory is a volatile prospect."

"Two? Oh yes, Devon is a twin. But small men make me feel like an ogress."

"So rescue is on the way."

She raises Her arm above Her head and arches the stradivarius curve of Her back.

"The seams of my pleasure craft need calking. From stem to stern. From nose to toes. As Commodore you must decide who is to pilot. I mean it, Dylan. It's up to you."

"We can sometimes control whether and when to shuffle and deal. But the way the cards combine is built into the deck."

"I trust you to decide those questions," She sez sincerely.

-138-

"Rotwang was interviewed on the Satellite World Show. . .Rotwang was introduced as the first Interplanetary Ambassador. . . 'We are all mutants now,' said Rotwang. 'We are no longer Homo Sapiens—but we are still humanoid. We can be anything we want to be—we must use the power of our minds and control the mutation. We must become the new people.' The next day's edition of the Daily Alien was ordered by over 1,000,000,000 people, and the world turned its giant ear to hear the message of Rotwang and the Aliens."

ROTWANG by Tim Hildebrand

IF THE FIRST TWELVE CARDS REFLECT THE PAST, THEN THE NEXT TWELVE. . .

Millbrook, N.Y., October 1963.

The two men were crouched on their knees, Japanese style, raptly concentrating on the unfolding parchment cards. The candle-light reflected off the bald forehead of the Yogin, and flickered on the three statues; the spinning Siva, the floating Dakini girl, the fused Buddha.

Ram Poona flipped to the seventh card—a hulking, hairy yellow-skinned hermaphrodite, paleolithic hominid holding a stone-axe is bending over looking at its own reflection in a pool.

The eighth card—a golden-skinned hermaphrodite sitting on a Chariot, Hir right-hand holding a pen (which in Steinberg fashion is drawing the outline of Hir own head).

"This one is modern enough to be from the New Yorker," said Dylan with awe. "How old are these cards?"

"The Orientalists I've talked to say that this style of handsewn parchment is at least two hundred, and more likely, several hundred years old."

The ninth card—two regal, golden-skinned humans coupled in the Yab-Yum position, each with a plumed pen in right-hand drawing the other's body.

On the tenth card a naked young, handsome man, green-skinned, stands in front of a mirror from which he is reflected as a beautiful young woman. Each is lustfully fondling the genitals of the other.

The eleventh card is a straightforward presentation of Mother-Queen and Father-King naked, green-skinned, on thrones surrounded by children.

The twelfth card—an enormous city square completely filled with human beings, millions of them jammed together, all facing the center of the plaza where an enormous stone lingam rose up from an enormous oval stone yoni. Both were green.

"That's amazing. It's a scene right out of the Third Reich."

"Yes. Quite prophetic," said Ram Poona, reclining back on his heels. "Now tell me. What do you make of that sequence?"

"It's a Tarot card summary of evolution. An amazing performance, if you're right about the date. Preceding Darwin, I mean. Do you agree?"

"Of course. But there's a lot more. I've studied this manuscript for a long time and at many levels of magnification. I'm beginning to understand why Siva-ji passed this on to you."

"Do you understand! This manuscript is a fucking Rosetta Stone and that's just for openers. Notice that there are twelve drawings. Don't you see? It's the Zodiac! The trick is that it starts with Pisces. Do you see it?"

The skinny Yogin was leaning forward speaking like a No actor, soft hissing intensity, eyes flashing. Raving.

Dylan scanned the twelve cards and nodded. "I'd like to give it more study. But I think I see what you mean. Aries. Taurus. Yes. And Gemini the otter! I see. There are low level correlations of content-analysis scans of the Zodiac language."

"It's also the twelve Divinities in the Greek and Roman pantheon. The I Ching. We'll go to that later. But next I want you to see the second half."

"There's more?"

"Sure. The first twelve are just the first half." Ram Poona leaned back again on his heels and watched the Minstrels face. A long period of silence followed. Dylan suddenly blinked and pushed his body forwards to look at the Yogin. "You mean . . . " he said slowly, "you're implying that . . . "

Ram Poona nodded smiling.

" . . . if the twelfth card is Aquarius and it portrays Hitler, Mao and the sexualization of centralized government . . . "

Ram Poona was smiling broadly.

" . . . then we're just now at the mid-point of evolution . . . "

"That's how I read it."

" . . . and the twelve cards on the other side will give us the evolutionary stages to come?"

-139-

"Q. What Does European WoMan Want?"

A. SMI²LE
Q. *What makes Her SMI²LE*
A. *Space Migration; Increased Intelligence; Life Extension.*
    With unlimited Space - Time - Brain you can make anything and everything sexy.

Joanna Pacula

AND THE ANSWER TO HER QUESTION?
WHAT DOES WOMAN WANT

Lausanne, September 1971.

The quartet sit silently around the restaurant table. Michel's eyes are bulging. Dee Dee's face is flushed. She squirms uneasily. Maya's soft face has become thoughtful. The Bard leans back in his chair and solemnly surveys his rapt audience.

"Heavy, eh?" he says with a thin smile. The three listeners heave a collective sigh. Maya whistles gently.

The Poet moves forward and empties his cognac glass. He offers a Rothman to Dee Dee and a Gitane to Maya. He lights their cigarettes and then his own. He continues the story.

"The Husband thinks for a moment and then starts a slow, undulating, teasing, amused tap-dance. He sings:

> Night or day?
> Why, you are the one . . .
>
> Day or night?
> You'll stir up fun
>
> Ask me, and I'll tell yah
> I want yah all . . .
> Winter, springtime, summer or fall

The Bride, surprised and pleased, lies back on her silken pillow watching this funny guy, her husband, pretend to dance and sing for her.

> No matter the hour
> You'll still be on time
>
> I'll love you tender
> Whenever you are . . .

My sigh is still a sigh
As time goes by . . .

The Bride smiles broadly and wiggles down into the pillows.

In time Gibralter may stumble
The Rockies may mumble
They're only made of . . . day . . .
Day and night
And under the fun
You are the one . . .
O'clock, two o'clock, three o'clock

The Husband is now whirling and stalking around the room like David
Bowie imitating Mick Jagger . . .

And . . .
If there were more
Then 24
hours a day

If there could be . . .
More than 62
Hours to woo

They'd be sent
In sweet content . . .
to boodle you . . .

The Bride laughs aloud. "Boodle?" she asks. "What is this boodle?"
The Husband nonchalantly adjusts his imaginary top-hat with his finger
and swings his imaginary Fred Astaire cane . . .

Wise guy or foodle
Christian or joodle
Pizza or noodle
Apple or strudle
Row boat or canoodle
My world will always orbit
Yoodle
As time goes by . . .

The Bridegroom bows and . . . with a glowing radiance on his face, says: "I can make no choice. You must decide, my Bride, when and how you wish to come to me."

At this point, the Bride lifts Her naked arms above Her head in a flinging motion of joyous abandonment. She throws Her head back and looking upward utters a soft cry of exultation. She then flung Her soft, smooth, curved arms around Her husband and looking in his eyes sent him a look of shining adoration.

" 'Thank you, my perfect husband. You have, with your total love, delivered us from the bondage of duality. By your devotion you have made it possible for us to live in beauty and love and wisdom every moment of every day, forever and ever.' "

-140-

"We find in West Indian VooDoo, a centerpost, a gaily painted pole very like the maypole that survives in Europe from Celtic pagan celebration. . .The gods are said to enter through the centerpost, and the dances for most ceremonies revolve around the centerpost. We don't find this in the accounts from Africa. It speaks of a definite Irish-pagan influence.

> *Michael Ventura in SHADOW DANCING IN THE USA*
> published by Jeremy Tarcher

OH DEAR! TERRIBLE TALK ABOUT SEPARATION!

Villars sur Ollon, October 1971.

"Did you ever imagine we'd be in this situation?"

"Yes, as a matter of fact. I previewed it several times."

"I knew it. Remind me."

"Once, at Millbrook, when you were still an innocent low-mass secondary, before my nova-flame-out . . . "

"Yes, I remember."

"You were standing in front of the mirror in the third-story water-room. And I made some leave-you remark."

"Probably designed to strike terror to my dependent girlish heart . . . "

"You turned and flashed a totally cool image, waved a flippant hand and said . . . "

"See you around?"

"It was totally out of the script. Like Shirley Temple shooting heroin. And

I saw you boogie free and footloose through all the dance halls on the avenue. Dancing across the galaxy in someone else's arms."

"You're so reckless," She says in awe. "Why did you ever let that sort of sequence emerge?"

"The next one was more powerful. We were using the ranch-house on the desert-mountain-top as launching pad. We were several parsecs out, decelerating slowly from near-light speed, sitting on the lawn, our backs together."

"I remember. Flying blind tandem formation."

"And suddenly we began to spin as though we were on a love-seat facing in different directions. Binary stars spinning faster and faster around our mutual center of gravity. And I knew that we'd be flung out into N-dimensional space in different directions. You, perhaps, shot across towards galactic center towards Provincetown. Me, perhaps, slung out towards the Lesser Magellan, orbiting Benedict Canyon."

"See you on the other side."

"And it's a long, long way around."

-141-

"Truth is 24 frames a second."

Carinthia West (20th Century Film Philosopher)

. . .THEN THE NEXT TWELEVE CARDS REFLECT THE STAGES OF THE FUTURE?

Millbrook, N.Y., October 1963.

Ram Poona held the deck of parchment cards in his hands and shot a happy grin to his companion.

"Are you ready to look at the future?"

Ram Poona, with slow deliberation laid the deck on the tiger-skin rug and flipped the thirteenth card.

The color was blue.

The figure of a hermaphrodite floating horizontally. A serene, blissful look.

"Thirteen is rapture? We've been there."

Fourteen was blue. A hermaphrodite Yogin, with flowing hair, sits in the lotus position on the back of a powerful winged horse which soars through the clouds.

"I know that one well," said the Yogin softly.

"I think I can guess what comes next."

Card Fifteen—a man and a woman fused in Yab-Yum coition floating on a cloud, radiating a halo.

"That's interesting. We seem to be dabbling in the future already."

"I think that's why The Old Man gave this to me to give to you. We're ready for the next stage."

Card Sixteen is light-blue, sky-blue. A beautiful female in free fall, through a sky filled with stars. Hir body is also filled with stars whose beams intersect in a web of interstellar radiation.

"The Cybernetic Hippy?" said the Commodore.

Card Seventeen, the same figure, sits in the lotus position in the star-filled sky. From Hir hands and from Hir head radiate bundles of shining rays. SHe is creating forms with radiation.

"The Cybernetic Yogin?"

Card Eighteen, a naked man and a naked woman sit in the sky-blue meadow of stars. Bundles of energy waves radiate between their and their bodies.

"Brain fucking?"

Card Nineteen—the Amino Acid Consumer is duplicated in ever-decreasing size, copies of Itself spiralling through the star-filled sky. The color has changed to violet.

"This one has something to do with DNA and evolution. But I don't really get it."

Card Twenty—the Amino Acid Engineer is creating organic designs, weaving star-rays, designing Its own body.

"I see. Nineteen and Twenty are computer generated, digital versions of Seven and Eight. That's fascinating. Do the first twelve stages predict the next twelve?"

Card Twenty-one—the Nuclear Lovers are now coils of energy spiralling around each other, weaving rays to form each other's faces and other organic forms.

Cards Twenty-two, Twenty-three, and Twenty-four portrayed silver doughnut-shaped clouds sprinkled through a jet-black field. Faint broken track lines of silver curved through the void "The Hindus ran out of High-Tech-Know-How?" asked Dylan.

-142-

"...practicing pagans from Ireland infused their beliefs with the Africans, mingling in VooDoo two great streams of non—Christian metaphysics. The snake, after all, was a holy symbol to both...
...In their beliefs and symbology the pagan Irish were closer to Africa than to Puritan England. This is part of our buried history, and as we bring it out into the light it will become more important."

> *Michael Ventura in SHADOW DANCING IN THE USA*
> *published by Jeremy Tarcher.*

DYING EMBERS! BLUE SONGS! SALT—WET TEARS! A RINGING TELEPHONE!

Villars sur Ollon, Octobeer 1971.

Their time-ship wrecked in the Alps, radio reception blocked by the planet's atmosphere, they realize that, however painful, the next step is to dissolve the structure which had brought them so far. Separate. Free the elements for new and more energized connections. A common grayness of waiting silvers their routine.

It's a time of drag and drab.

They lie at night, entombed King and Queen, royal mummies, strapped to the surface of the cold water-bed which carries them into the uncharted swamp of the future.

She has taken to sitting with her back to the glass doors gazing out to the sky.

He spins aimlessly with increasing acceleration flashing distress signals.

One night sitting in front of the fire he pokes the dying embers. "And so love dies," he sighs. (He never felt it less.)

She leans forward, that blues-song to unsing, and he feels Her face salt-wet against his cheek.

The phone rings. She looks up in expectation. He answers the call.

"Johan ... Why that will be perfect. We'd love to see you. Sunday's fine. I'm leaving Monday for a week but that won't matter ... Oh no. You can take care of Her while I'm gone ... Well I can see you when I return ... Well let me decide. Come Sunday ... "

She looks up wide-eyed. "Well?"

"Your cousin's whistle," he says laconically.
"He's coming Sunday! Alone?"
"Robin and Devon are coming with him."
"That's the way you want it?"
"Solve et coagule."
"What will people say?"
"I am at a loss for words." he sighs.

-143-

"One night Rotwang dreamed that someone had written a book about him. It became the best-seller-of-the year. The author quickly set to work and wrote 3 more books. **The Return of Rotwang. Rotwang Goes Over,** *and* **Guide to Rotwang.** *Over a million copies of each were sold. Both Rotwang and the author, Tim Hildebrand, were able to retire on the royalties, and lead a life of careless love, peace, and goodwill."*

ROTWANG *by* Tim Hildebrand

BOYISH VIGOR! SEXUAL MAGNETISM! ATHLETIC CHARM! SMOULDERING GLANCES!

Villars sur Ollon, October 1971.

They meet the arriving elements at the Aigle train station.

Robin appears first. She is a soft, round earth-infant, teen-aged Prosperine, from Laguna Beach. A strong element.

The Sly Mercurian leaps down to the platform and immediately splits into two disparate youthful forms.

Devon and Johan.

Devon, who, for some mysterious reason, has been assigned the Mediterranean valences, becomes a small, sensitive entity. Smart but low self-esteem.

Johan, who has been given the positive charge, unfolds into an aluminum giant, glowing with boyish vigor. His enormous face, now beams with frank, look-you-right-in-the-eye, self confidence.

Devon slides to the side of the molecule watching silently. Robin, his consort, edges towards him smiling happily. Johan is all over the platform slashing bullet shots into the corners of the court, wrestling with the baggage, flogging the porter with evangelical sexual magnetism in pidgin

English, embracing his host with athletic charm, overwhelming his Hostess with smouldering glances.

Poor Dylan watches the performance with mild incredulity. She observes with an amused maternal smile.

Their eyes meet.

"What energy," she murmurs. "Thank the G.O.D.S. for youth."

"You're just a girl at heart," he agrees.

-143½-

"All of them--the many Africans who created VooDoo and the 40,000 to 80,000 Irish who gave to VooDoo some of their flourishes and sorcery--would have their revenge. Jazz and rock 'n roll would evolve from VooDoo, carrying within them the metaphysical anditote that would aid many a twentieth century Westerner from both the ravages of the mind-body split codified by Christianity and the onslaught of technology. The 20th century would dance as no other had, and through that dance, secrets would be passed. First North America, and then the whole world, would--like the old blues says--"hear that long snake moan."

Michael Ventura in SHADOW DANCING IN THE USA
published by Jeremy Tarcher

WEARY EAGLE. PREDICTABLE ORBITS. SOFT SANDALS ON FLEET SILKEN FEET. SHE IS READY FOR THE ROAD.

Villars sur Ollon, October 1971.

He is slumped back on the sofa, weary eagle, his nakedness covered by a soft sheep-lined leather coat. She swoops back and forth packing for departure. She pauses to regard him tenderly.

"You never looked better," She comments.

"I never felt less."

She looks out across the valley and sighs. "This is the most beautiful place on earth. You'll not forget these mountains and what I told you?"

"I don't plan to forget."

"And there's nothing to forgive."

"Our orbits are predictable."

"Remember everything that happens."

"Yes."

"Are you jealous?"

"I'm inert."

"You'll be all right?"

"It feels like all left."

"You're doing this, you know. I don't want to go."

"I'm doing nothing."

"Exactly. You'll think of me?"

"Yes."

"As I lie cozily in the Devil's arms?"

"Are you crying?"

"You'll remember? All ways? All ways?"

"You can't say it hasn't been fun."

She leaves the room swiftly.

In a few moments She returns. She has dressed perfectly for the voyage. Soft sandals on fleet silken feet. Tight blue jeans. A woven blouse. Her leather travelling bag swung casually over Her shoulder. She would not be out of place at any time in human history. She twirls gracefully and shrugs in farewell. She is ready for the road.

-143¾-

"The Human Brain is composed 10 billion-billion working parts."

Sabrina Guiness

THE YOGA KNOWS A BEAUTIFUL YOUNG LADY NAMED PRINCESS BARBARA, A VERITABLE DAR DAR!

Millbrook, N.Y., October 1963.

The twelve "future" cards are now exposed. The two sit silently studying the sequence. From time to time the Yogin carefully rearranges the cards to expose the first twelve pictures, prepares a chillum or lights a fresh candle.

"Now you know why I came here. First to remind you that tantric fusion is the posture from which the future is explored."

"That message is hardly new," sez Dylan. "There are dozens of tantric handbooks in the occult bookstores."

"But they're written by wrinkled Hindu scholars translating pedantic instructions about matching penile length to yoni size. And the up-scale computer people don't read them. This map tells us what comes next."

"Stages beyond the body?"

"No. Fused bodies, eroticized, become the time-ships of Info-Space."

"Blissful bodies can't get us zooming around the Cyber-Brain."

"But they can eroticize the electronic. That will get us off."

"Computer will help us understand and explore the universe of the brain. Amazing. These Ganges guys knew this back in the 19th century."

Ram Poona looked very pleased with himself.

"Hmmm," sez the Minstrel thoughtfully.

"Oh, by the way, I talked to Sylvia today. She's in New York. I wondered if she could join me here?"

"Of course."

"And She'd like to bring a friend. Is that all right with you?"

"Sure," sez Dylan hopefully.

"Her name is Princess Rosamund. She's a high person. And beautiful. And they say she is a Veritable Dar Dar. The cards seem to indicate that you will love her forever.

-144-

"From the first the music has felt like an attack on the institutions.

From the first it moaned and groaned furiously all the length of its great long snake, and has never been afraid of venting its own passion. 'If I told you what our music is really about, we'd probably all get arrested', Bob Dylan told an interviewer in 1965. . .the music has frightened its very own dancers, so that many don't want to be challenged in that way. . .They let the music become merely a memory of their own youth. It speaks through the body and invokes the spirit. And some of us have felt, since the first day we heard it, that this is the aesthetic we have to live up to. No matter how the deal goes down."

Michael Ventura in SHADOW DANCING IN THE USA
published by the Master Bookman J.P.T.

WELL YOU CAN'T SAY IT HASN'T BEEN FUN

Villars sur Ollon, October 19, 1971.

Mid-day.

He hears shutting door, shifting gears, vanishing whine of motor. The Doppler-effect blues.

He sits watching departing swallows write Thank You Notes on blue-linen sky. His life-indicator dials flick like death-watch beetles pitifully near zero. Carrion memories buzz in his head. Well you can't say it hasn't been fun!

At 12:15 he drives the VW van to the Police Station to sign the register.

"*Comment va votre femme?*" asks the Chief affectionately.

"*Comme toujours.*"

"*Comme elle est belle!*" sez the Chief.

□ □ □ □ □ □ □ □ □

And here comes Anna Kate! Riding into town cushioned on the soft leather of Nigel Featherbone's Ferrari. A silver scarf at her throat fluttering behind in tongues of flame. She is a legendary emissary from Texas, a land once drained, now again in Renaissance, herself of illustrious title but now too far into the future to control the power.

She's dressed in a white auto-racer jump-suit with *Mobil* scrolled in blue across Her back, a dress for atmospheric changes, sudden acceleration, quick pit-stops for chemical-fuels, a costume to reflect radiation and mirror star-light as She smiles, preoccupied but without self-indulgence.

So DA DUM DUM DUM for elementary talks, She's a 21st Century Fox, all right but there's no room in Her womb for mundane affairs, nor will She spend more than a casual franc on the Swiss ski-village landscape, the wood-carved gabled houses, the narrow shop-lined street from which rolled down the green-pasture slopes, beginner, medium, advanced, whispering *come tumbling down, slide down . . . forget your hopeless search . . . we want to roll you, rolllll you* . . . but, oh no, not Anna Kate. She has boogied naked on the glass table-tops and run hand-in-hand under the crazy moon and lay back, open to the archer's bow, grass stains on creamy thighs. But the goaty physics professor could never make Her come and now he had taken to calling collect, begging loans for old times sake.

She motions Nigel to pull the car over to the curb and She leans out the window, waving to a young woman with long blonde hair.

"Hallo! Betty Ann!"

The woman stops and examines the car with hands on hips. Her face glowed with an amused vulnerable expression. "My Gods," Anna Kate whispered, "She's stoned."

"My name is usually Belle."

"Oh, sorry." Clipped Tex-Brit accent. "I thought you were someone else." Anna Kate pauses and smiles winningly. "But perhaps you can help us."

The girl walks towards the car still smiling curiously.

"Maybe I can."

"We're in town looking for . . . "

"Yes I know. I am too."

"Do you know where . . . "

"No. I've been trying to find out. No one will talk about it. Anyway, today's not the day. I just saw the car head down the mountain."

"What kind of car?"

"A brown Volvo."

"Let's hit it, Nigel. We'll catch him on the Geneva freeway. Want to come with us, Belle?"

"No, I've decided this isn't the right time. But good luck."

Nigel Featherbone swings the Ferrari half-circle, reverses and roars away, just missing the yellow Porsche slowly coming along the narrow street.

☐ ☐ ☐ ☐ ☐ ☐ ☐ ☐ ☐

Dylan drives to the village center and parks the yellow Porsche in front of the tobacco shop. Looking out he sees the body of a young female biped approaching along the sidewalk. Her head is hidden by the overhanging shade curtains. It is a lush, Levantine body cased in tight blue jeans worn below the generous curve of hip. The gait in undulating. A five-brained creature! He watches his own sluggish but unmistakeable response to the somatic signal. Her headless body floats closer, innocently (?) unaware of his voyeur reception. He studies the blissful Semitic face as She passes. Another grounded rapture victim, no doubt about it.

She's undeniably a Woman. So Dylan knows what she wants.

EEGH IN RTVY

-POST SCRIPT-

"ILY, B"

The Author

CAN THIS BE THE BEGINNING?

Villars sur Ollon, Oct. 19, 1971

The balding, pot-bellied waiter in Le Sporting, standing in his accustomed post next to the cashier sees the Fugitive through the window. He glances to the corner, checks the time on his wrist watch, extracts small notebook from shirt pocket and writes.

The Bard, Dylan, walks across the street and enters the cafe. The waiter trots forward to pump his hand. "You search Monsieur Hyatt, Monsieur Dylan?"

"Oui."

"He waits in the corner."

Hyatt rises to his feet. The two men shake hands.

"You look sad," sez Hyatt.

"I'm bored with being chased by government agents with pit-bull attitudes," says Commodore D.

"Yes, it must be exhausting," agrees Hyatt mechanically.

"How do you explain these guys on government payrolls who make everything so mechanical?" What a dumb thing to say, he thinks.

Hyatt must be thinking the same thing. "Ah, Maestro, it's your day for conspiracy theories?"

"No. I just wonder how these mechanical officials explain to themselves and their dependents what they are doing."

"Very simple. They have their religious explanations. The white male service-academy protestants who run the system are aware that the Individualism and Self-hood you advocate is the ultimate threat to their domination. They know that auto-control of the brain, self-piloting of the mind will put general motors out of business."

Dylan lights a Gitane and purs Heineken into his glass. It's one of those chess board confrontations so pleasing to men of the Industrial Age.

There is a long pause as both men review their databases. Both sigh inwardly and smile outwardly.

"Tell me, Hyatt", says the Brain Damaged Bard. "You know these guys. What pleases them? What motivates them? Being part of the hive? Feeling like a necessary cog in the great machine? The warm, comfy security that comes from winning the approval of the collective? Certainty? Unquestioning conviction that their system is good and all the others evil?"

"It's our religion. You know that," sighs Hyatt. "God and Devil. We call it Godly when it's good for us. And it's evil if it's not good for us. Now that's a simple, practical and effective theology, you must admit. Is it good for us WASPS? For us Jews. For us Armenians? A moron can understand it. The ants do it. The bees do it. Even service-academy-educated fleas do it. It's called monotheism. The Celtic—Irish are the only whites who don't run their hive this way. And look at what's happened to your head-strong gene-pool. Scattered all over the world, you are. Look at yourself, Dylan, your poor family uprooted and your dear children abandoned and you, a powerless exile."

Hyatt is pleased with himself.

"It's also called religious-kook fanaticism," says Dylan. "A genetic disease which has killed more humans than the plague and old age. You're fanatic. Because you can't yield on a single point. Or the diabolical simplicity unravels. And it becomes complicated. There can be no tolerance or compromise because you can't make a deal with genetic rivals, AKA the Devil."

"Yup," says Hyatt, nodding. "There is one God, the Father, and he has selected my ant-hill cult to be His agents. Hey, don't knock it. This Christian religion pays off. It's done well by us for 2000 years, hasn't it? Hyatt is holding his plump left hand in his right, stroking his gold ring with his right thumb.

"The crazier the slogans. . ."

". . .the greater the test of idiotic, submissive, insectoid loyalty. You got it, Dylan. In a monotheistic religion no one gets rewarded for independent thinking and creative innovation. You get 100 million Arabs chanting a one-god motto and 100 million christians chanting a rival one-god slogan and you got a lot of business cooking for the military and arms industries on both sides. Hive psychology. Sure works like a charm, you gotta admit that."

"And when a genetic agent comes along to question the hive system . . ."

"Well, that's where me and my spook-crew come in. We're actually quite interested in scanning new, dissident opinions. Our hive way of learning is to observe what intelligent, independent thinker-bees, like you, come up with. And then we factor your heretical thoughts into our hive survival options. That's why we read your books so carefully and why we make sure that they don't circulate among the general public. It's a damn shame that you're financially crippled because we won't let your albums hit the hive best-seller lists. That's just the system. We take charge of the money, honey. It's a sticky job, but someone has to do it."

Hyatt is very, very pleased with himself.

"But it's actually quite flattering to you, Dylan. You could call us, in Counter Intelligence, your most devoted fans. We hang on your every word. If we don't your words could disrupt hive-discipline. In a way you could consider yourself one of our most valuable assets. Does that please you at all?"

"Thanks a lot," sez the Exiled, Impoverished, Wifeless Minstrel.

□ □ □ □ □ □ □

Author's Note: For those psychologically hip critics who think Dylan is a cold, unemotional fellow -- good head, good genitals, no heart, no guts --please be advised that his mood at this crucial moment is sad, heartbroken, poignant, wretched, dejected. Hey, believe it, doctor, he really feels discouraged, down, forlorn and gloomy. You critics who go rushing off to spill self-pity on the tearstained couches of psychotherapists, hey, you have never come close to Dylan's deep melancholia, his joyless, mournful, pathetic despondency during this enounter with the enigmatic, cool Christopher S. Hyatt, Ph.D., the ultimate Hive Master Guru Manipulator.

□ □ □ □ □ □ □

"You're quite welcome, "says Dr. Hyatt.

The silence is broken when the courier vents an enormous exhilation of breath.

Disinformation, in the guise of sincerity, is about to emerge from the closet. The holy Dr. Hyatt bobs his head up and down in fake resignation.

"All right. I'll lay our cards on the table, Dylan."

"Your cards? And its your shuffle and your deal?"

"Excuse the metaphor," sez Hyatt dryly. "The undeniable facts are that your predictions, which seemed hallucinatory and impossible to us five years ago, are coming true with shocking accuracy."

Hyatt lifts his plump face to gaze deeply into Dylan's eyes. The heavy artillery of flattery is about to be wheeled into action.

"Yup. Congratulations! Thou has conquered, Galileo. And, poor Dylan, you don't even realize it! Ha ha! You have swallowed our propaganda. So let me cite you some demographic statistics."

Hyatt pulls a note-book from his pocket and pretends to search.

"According to hard-data from the best western intelligence sources, including the Israeli. . .let's see. . .we'll start with the Middle East. . .the following influential young men and women have brain-washed themselves, declared their individual independence and deserted the gene-ship. Iran. . .seven members of the royal family, five male, two female. They are, of course, the best educated, the most sophisticated. Exactly the people we have been grooming. Hundreds of young scientists and administrators. To them becoming westernized means personal freedom, rock n' roll, blue jeans. Got it?"

"Gotcha," says the Fugitive, skeptically.

"Saudi Arabia. . .eleven out of fifteen most promising princes. Hmmmm." He flips pages. "Well, to summarize, in every pro-western Islamic state the elite youth is receiving your Satre-ian signal of selfhood."

"How interesting," says Dylan, yawning.

"Let's move to conservative Spain. That was a shocker. We couldn't accept these figures until we re-checked them. Of 132 of the most promising young people, I'm talking about the aristocracy, whose families own and run the contry, 88 have copied and adopted your signal of individuality. Talk to them about power-politics, the Cold War and industrial economics and they laugh in your face. When Franco dies Spain will go marijuana rock 'n roll in a week!"

"How nice for them", murmurs the wary Fugitive.

"In Italy the trend is even stronger. But Italian, mongrel cynicism has always resisted genetic loyalty. France. Scandinavia. Same thing. You get the picture?"

"These young people just don't wanna work on Maggie's Farm no more." says Dylan.

Hyatt looks puzzled.

"What do they seem to be for?" asks Dylan.

"That's a hard question. It gets vague. They don't follow leaders. They watch their parking meters. They talk about individuals piloting their own lives. Neuropolitics. Exo-Psychology. They seem to believe that a hard rain is going to fall. Feminine concerns about what woman really wants. They're passionately anti-military and anti-clerical, of course."

"Of course."

"For security reasons I can't give you specific details from other countries except to tell you . . . let's see . . ." Hyatt is adding figures on a paper napkin. "Of approximately 1000 of the most promising young scientists and political administrators in the core democracies—Germany, England, America— over fifty percent are committed to the planful and apparently successful use of your neurological methods and to the general philosophy you have been broadcasting."

Dylan is rolling his upper lip against the smooth, silk moistness of his full lower lip and nodding thoughtfully. "How about South America?" he asks idly.

"Spotty, but the trend is there. It is a genetic thing. The more aristocrats, the bigger your majorities. In the bourgeois socialisms and democracies, the smaller. Another strange twist. In the foreign offices and among the diplomatic corps your triumph is complete. It's a scandal! Seventy-three ambassadors that we know of. Most of the wives too. Hundreds of consuls and attaches. And . . . well, you might as well know the worst, three prime ministers, six rulers, four foreign ministers."

"But nothing among the military?"

"Among the younger officers. But so far that situation is in hand."

The Commodore examines the palm of his hand and smiles.

"The conclusion is obvious," continues Hyatt. "Your game-plan has succeeded. The significance of these statistics was slow in dawning because it was hidden under the Generation Gap and scattered globally. The shocking fact is that the use of your brain-change technology is most pronounced among . . . "

"The sons and daughters of the ruling class."

"Precisely."

"So what is to be done? Michel was right. It's apparently too late to kill me."

"Don't think that hasn't been discussed. It was decided to convince the world that you were mind-blown. Crazy. Your flight to Algeria was a delightful gift. Algeria! That was better than San Quentin."

"But the crazy jacket won't work. They'll just assume that I made a mistake in reality selection. One brain-crash of a veteran test-pilot can't ground Trans-World Airlines."

"Yes. We realized that soon enough."

"So what to do?"

Hyatt glances up with a sudden move and then throws his pen on the table in well-acted exasperation.

"Please, my friend, don't play with us. I'm serious. I repeat my question: don't you know why we in the Intelligence Community have been following you around?"

"Why?"

"Because we're waiting for you to answer the question we have tried to answer for 2000 years. Please, Dylan, tell us: what does woman want?"

Dylan whispers one word.

Hyatt takes a deep breath.

"Now! Here's the kicker! Would you believe you have receivers behind the Iron Curtain?"

"In the Bloc?" asks Dylan, teasing Hyatt with Company Jargon. "I've been expecting that."

"Well the Intelligence Agencies haven't," snorts Hyatt. "This SELF nonsense started popping up in the more restless satellites. Poland, of course, for starters. The familiar pattern of youthful rebellion. Rock 'n' Roll. Blue jeans. Marijuana. Non-military hair. Amused disregard for authorities. Wholesale defections of Polish intellectuals, artists and Bohemian hooligans. Roman Polanski. Gene Gutowski. Joanna Pacula, the most beautiful and graceful woman in the People's Republic."

"Czechoslovakia, of course, is the most avant garde satellite. Milos Forman. Roman Polanski. Kundera. Once again, the global symbols of this new order. Long hair. Rock music. Stoned smiles."

"Hungary, I'd guess," says the Bard.

"Hungary, naturally. Yugoslavia. East Germany. But, I'm glad to say, little restlessness in Bulgaria, Albania, Romania—they stay loyal to tradition."

"Seems to me you've left one country out . . . ?"

"The Motherland?"

"What word from Moscow?" asks the Philosopher. "Let me guess." He simulates a mocking smile. "In the Soviet Union it's the children of the party officials. They listen to the European radio stations and can afford black-market records. And their parents are watching X-rated movies on video tape. Right?

"Right," says Hyatt soberly.

"The kids of the diplomatic corps and the foreign service. They have lived in the west. They've seen American TV and Easy Rider and The Graduate. Right?"

"It's true," admits Hyatt.

And the kids of KGB officials. I bet that surprised you."

"Oh! How do you know that?" asks Hyatt.

"Makes perfect sense to me," says the Bard. "There's one Soviet group that knows exactly what's happening in the free world. The KGB. They have the confidence to say what no one else can admit. Stationed in Paris, they read *Actuel* and *Le Monde*. In New York they read the *Village Voice* and the *Wall St. Journal*. They're better informed than most Americans about what's really going on. They're detached. They're hip. And, you better believe that their wives and children are too. They know that the old world of Super-powers and Cold Wars and imperialism is over.

Hyatt nods his head somberly.

"It's true. Listen to this quote from a top party member. Guy's name is Aleksander Yakovlev. He was ambassador to Canada. "Fundamentally what we intend to do in the Soviet Union is establish self-government. We are moving toward a time when people will be able to govern themselves and control the activities of people who are leading and governing them.

" 'We are,' writes Yakovlev. 'talking about SELF-government, SELF-sufficiency and SELF-profitability. SELF-this and SELF-that. It all concerns de-centralization of power, opening up, glasnost.' "

Hyatt lays the paper down and grins. "Can you believe that kind of talk?"

"I've been waiting for some years," says Dylan. "But how can he get away with writing that?"

"Apparently there's a second echelon of Soviet leaders and intellectuals, younger guys, too young to have been in World War II. Their writings are circulated as memos or as underground samizats. Much of the stuff is plagarized from your writings about selfhood. Sartre too. They use all your buzz-words except SELF-indulgence. They're not ready for that."

"Wonderful. Got any more?"

"Yeah. Here's a cute one. It's a song which has become an underground hit in the Soviet Union. Hundreds of garage bands playing it. It's called: "I have no intention to work on Breznev's agricultural commune, any more."

"No shit."

"No shit. Want to hear the words?" Hyatt shuffles papers and clears his voice.

> *I refuse to work on Breznev's Agricultural station any more. . .*
> *I refuse to work on Breznev's Agricultural station any more.*
> *He hands you five kopecs.*
> *He hands you ten*
> *And asks you with a smile*
> *If you are enjoying yourself."*

Hyatt coughs self-consciously. "The five and ten apparently refer to five and ten year sentences to Siberia," he explains. "There's a lot more. About not working for Breznev's mother or Breznev's Father. Apparently the National Guard is stationed around the door of his dasha."

Dylan is grinning broadly. "So Maggie goes to Russia."

"What's that?" asks Hyatt.

"Aren't there any songs about 'don't follow leaders, watch your parking meters'?"

Hyatt looks. "Yes I told you. There is just such a song. The CIA has been puzzling about that. There are, as a matter of fact, no parking meters in the Soviet Union."

TO BE CONTINUED

PERFORM THIS BOOK!

There has been much talk by computer-utopians about "Interactive Fiction." Paper-made books, of the sort you hold in your hand, are not interactive. They cannot respond to input from the reader. In computer jargon a book printed by machines which impress inked-letters on sheets of wood pulp are ROM (read-only).

Electronic books present thoughts in the form of clusters of electrons which can be easily changed by the reader. Reader access to the book is called RAM.

This book, *What Does WoMan Want?*, provides the source text for an interactive-computer program. This is one of the first novels designed by an author not to be passively read by the reader but actively performed.

Timothy Leary and Cyberpunk Legend Alan Mark Launchett have developed a PERFORMANCE BOOK. This is a book-on-a-disc, an electronic version of *What Does WoMan Want?* which engages you, the no-longer passive reader, in a mind-game with the authors.

PERFORMANCE BOOKS work like this:

-1-

Use the form at the back of this book to order your Book-On-A-Disc Software (from Falcon Press PERFORMANCE BOOKS, 2210 Wilshire Blvd., Suite 295, Santa Monica, CA 90403). Indicate whether you wish the Amiga Software or the PC Software. The Performance Book-On-A-Disc is $15 (plus $3 handling).

-2-

While waiting for your Performance Software to arrive you read *What Does WoMan Want?*

-3-

When the disc arrives you boot up the program on your Amiga or PC. Next you reread the first "Inning" of the book (around six pages).

Then the author serves you twenty thought "Pitches," tricky idea-screwballs, cognitive curves. You exchange mind-strokes with the author. You answer (or wisely decline to answer) questions, puzzles, teasers about this "Inning." At the end of each "Inning" you are scored on ten dimensions of Mental Proficiency

Instant replay allows you to improve your mind strokes until you have mastered this "Inning" of the book to your satisfaction. You solve puzzles, revise the action, compare your reactions to the six pages with those of the author.

You can replay each chapter and improve your mental performance on ten dimensions of Mental Ability.

WARNING!

There is no authoritarian teacher scoring your reactions. You are the referee, field-judge, umpire. You track your performance as it changes over the 64 "Innings."

Your performances occur in the privacy of your own mind. (This absence of a judgmental teacher tends to bother some players, but after a few trials you will never want to go back to the old author-reader, teacher-student relationship.)

-4-

At the end of each "Inning" of the book, you can choose to write in your answers to two Super Questions on the Mind Game Entry Form (which comes with the manual), and compete with other non-passive readers.

Since there are 64 "Innings" to the book, there are 128 Mind Game Questions. Everyone who mails in entries will receive answers and Certificates of Mind Skill. To increase the excitement of participation, authors Leary and Launchett are donating 15% of the profits from the sale of their PERFORMANCE BOOK to be awarded as prizes to outstanding player proficiency in the Mental Performance Mind Game.

NOTE: Enrollment in the Mental Performance Mind Game is void where prohibited.

ORDER FORM

To receive your Performance Book-On-A-Disc, complete this form and send to:

Falcon Press PERFORMANCE BOOKS
2210 Wilshire Blvd., Suite 295
Santa Monica, CA 90403

Name ————————————————————————————

Address ————————————————————————————

City/State/Zip ————————————————————————

I am ordering: Amiga Software ☐   PC Software ☐

Please enclose a check for $18 ($15 + $3 Handling) made payable to: **Falcon Press Performance Books**. Participation in the Mental Performance Game is void where prohibited by law.